Finding the Light

A memoir

J.E. Mackie

This book is a work of non-fiction. All names have been changed in order to protect the identity of those within the book.

Printed in the United States of America

First Printing:
Vanguard Premier Publishing

ISBN- 978-1-7333415-0-9

CONTENTS

CHAPTER 1

After the initial shock, the nervous chatter began the instant the voice over the intercom quit broadcasting: "Teachers, we are on full lock down. Please keep your students in the classroom until further notice." The Columbine massacre had occurred only months before, so this pronouncement instantly put everyone on edge. I tried my best to keep things as calm as possible and keep the discussion of the psychosis of Hamlet going without letting the students digress into speculation regarding the reason for the lockdown – nothing short of a miraculous accomplishment. After all, there was no fear in the intercom voice and they hadn't used any of the special codes used to inform us that there was an actual threat on campus, but I had to admit, I was just as nervous about whatever prompted the lockdown as the students were. Thirty minutes later, another voice came on to give us an all clear and have the students move on to their next class. They asked the students to try to avoid all the emergency personnel working near the student bathrooms on the north side. That wasn't a well thought out request because it was like drawing moths to the flame.

Most of the students were tardy as they began to straggle in for the next class. It was hard to read their emotions and their hushed whispers to infer what they had heard or seen, so I just asked. Apparently, a senior student in the special education department had fatally shot himself in the student bathrooms. My lesson plan for the rest of the afternoon no longer mattered. The students obviously needed time to process the information. As they began to talk about the student, they described him as a stereotypical loner that always walked closest to the edge of the walls. He always wore black ragged clothes with unkempt hair. No one ever included him in a group and he was never seen with other students. Suddenly, they were talking about times when they knew they had seen him bullied or made fun of and no one did anything to stop it. They started talking about how easy it was to join the teasing because everyone else around them was doing it. Guilt started to settle in around the room as they realized that their silence helped to cause someone's death. The impact and severity of bullying finally started to be a reality.

That experience changed the emotions on campus. Students became more tolerant; more aware of the other students around them; more aware of their own actions. Regardless of the suicide, I knew I had made a connection to the students that year. A teacher can feel when a class gels together, but this year the connection was on a whole other level. With a month or so left to go in the year, the administration had gathered the senior class to do team building exercises to help them grow closer together as a class. As I stood at the edge of the gym and watched, I grew more and more frustrated. After the connections I thought were made in my classroom, it frustrated me to see that my students were not taking the bonding exercises seriously. For all their big talk and what they supposedly learned from the experience of the boy killing himself, I suddenly couldn't see a difference in their behavior now compared to before the other student's death. The groups were segregated throughout the gym, raucous boys were pushing other kids around and knocking other kids' hats off – girls pairing up and whispering in each other's ears as they made snide remarks about other groups of girls. Faced with the anticipation of graduation, all the progress we made that year seemed to dissipate.

The next day, I sat my classes down for a heart-to-heart chat. I tried to explain to them that in less than a month the only things they had known their whole life was about to change. The people and relationships they relied on would change dramatically in a few short months. I also tried to explain that while for some students graduation will be the best day of their life up to that point, for other students it could be a very trying time, and they need to remember to be aware of those around them. To help explain my point I shared with them the following short story:

A Sandwich and a Poor Excuse

Most seniors want to spend graduation day hanging out and celebrating with their friends. I would have loved nothing more than to do just that. While others in my class were attending the principal's senior breakfast, I was at the local university attending class and preparing for my finals the next day.

In between Health 101 and my U.S. Constitution class, I was at least able to attend graduation practice which conveniently was being held on the university campus since the ceremony would be held there later because our high school auditorium wasn't big enough. Why they called it practice I don't know because it really should have been called the lecture on "what not to do" that evening. There was no actual practicing involved. Anyone who was deserving of graduation should have known everything they were saying anyway, so my mind drifted to other things.

Throughout high school I was your typical over-achiever. I participated in almost everything from sports, to the arts, to an elected position in student government. I never considered myself popular, or one of the "in" crowd, but I thought I knew most of the people in my graduating class. There were only 247 of us. But there I sat between two people I had never even seen before. Was it a fluke? Had the two long haired, unshaven boys surrounding me gone to some alternative high school to get the required credits then at the last minute transferred back to my semi-reputable school for graduation? I would never know since I was not about to strike up a conversation with these twin-towering, druggernauts and start trying to make new friends now. Sitting between them, I started to realize that life in my small pond was about to change exponentially.

Others that I considered part of my pond were on stage and when I realized the cavern of space between us, something inside me went thud. I was not part of that pond anymore. They were on stage and I was in the audience, just an identical copy of everyone else around me. What was I doing sitting out here? I had sat up on that stage for all three of the graduations before mine. In addition to the student government, the choir and band were both on stage. For three out four years I was in that choir. Why, in the culminating year of my high school experience, was I sitting out here rather than on stage?

The answer: I made the decision to give it all up. I skipped out of my senior year of high school to speed up my college education. At the time getting a head start on college seemed as if it was the best thing to do, but now that I was just sitting with everyone else in the audience, not being on that stage and missing all those experiences of my senior year really started to bother me. The spot where the thud hit was now starting to ache. I knew there were people up on stage who did not want to be there, underclass students, who were only there because it was part of their grade. I knew because that is how I had felt last year too. They were fidgety and rambunctious. Anyone could read their dislike from the back of the auditorium as they were whispering to each other and cracking jokes. Were they aware they held a precious position sitting on that stage? Were they aware they were creating someone's memory? I doubt it; they just wanted to be anywhere but there. I would have done anything to trade places with any one of them.

Back in my U.S. Constitution class an hour later, imaginary images of laughing friends sharing giant ice cream sundaes at the senior social eclipsed the lecture that I was supposed to be concentrating on - totally defeating the point of actually going to class. This was different from graduation practice, now I really needed and wanted to pay attention since this was the last review before the final tomorrow, but I couldn't bring myself to do it. As soon as we were excused, I bolted to the ice cream party. Apparently, it doesn't take too long to eat an ice cream sundae because when I arrived there were only a few stragglers gathering up all the pieces of popped balloons and torn streamers littering the ground. Feeling sorry for the one or two people left to care for the immense mess left by my thoughtless peers, I stayed to help clean up. By helping clean up, I was hoping it would feel like I had at least been there and shared the experience, but instead I began to feel more like the discarded wrappers I was picking up. I realized I did not belong to this graduating class. This day was not only the culmination of twelve years of school, but the culmination of a weeklong calendar full of special activities, and I hadn't been able to attend any of them. I hadn't been able to share in the joy and sense of relief that my classmates were feeling.

Moment by moment, I was losing my connection to what had been my life for the last four years. The world was closing in around me and I was in a solitary bubble whose surface could not come in contact with the outside world. I didn't have time to talk to anyone at practice since I was between classes and no one seemed to care that I didn't make it to the social. No one called to see where I was or what I was doing. Everyone was in their own bubbles, far away, sharing this day with whoever was important to them. My bubble didn't coexist with theirs, so why would anyone even care if I continued on with the rest of the planned activities of the day? I would just be another nameless face in the crowd. Would my classmates even notice if I crossed the stage? Or even care if I did?

I went back to my house on the hill and holed myself up in my room - feeling safer in my little cocoon. I sat on my bed and stared at my phone waiting for someone, anyone to call. Heck, I probably would have been happy if a telemarketer called. I tried to open my books and study for my finals, which was what I told myself was the reason behind going home rather than reaching out to find my peers, but the attempt was useless. I would read the same paragraph over and over with no idea what the words were saying because no matter how I tried, I couldn't bring myself to focus.. Eventually, the words just became a giant blur on the page as tears welled up in my eyes. I tried to deny the sorrow and fight back the tears, but the hurt was too overwhelming. Giving in and wanting to escape, I closed the book and slept.

Sleep was like watching a fast-forwarding replay reel of high school in my mind. Like flotsam from an overflowing dam, images rushed into my dreamscape. I relived serving seven straight points against our rival school in a volleyball match, spending hours with the other student officers planning and decorating for the junior proms, totaling my teacher's car during a debate tournament, painting the set for the school musical, my first performance with the marching band, and the multiple choir trips to California.

Against my will, the nervousness created by my usual commitment to attend to my obligations joltingly roused me from my sleep. Rushing out of my room in a panic, hoping to find my family anxiously getting ready to go with me to the evening's festivities, I was astonished to find the house still empty. Assuming that my family must have been caught up with last minute duties at work, I began preparing for the night anyway. I didn't have to worry. My dad was one of the teachers at the school. He was required to go.

I turned on the curling iron, set up the ironing board and threw in a TV dinner. Whenever I had awoken in the mornings after a fitful night of dreaming, I would always come out and tell my father about my dreams. Having no one to talk to now, I started recounting and analyzing them for myself. I had established quite a remarkable resume for myself, and other people always seem to be impressed. Now, realizing that I was experiencing the culmination of these four years alone, I started to wonder why I had worked so hard. I had this amazing resume, and no one was there to celebrate it with me. I didn't even know where my family was. It didn't seem like anyone cared I was graduating besides me, so why was I even continuing to get ready? With a heavy heart, the realization dawned on me that regardless of how I felt about things, I always did what other people expected of me. At the very least, my name was on a card someone was supposed to read and there was a gown to return and a diploma to pick up and even though I didn't know where they were, my family would be expecting to watch me walk across the stage. I continued to come up with reasons to justify to myself why I needed to go, and then as I leaned in to put on my mascara, I stopped short. Looking into my own eyes, searching my reflection, there was a moment of clarity when I realized that my drive to go was less about obligation and more about my need to receive recognition from others - the acceptance of friends and family. After all, due to my academics, I was one of only two students to receive special accolades after my name was to be read that evening.

But I started replaying those memories one more time, and I realized, I didn't play volleyball because I wanted to. I played volleyball because my step-brother played three sports and my father was a high school coach. Athleticism was expected. I didn't run for student government because I cared about the school. I just wanted more people to like me. I participated in performing arts because people came to watch them. I knew my talent was less than mediocre. I never got a lead or a solo. My mother had told me my whole life I couldn't sing. I was just rewarded for being less absent than anyone else. The whole reason my teachers chose to do a choir musical revue my senior year rather than a traditional musical was because I wasn't talented enough to carry a show and the more talented people had severe absenteeism. They didn't outright tell me that, but reason for their decision was obvious enough to me. The bottom line was all my accomplishments were meaningless. I was just a number – no different than the hundreds of thousands of students graduating high school this month. This graduation wasn't special or different from any of the others I had attended. What was supposed to make this one so special? Me? Clearly, there was nothing special about me. I wasn't even important enough for anyone to call and check on me. What would really be the consequence if I didn't go? They would pull my name card out of the stack and move on to the next student and my diploma would be returned to the school to be picked up whenever I got around to it. Only the name reader would even know I had been skipped. Life would have gone on without me as if I had never even existed.

I started to see the only reason I had filled my life with so many activities was because they were the savior from the isolation I was feeling right that very minute. I did all these great and wonderful things in order to gain acceptance, to be recognized and to have friends, and here at the end of it all, I had no one. Apparently, not even my family. It was at this realization of the fruitlessness of my efforts when I noticed the shelf of medications. That is when the idea struck me that just like no one noticed I wasn't around for any of the social events today, no one would notice if I took those pills. On the most important day of my life so far, no one seemed to be aware of my existence. What difference did my life make? Even as I was contemplating the deed, scanning the different medications on the shelf, I was finishing my preparations for the night. The dichotomy of the situation wasn't lost on me. It was partly my obsessive need to fulfill obligations and partly holding on to the belief that my life had to matter to someone that made me put the pills in my pocket rather than reaching for a glass of water to help swallow them.

Dressed and ready to go, I waited at the house for as long as I could. In the days before cellphones, I had no way to know where or how to reach anyone, so I had no idea where my family was. I could not wait any longer; no one had called; no one had come home, but I had to leave if I was going to make it to the ceremony on time. I drove the ten miles to the university, swerving mindlessly as I felt the bottle of pills in my pocket. I held the wheel loosely as the cars in the nearby lanes honked when I swerved thoughtlessly into their lanes. I didn't care if I crashed.

I didn't want my gloom to make me stand out from everyone else, so as I approached the building and started to encounter my peers lining up, I presented a smiling, problem free persona, as I wandered through the sea of red and blue gowns, scanning the surrounding crowds looking for my family hoping they had planned to meet me near the auditorium. Of course, I was surrounded by plenty of people I knew, people who I had sat next to in class, passed in the halls or performed with onstage, but no one said much more than a cursory, "hello" since they were engrossed in their own little clicks. I stood at the edge of the throng, unable to focus on their social chatter, searching among the crowds and bobbing mortarboards for my six foot four-inch-tall father who usually loomed over a crowd. When the time came, like a robot on cue, I reported to my assigned place in line. Everyone around me was worried about how their cap looked or how it was going to stay on their head. Boys complaining about ties choking them and girls worried about walking in their heels. Random shouts to "turn this way," or "smile" as families all around were capturing Kodak moments. I was a statue in the wave of motion around me in a time lapse photo - mobs of familial paparazzi surrounding us with strobe like flashes. I felt like I was moving in slow motion in the time between flashes. When the music finally started echoing out into the halls, we began our procession into the auditorium. The students in front of me were waving to their friends and family fervently as if they were a departing European immigrant on the deck of ocean liner setting out for the Americas, never to see their family on shore again. As I scanned the faculty seating section, I realized I had known some of these teachers my whole life, and after attending graduation for three years, I knew just where to look to find my father since the coaches always sat in the same place. There, on the end, was the empty seat where my father should have been. I started to scan what I could see of the people seated in the auditorium, since he might be seated with the rest of the family instead. Instead of finding the familiar face I was searching for, all I could discern was a sea of nameless, unknown faces.

One way I am not that different from any other graduates is I cannot remember a thing the speakers said that night, but I am pretty sure everyone around me was having a much better time because occasionally the crowd would burst into laughter. Each time, I would use that commotion to turn around to check to see if my father had taken his seat yet. Every time, no. I began to get nervous, the wetness of my palms starting to imprint on the fabric of my gown. It was time to prepare for our walk across the stage. I took one last glance to his empty seat before we walked backstage. I waited apprehensively for my turn. Before heading out on stage there was a teacher waiting to greet us to make sure we timed our entrances perfectly. I felt embarrassed to ask, but I had to know: "Can you see my father out in the audience?" I did not have to tell her who I meant; everyone knew who I was.

She searched through the audience, and came up with the same inevitable answer, "No, darling." With my heavy sigh, she could hear my heart break.

I walked on stage, passed the drama teacher who had been the most influential teacher to me in my four years. I stood on the huge 'X' marked on the floor and trembling, stared blindly into the audience. His familiar voice rang out, "Elizabeth Hunt. National Honor Society. Sterling Scholar State Finalist." In the awkward, ensuing silence, I heard a man cough in the balcony. No one clapped. No one yelled - not even previous band or choir peers. Not even an obligatory clap from teacher. It felt like a walk to the electric chair, a "last mile" as I turned to walk across the stage - in silence - to shake hands with the principal and all the other dignitaries. Unconsciously, we exchanged courtesies. The only thing I was aware of at that moment was trying very hard to hold up the appearances that all was well, trying not to cry or completely collapse in front of an auditorium of strangers under the weakness I felt rushing over my body. Staring at the ground, I forced my feet to propel me forward to my seat. I sat there, face forward, staring intentionally at nothing but the lights on the ceiling. The harsh theater lights burning my irises. Finally, the moment came when all the grads threw their caps in the air - that was the moment I would be able to finally go find my father - to run to his comforting arms and find out this was all a bad dream and he had just sat in a different seat since he had come late.

It was the coaches' jobs to collect the fake diploma they handed us on stage and to hand out the real ones when we returned our gowns, so the second those caps went flying into the air, I went flying out of the building to where the coaches would be waiting. I did not see my father, but maybe he had gone to the bathroom, after all, I was rushing out of the building before the caps even hit the ground and was the first one to arrive. "Have you seen my father at all tonight? Did he mention anything about what his plans were to you?"

Uncomfortably looking around at each other, hearing the devastating heartbreak in my voice, one of them bravely spoke up using the most solemn tone I had ever heard, "No, Elizabeth." There was an awkward moment of shared silence as I handed them my gown and they handed me my diploma. As I turned and walked away, I could feel their pitiful looks resting on me as the mob of students rushed passed me, jostling me out of the way as they crowded their way toward the tables. The coaches felt sorry for me – even they didn't understand why my father wasn't there. "How could he do that?" I heard above the din as I walked away.

Walking sullenly back into the lobby of the auditorium, I climbed half way up the staircase leading to the balcony. I sat alone on the stairs and watched the sea of mingling people yelling and crying out in exhilaration. Cameras were flashing, flowers were getting squished and balloons were popping, and there I sat, a lone spectator. No one greeted me, no one waved to me, no one hugged me, no one took my picture. It might as well have never happened.

No matter how hard I tried, I just couldn't stop them anymore. The tears began to roll down my face. Even though no one had noticed I was there, I could not let myself be noticed now, so I fled. I had to get away before the tears became a flood. It wasn't enough to find a corner to hide in. I couldn't even stand to be in the same building. I had to escape the happy, giggling, ecstatic sounds. I ran to the first dark corner of the first open building I came to when the dam finally broke. I was crying so hard I was convulsing and gasping for breath. I don't know how long I was there, but eventually the lights in the building started turning off one by one because, of course, no one knew I was there.

As I started to walk back to the auditorium, just like it does in the climax of every sappy movie, it had begun to rain. While rain had been forecast for the evening, I didn't have a coat or umbrella, and the gentleness of the rain somehow felt comforting, so I didn't try to run or cover my head. I embraced the rain as it surrounded and enfolded me like a welcomed friend. Walking slowly, I allowed the rain to drench every fiber of my being. By the time I had returned to the auditorium there were only a few stragglers still clearing the building. If they happened to notice me, they wouldn't have been able to tell that I had been crying, every part of me was wet. It felt as if the rain was there just for me, warming and consoling me. It was dark, cloudy and cold, and I was probably the only person that night who appreciated it. It was raining on everyone else's party for a change, not mine.

My big night, my big rite of passage was over and I had spent the entire day alone. As I got in the car, I remembered the pills. When I arrived at the auditorium, I had taken them out of my pocket and left them on the seat in the car, and there they were blatantly staring at me. They were calling me, challenging me to take them. I stood in the rain with the car door open, staring at them, realizing I could have taken them. No one would have noticed. There was no longer any justification for not taking them. I don't know how long I stood there supporting myself on the door, trying to find a reason to ignore their call before the despondency overwhelmed me and I just *picked up the bottle and got in. Once I was closed in the car the with them, the pills seemed to scream louder to me, "Just take me now and all the pain goes away. You'll never have to remember any of this. You'll never have to see any of them again. Take me now and no one will ever hurt you again. No one cares about you. No one cares what you do. No one will miss you when you are gone. Look around, no one is here for you now. Just take me now and all of this just goes away."*

It sounded so good. Never having to be hurt or alone again. If only I had something to wash them down, but then a little voice deep inside would argue, "No. It just can't be true. You must matter to someone. Someone has to care. You don't know what happened. What if something bad happened? What if there was an accident?"

I shook my head hoping to clear all the negative thoughts. Yes. What if there was an accident? That would explain things. Trembling, I started the engine to my car. I didn't need the pills - just reckless driving in the rain. I moved down the road, water inundating my windshield with splashes caused by the cars rushing passed, annoyed by my pace. I was enjoying the gentle rhythm of the wipers. They seemed to be washing my life away for me right in front of my eyes.

The car seemed to drive its self. It arrived in front of my house from its own memory. It had to be at least eleven o'clock; usually everyone had gone to bed by now, yet all the lights in my house appeared to still be on. Based on the subtle shadows of movement, I could tell people were still up. The dog had heard me pull up. I could hear his barking from the curb. I couldn't hide out in the car. He had given my presence away. Checking the mirror, I made my wet wreck of a self as presentable as I could. If no surprise accident had befallen any of them, my illusionary act of happiness as I walked into the house would be the only way to hide to the pain. There was no way I wanted them to see the hurt they inflicted on my heart. I opened the door to the house and waited for the response. "Hon, is that you?" Instantly followed by a babbling of excuses, "Hey, I am really sorry I could not make it, but I got sick. You know how it is. You understand." Following his voice, I entered the living room to find my father sitting in his big Laz-y-Boy recliner, a thirty-two-ounce cup of Mountain Dew in his hand and my twenty-two-year-old stepbrother lying on the floor holding the dog at bay with his girlfriend at his side. My step-mother came around the corner from the kitchen and handed my father a toasted BLT sandwich. "Do you want one?" she asked.

"No, thank-you."

"So how was it?" he asked, as he took a bite of his sandwich, the sound of crunching toast and crisp lettuce cutting through the air as a glob of tomato seeds dropped onto the plate.

"Fine. The most interesting graduation I have attended," I said as I turned and walked into my room and locked myself inside. No hugs, no presents, no congratulations, no balloons, no cake, no flowers, just a sandwich and a poor excuse. I might have been able to accept his story if only his apparent lie had been even a little believable. I had gotten home in the early afternoon and was home most of the day. If he had been so sick all day, where had he been all day? I am sure his administrators would have let him come home so he could gather the strength to come see his baby daughter, "his" only child, achieve the noble rite of passage his career was based on. I mean, if he was so sick, how could he go to work all day and still be up at eleven, happily socializing with the rest of the family while having a late-night snack? When I am sick enough to miss important commitments, I am curled up alone in my dark room, restlessly trying to sleep due to medication and exhaustion, unable to eat with a pot at my side because I can't keep anything down.

I kind of paused for a moment, digesting his excuse, waiting for someone in the room to ask me why I thought the graduation was so interesting, but the moment passed and as I turned to leave the room my step-brother began to talk about his day like there was nothing different about this day than there was any other day, and for him I guess that was true.

I made my way to my room, put the bottle of pills on the dresser, sat on my bed and stared at them. My family had no clue what I had felt or gone through that day and they never would. Their lives that day went on unchanged – just another day, yet mine changed forever. I learned to never count on anyone, even family, to ever be there to support you. I learned that you need to do things for yourself in life because no one else cares about what you do. In the end, your accomplishments mean nothing, and no one will remember them, but also I gained an immeasurable amount of strength that day knowing that I can survive irreparable pain. Like most graduates, I began a new life that day, but unlike most graduates, I didn't leave high school with the optimism and happiness (or even the fear or dread) of finally beginning my life path. I left knowing that it doesn't matter what I feel because there is no purpose or meaning in life because no one cares what you do and in the end no one will remember. You just have to put one foot in front of the other and keep going whether you want to or not. I put the bottle of pills on my dresser and got ready for bed. I had eight hours before my final exams in the morning and needed to rest.

By the time we got to the end of the story, students were squirming in their seats. A few had puffy red eyes. I had clearly touched a nerve with a few of them, but then I dropped the bombshell.

"Did you notice who the author was?"

"No, there isn't one listed."

"Nope. That's because I wrote it. It is my own story about my own graduation."

Silence fell over the room; suddenly students averted their eyes and looked at their desks. The reality of what I just shared with them began to sink in. Students never seem to look at teachers and consider the fact they are actually human. They can't imagine their teachers shopping, socializing, or doing anything outside of a school building. They don't remember we were once in their shoes and lived through some of the same experiences. They don't think we have bad days or rough times. We are trained not to bring our personal lives into the classroom, so they don't see us as feeling human beings. Since I was willing to share this emotional experience with them, it seemed to suddenly open their eyes to make me real to them. Some of them stared at me in awe realizing many of their assumptions about me were completely false. I was not the happy-go-lucky, optimistic, light hearted teacher they thought they knew. There was darkness lurking under the surface.

I wondered if this one story could seem to have such a profound impact, what would happen if they knew the rest? With a flair for the dramatic, timed perfectly for the bell, I said, "Remember to be aware of those around you; remember it's all about to change; remember to savor the moment of your friends and loved ones now. Remember that each person has a story and don't be too quick to judge. Have empathy for others. These are the greatest lessons I can teach you."

BRIIINGGG... on the end of my words the bell rang. After a normal lesson when I think we have had life altering discussions, my heart always dropped when the bell would ring and the entire demeanor in the classroom would instantly change back to focusing on the teenage social life like the profound thing I had just taught never happened, but in what seemed like a whole new level of respect, this day, the students filed quietly out of the room.

A few days later my principal asked me to come to her office. Any time your boss calls you into the office there is a moment of fear that strikes when they ask you to close the door behind you.

"Have a seat, Elizabeth. How are you?"

Sitting awkwardly, I mumble, "Fine."

"Great. Well, I called you in today because I have just had a very unique experience. In the ten plus years I have been an administrator, I have never once had students come in and specifically request a speaker for graduation."

In my head, I am thinking, "Okay, so what does this have to do with me?"

"Elizabeth, did you share a story with your students about your own graduation?"

I cautiously answer yes because now the idea behind the meeting was beginning to take shape. She wanted to talk about the story, but I still didn't understand what that had to do with a graduation speaker. Was I in trouble or not? Had sharing my story gone too far?

"Well, your students were so moved by that story, that they came to me asked if you would be one of the speakers at graduation."

I didn't respond. In the span of a few seconds, multiple thoughts raced through my mind. "Wow, my students were really moved? Thank God I am not in trouble. No way I will speak at graduation! Speaking at graduation would be interesting. I wonder what they think I would say? Was this just their pity?"

"Um...," was the only thing that came out of my mouth.

"You should feel honored that the students like you enough and respect you enough that they made this request, and it says something about you as a teacher that you have been able to connect with your students so well, but don't worry."

It was hard to concentrate on her words, until she said, "But."

"But? There is a but?"

"But we have already arranged for all our speakers this year, so instead the students agreed that they would be happy just to have you read their names as they cross and maybe you can give a speech next year." Wow, okay. Reading names? That is not nearly as scary as an actual speech. No problem. I had a whole year to worry about a speech, but l didn't know then, that there wouldn't be a next year at that school.

I left her office feeling like I had just run the gauntlet having gone through so many emotions in such a compact period of time, finally settling with gratitude because my administrator felt I had been able to have such a strong, positive, impact on the lives of my students.

CHAPTER 2

There were nights I remember sitting in bed with my husband and wondering how I would find out that my mother had died. I always wondered who the person would be to call me. My mom was a single lady who lived alone, 400 miles away and had very few friends. I always thought that some day when I was old, I would get a phone call from some stranger that would tell me my mother had been in the hospital for some time and had just lost her battle with...*fill in the blank with your choice of illness.*

How would I feel when I finally heard the news? My mother and I had a very strained relationship. To say we didn't get along would be an understatement, so I wondered how I would react. As a college student, when family called to tell me her father had died, I crumpled into a ball on the floor, sobbing, unable to respond to the person on the other end of the phone line. Would I cry like that for my mother?

But then it happened. One Sunday night in May, I had gone to bed and was sleeping soundly when the phone rang about eleven forty-five. The caller ID read LVPD. My mother wasn't the only person I knew in Las Vegas at the time, but even before I heard the voice on the other end of the line, I knew it would be about her. In that split second before the officer began to speak, my mind instantly assumed she must have been in a car accident coming home from somewhere – not what was coming next.

"Hello. Are you Elizabeth Mackie?"

"Yes."

"Are you the daughter of Joy Wexler?"

"Yes."

"This is Mr. Hendricks from the Las Vegas Coroner's office. I hate to be the one to tell you this, but we were called to do a welfare check on your mother's home and when we went in, we found her lying at the bottom of the stairs. It appears she has been dead for quite some time."

Woken up from a sound sleep to that? My mind went blank. It took me a few moments to process what had been said. I sat stunned – frozen – without any emotion at all. There was no overwhelming wave of grief; there weren't tears or gasps of shock – just silence. After what seemed like a few minutes, I remembered there was someone on the other end of the line waiting for a response. Clearly the officer had experience delivering this kind of news since he patiently waited. I blurted out the first thing that came to my mind.

"Did it appear to be natural causes?"

Who knows what would cause a 65-year-old woman to be found at the bottom of the stairs? A simple slip and fall? A sudden heart attack? A violent intruder?

"Well, Mrs. Mackie, that is what we wanted to talk to you about. How was your mother's mental health?"

Ah! Those words told me everything I needed to know. Without him actually saying it, I instantly knew what had happened.

I explained to the officer, "She has tried to kill herself before, a few years back and the last time we talked she was very distraught over having to put her dog to sleep."

At this point the coroner proceeds to tell me about the nervous church friend who called the police to have them check on my mother. She had known about my mother being depressed about her dog being put to sleep but hadn't spoken to her in a while and hadn't gotten my mother to answer the door or phone in a few weeks. The church friend was the one who told the officers to locate me. Then he went on to tell me about the huge, mostly empty bottle of vodka they found in the fridge and enormous array of empty pill bottles found on the counter. They would do medical tests to determine cause of death, but all indications pointed to suicide.

We started to talk about the timeline of events of what appeared to have happened and what I needed to take care of as soon as possible. The coroner went on to tell me that according to the decomposition of the body, they felt that she had been dead for possibly six weeks. The church friend said her last contact had been in early April, and the last phone call or email my mother sent appeared to be to me just after my birthday in mid-April, which matched the timeline and implied that she had lain there dead at the bottom of the stairs for six weeks.

Her body was unrecognizable, and although he went into the gory descriptive details about what that meant (and I mean gory), I will spare readers that trauma. Needless to say, they would need to match dental records to officially identify her, then complete an autopsy and toxicology report.

It was all a business-like call telling me where to go to get her stuff and how paperwork would be processed. Since I was the only legal next of kin, it was expected that I come to Vegas to pick up her possessions and take control of the house.

It really was a bit much to absorb in the middle of the night after being woken from a deep sleep, yet my adrenaline was pumping so fast after the call that there was no way to go back to sleep. Being so far away in the middle of the night there was nothing I really could do at that exact moment except wait until morning. Still in shock from the horrific details, I just lay there running through a checklist of everything that needed to happen next. There were still no tears.

My immediate concern was for my students. I was in charge of making the school yearbook. I was teaching at a small private school and we weren't using a professional yearbook company. I was the yearbook company - me and my Microsoft Publisher skills. I had finished all the pages for the book, but still needed it copied, bound, and distributed. Two hundred students' yearbook day would be destroyed if I didn't come through with my commitment. School was out for the summer in four days and the school was officially closing its doors forever, so it had to go home with students before then. Taking time off was not an option. Lack of focus and dedication was not an option. How would I have time to explain everything to the family, get to Vegas and get the yearbook done all at the same time? I had all the files on my computer and still had to find the easiest method of getting the book copied and bound because my vision for the book was more than simply using cheap photocopy paper from the teacher workroom. I wasn't going to sacrifice my vision and the quality of the book for two hundred people just because one person they didn't know had died. With all the end of school happenings the other teachers were responsible for, I felt like I couldn't ask anyone else to add more things to their plate. Besides, I was the computer teacher and only took the job after seeing how little the rest of the staff knew about working with computers. I was the only one with the knowledge to complete the project. Explaining to anyone where everything was and how to put it together would take just as much time as just doing it myself. I had to put on the optimistically happy mask of teacherhood and get the job done regardless what was going on in my life outside the school walls.

When the rest of the household woke up, I followed all the normal routines. I took the children to school and then went promptly to my grandmother's care facility. She and I were the only two of the immediate family left within a fifty-mile radius of where my mother had grown up. As a result, even though I was in my early thirties, I had been the one called on to take care of my grandmother the last ten years of her life. My grandmother had just turned 90, and recently the calls I received to assist in her care because she had fallen, or needed special supplies from the grocery, or a driver to the doctor were happening more and more frequently. I felt I was spending as much time caring for her as I was my own four young children; however, at her age, I had been steeling myself for her death, and now I had to sit her down and tell her about her daughter's death. I didn't go into the gory details with her either, but I told her upfront about the pills and alcohol and the idea it was potentially a suicide. Knowing how she felt about suicide, I tried to ease the blow by explaining we would have to wait for the coroner's report for confirmation, and until then nothing could really be confirmed. My grandmother reacted just like I did. She didn't seem surprised, nor did she break down into tears. Her first-born child had just passed away and her first reaction was to blame herself. She calmly said it was her fault and that she had caused it because they hadn't spoken for the last eight years.

I can't remember exactly what had caused this particular family rift. After all, there was always some kind of rift over something, and I never knew exactly who was speaking to whom at any given time, but eight years ago my grandfather had died. There were differences in opinion over the quality of his care after he slipped and broke his hip and differing opinions in regard to handling his funeral. My grandfather and one of their daughters were Catholic, and my grandmother, my mother and her brother were members of the Church of Jesus Christ of Latter-Day Saints (L.D.S.). It was my Aunt Lydia, the youngest child, the Catholic one, and the one who lived the closest, and who had the closest relationship with her parents, who had helped her mother throughout that difficult last year of my grandpa's life. Aunt Lydia had never really known my mother very well. My mother was sixteen years older than Lydia and had moved out of the house by the time Lydia was five years old. The older, stable, well-established couple who raised Lydia, was not the same young, insecure, abusive couple that raised my mother. The differences in the realities of growing up for these siblings created a completely different world for each of them – a world that made it very hard for one sister to understand the other.

My grandfather had fallen and slipped on the ice one winter and never fully recovered. Arguments as to *how* he was cared for, *where* he was cared for, and *when* he was cared for were just the beginning of the family falling apart. Next it devolved into *who* was to be told about his impending death and *when*, and *who* was allowed to visit and *when*. These were all big bones of contention between my mother and everyone else. Arguments over who presided over the funeral, who could attend the funeral, who dedicated the grave and where the family would be served a meal afterward were intense. Everyone knew the stubborn difficulties my mother would cause, and so they tried to leave her out of the loop all along the way which only served to make things worse when she found out. Even though she had barely had a relationship with her parents since she had moved out thirty years before, my mother still felt she knew best how everything should be done because she was the oldest. She expected everyone to defer to her, and that wasn't how things went. Rather than helping my grandmother and trying to make things pleasant for everyone in that challenging time, all my mother did was add tension and strife. My grandmother didn't handle her husband's death well. Time never healed the wound of her loss, and the family never got over the difficulties my mother caused during that time.

My grandmother felt that because of my mother's death she was being punished and said the idea that my mother had potentially committed suicide would be a family embarrassment. She went into full denial, refusing to believe that the police had found large empty bottles of vodka around the house. Her denial didn't surprise me. I had tried to tell her for years that I knew my mother was an alcoholic and how she had bottles hidden all over the house, but no one in the family ever believed their faithful daughter/sister/niece/cousin would drink since it was such a sin within The Church. Since it was easy for my grandmother to deny that my mother might have been drinking alcohol before she died, it was just as easy for her to deny that she intentionally took every pill in the house as the coroner had implied. "If she had died because of an overdose, it must have been a mistake of mixing pills she shouldn't have," but even that wasn't the story I was allowed to tell the rest of the family. I was expected to say: "The reason for her death was inconclusive."

After we talked, I waited while my grandmother called Lydia. She lived an hour away, but she immediately took the day off work and drove up to meet us. It was clear Lydia had been on the phone during her whole drive up because it wasn't long after we ended the call with her before our phones began to ring. As soon as we would end one call, our phones would ring again. News was spreading through the family. Everyone wanted details, but the reality was, other than the part grandma didn't want me telling everyone - there were no details. No one knew when it happened or how it happened or why it happened. It just happened.

There is a standard manner of death that seems easier to accept. Someone either has a tragic sudden accident or they are under a doctor's care and they pass away. For either of those ways the body gets released to the funeral home and the funeral is usually planned within a week or so. Deaths that occur where the person needs to be identified and an autopsy is required to determine the cause of death take a lot longer. Everyone calling wanted to know when the funeral was going to be and trying to explain that there was no way any kind of timeline could be provided made people abrasive. After all, how were they expected to make plans?

At the time, The Church of Jesus Christ of Latter-Day Saints strongly discouraged cremation since they believe the body will be resurrected at the second coming. Trying to explain that the coroner would not even let me look at my mother's body because of its horrendous condition which meant no open casket was possible because there could be no embalming to preserve the body because it had already decomposed so badly, making cremation the only option was not something family members could understand. (Besides, transporting ashes across the state line is much easier than transporting a body across state lines. Strange little things like that are learned in strange events like these.)

It was disturbing that my grandmother and aunt didn't want to talk about the reality that there were alcohol and pills found near my mother's body. My grandmother and aunt seemed embarrassed, like my mother's suicide would put a black mark on them. Rather than trying to understand the reason why my mother might have done this, they were more worried about how other people would judge them. Neither of them had spoken to her in eight years, so I couldn't understand why either of them thought it had anything to do with them. Their reaction seemed exceptionally self-centered. Maybe it was because they felt responsible, like they hadn't done enough for her because they hadn't talked to her in eight years, but I had maintained my relationship with my mother – at least superficially – throughout my whole life. I understood exactly why they had stopped talking to her because I knew my mother had always been a mentally unstable woman. Her taking her life was more a reflection of her mental instability. Living with her as her daughter made the mental illness easy for me to see, but just like the alcoholism, no one else in the family ever believed me when I tried to tell them.

I knew exactly why the rest of the family had stopped talking to her and I didn't fault them for it. My mother was a very abrasive person, who was exceptionally difficult to get along with. She always had to be the center of attention. She always had to be the best one in the group. She always had to be the one who knew more than everyone else. She was always right. Everyone was expected to worship at her awesomeness, and as a result she was cruel to every person she encountered because no one could worship her to her liking. At some point, you had to draw a line to protect yourself. I understood that better than anyone.

In order to protect myself, I had left her when I was a teenager to live with my father. No one in the family would believe the stories I told about our life together, but eventually my father could no longer deny that I needed help. To everyone else in the family, I was a precious gift given to my mother that she had wanted her whole life. To everyone else, everything she did, she did for me. To everyone else in the family, my mother was to be honored and respected by me just because she chose to be my mother. To everyone else in the family, I was the disrespectful problem child who ungratefully left her. Everyone else refused to see the alcoholism and abuse I suffered from her for years.

I hated this woman people called my mother. More precisely, I hated the woman who raised me as her daughter because she wasn't my mother. I was adopted. But in the cultural belief in the religion in which I was raised, motherhood is the entire purpose and meaning of life for women. Motherhood is placed on a pedestal and it assumes all mothers are full of an endless, undying, unconditional love for their children. 'Families are forever' and 'there is beauty all around when there is love at home.' Honoring your mother is a commandment. Hating your mother really wasn't an allowable option. If you tell people you hate your mother, they treat you like a pariah. "If you don't love your mother, the problem must be with you. You must be cruel and heartless - not your mother." It didn't matter how much she drank or how many times I was beaten or thrown out of the house. I was the cruel one.

My whole life I agonized over what I should do for her for holidays and special occasions. It felt like sending gifts to an abusive jailer after being released from prison. Yet, every year my father (adoptive) convinced me to send her a present, telling me it was the right thing to do just because she was my mother. One year when money was tight, I made her embellished wooden blocks. I individually cut, stained, decoupaged, and bedecked them. On each block, I pasted a letter of her last name (W-E-X-L-E-R) to use as decorations for her house. Wooden blocks for decorations like that were all the rage at the time around where I lived. After receiving the present, she didn't talk to me for months afterwards, so I knew I had done something to offend her. When we finally did talk, she said, "What kind of junk are you sending me? Crappy wood blocks with random letters? Are you *trying* to be insulting?" When I explained that I had handmade the blocks and they spelled her last name, she finally understood the gift, but she had spent months harboring anger against me because she didn't "get" the gift, thinking I had sent her junk. Apparently, as a working adult, giving homemade gifts was unacceptable. I thought the gift was thoughtful and well-intentioned considering what I could afford as a recent college graduate, but her misunderstanding was my fault because I didn't include a note to explain what the blocks were. I didn't think it would be that difficult to figure out. The blocks were all the rage where she lived too. After all, how many words would she know with an 'X' in them? But that's just how it was with her. I never knew when something would set her off. The only safe thing to do was keep your distance. Most people won't willingly walk across a mine field – even with protection - but any interaction with her was always like walking over a minefield. You never knew when your body would be blown to smithereens. Every choice of your appearance, every word spoken, every movement of your body could incite an explosion at any minute and you rarely saw it coming.

Every adult in my life had told me for years that regardless how I felt, I shouldn't cut my mother out of my life, "because she was my mother," so I had to learn how to accept her insulting and unpredictable behavior. I learned how to attempt to side-step the mines, and if forced, how to pick my battles carefully so the least amount of damage would be done by the flying shrapnel. But after all those lectures and long nights of telling me not to cut my mother off, they all ended up being hypocritical because in the end everyone else in the family did totally cut her out of their lives.

Her birthday was in March and that last year of her life, I had gone through the usual dilemma. Do I send a gift or not? We had not gotten along for a while, so I decided not to. A month later was my birthday and she sent me some flowers. It was an impersonal gift with a simple card saying, "Love, Mom." The impersonal-ness of it made me feel it was not worthy of opening up the lines of communication to call and thank her. If she knew me, she would know that I think flowers are a stupid gift, since all they do is die in a week. But she doesn't know me and when I didn't acknowledge the gift, she sent me an email to see if I got them and I replied with a simple, "Yes." I didn't say thank you. I wasn't thankful. Most of my childhood she had forced me to say things I didn't believe. Not letting me go to bed at night before telling her I loved her after she had added new bruises to my backside is a good example, so as an adult I tried to refuse to say things I didn't believe. I didn't want the flowers and I didn't want to talk to her, but that didn't stop her from reaching out to reprimand me for not treating someone who had given me a gift more kindly, berating me for not gushing about how beautiful or wonderful they were. She was oblivious to the hypocritical nature of it all. I knew this point was lost on her and I knew this would blow completely out of control, and she wouldn't let it go if I didn't write back and just bend the knee with humbleness and apologize for my inequities and poor judgement. For the sake of being able to back her down from a nuclear explosion and maintain the relationship, I conceded.

To give her my humility, that she didn't deserve, as a method to keep the peace was normal:

Mom,

I sincerely apologize for not acknowledging the beautiful flowers you sent me. I appreciate the thoughtfulness, time and effort you took to recognize my birthday. I promise that in the future I will try to do a better job of being more respectful. Again, I apologize.

Love,

Elizabeth

Just another time I had capitulated to her in an effort to keep the peace, only to have my efforts thrown back in my face.

Elizabeth,

I'm sure you don't give a "rat's ass," but I'm going to tell you anyway. I had to put Emily to sleep yesterday--one of the saddest of my days. She had Cushing's Disease the last three years that eventually led to liver failure. She was suffering so, but it still was one of the hardest decisions in my life to have had to have made. I should have done this months ago, but I was selfishly holding on to her for as long as I could. She was truly my best friend and she went with me through some of the hardest times of my life. She was just barely 13 years old. Being unreasonable about this, of course, I wanted her to live forever.

Love and enjoy your pets every day. They are truly the only ones that love you unconditionally and will always be loyal to you regardless of what life throws at you. They offer you the purest of love!"

How do I respond to that? "*I know you don't give a 'rat's ass.*" Without those words, the letter could seem like caring and thoughtful advice, but those words speak more volumes in defining the tone and meaning behind all the rest. Those aren't the words of a Hallmark card type of mother. That is not how a kind, gracious, 'there is beauty all around' mother, opens a letter! If she really thinks I won't care, then why is she bothering to tell me? Everything else after those words is nothing more than manipulation. Manipulation to get me to drop everything and turn all my focus to her so she can wail and cry about her sad and horrible life. Losing a pet is sad, but it isn't the worst thing in the world. Pets tend to be more replaceable than people. I realize that is exceptionally harsh, but it is still true. If my Labrador Retriever dies, I can go to a breeder the next day and get another one who looks just like my old one and is likely to love me just the same. If my husband dies, I can't go the husband store and get another one that looks just like him. Therefore, her subtle digs about only a pet being loving and loyal seemed a bit obtuse. Did she really not see that I would see those words as insults about our relationship? How could she think they would endear me to her? Almost every line of her letter read as an insult but, sadly, years of experience had taught me she didn't see anything about what she wrote to be insulting at all.

I mean, putting a dog down was really the hardest decision of her life? Harder than choosing to adopt a child? Harder than walking out on three husbands? Harder than moving across country twice? Harder than...I could go on and on. And this dog had apparently gone through the hardest times of her life. Really? She didn't get that dog until years after I left - so forced infertility while in the midst of miscarriage, adopting a child, two divorces, a husband's cancer and my running away were apparently a breeze compared to what she had gone through the last few years. Granted, she went through another divorce (to a man she had only been married to for a year) and was forced to retire due to her ethical misconduct, and had her fair share of financial and health problems she brought on herself, but by saying those years were harder than the life she put me through? I just couldn't believe it. The level of obtuseness in her words was too much for me. I got it; the dog meant more to her than me. I was replaced by a dog. A dog who was loving and loyal, and I was not.

I traumatized over how to respond to this email for a week. I talked to my husband, my friends, my mother-in-law, my father and step-mother, all for advice on how I should respond. I was sad about the dog; I love animals. I have a veritable zoo at my house, but it is just a dog – a dog that I had no personal relationship with, but her opening line was a clear challenge for me to respond, so I had to. After years and years, I was tired of this constant, even if subtle denigration. Dr. Phil says, "teach people how to treat you." If I allowed her to insult me, especially because she was unaware she was doing it, she would just keep doing it. Not telling her how inappropriate and unappreciated it was, would just give her permission to do it over and over again. This was my response:

"I am sorry you had to put your dog to sleep, but I really do not appreciate the tone with which the email started. If you eventually want to build a relationship with me, that is not the way to go about it. Again, sorry about Emily."

It was honest, short and mostly to the point. She would never see the insults in her comments, so there was no point in saying anything about those. The response that she sent me next, for all that anyone can tell was her last communication with another human being – ever. It essentially was her suicide note:

"Since I appear to be the only one trying in this relationship, it seems a funny thing for you to remark on how I started my sentence. You have never given me a reason to see you in a different way. I never and I mean never see your efforts. Why should I respect you? I guess you think you are owed it, but those days are gone. If you can muster yourself to do so, give my grandchildren my best!"

Maybe I should have just ignored her like everyone else had because, apparently, defining how I would like to be treated in a relationship is not making an effort to have a relationship. I should have known it didn't matter what I said or did because unless it was doing and saying what she wanted me to say, the way she wanted me to say it, I wasn't doing it right. She didn't see that the mere fact I was still talking to her (unlike everyone else) as effort, so from her perspective, she was right. She couldn't see that my detachment was a direct result of the way I was raised by her. Yes, I never went out of my way to initiate interaction; however, I never denied her anything. If she wanted to see her grandkids, I never told her no, but she would get all bent out of shape because I never invited her over or went to visit her. I didn't invite her because I didn't want her toxicity around my children. Every time she was around, the world exploded.

She saw the world the way she wanted to see it and it only revolved around her. She clearly didn't see the hypocrisy with her comment about respect. She expected me to respect and love her unconditionally, just because she was my mother, but apparently, it was wrong of me to expect the same treatment from her just because I was her daughter or even better just because I was a person.

As a school teacher, I firmly believe in trying to show respect to everyone, regardless of their age. It is one of things that has always made me a good teacher – a teacher that students want to have. When you walk into my classroom, you have my respect; you don't have to earn it. You can lose my respect because I can't respect someone who lies, cheats, or hurts others. As long as you are good person, with some sense of personal integrity, I have no problems. But my mother was not a good person at heart. She lost my respect, and she needed to earn it back.

She never once thought she was to blame for any of things that happened between us. She never apologized for the hurtful things she did to me. She was always without fault and I was always reminded that I was the compulsively lying, problem child. Our relationship was the classic definition of irreconcilable differences. From years of communications like those emails, I knew there was nothing I could say that would help her to see where the faults in her argument were, so I didn't respond to her last email. There was no point. There was no convincing her I was not the horrible monster she made me out to be. Everyone else in her world was always the horrible monster. The fact I was the only person left in the world that still talked to her, and the effort I had made to try to move our relationship in a more positive direction by trying to show her a better way to communicate with me was completely lost on her.

Then the phone call from the police came, and the timeline indicated that her demise came shortly after that last email. Apparently, my last email was so insulting to her that it was worthy of causing her death. It felt like my mother was still trying to lash out and punish me for not doing all the things she wanted. She was the poor, picked on, unloved mother. It reminds me of the scene in *To Kill a Mockingbird*, when after being disciplined by Calpurnia, young Scout throws a childish tantrum and says, "One of these days when she isn't looking, I'll go off drown myself in Barker's Eddy and then she'll be sorry." The only problem was, I wasn't sorry.

Monday, I had stayed home from work to talk to the family. Tuesday and Wednesday, I went to work scrambling to put the finishing touches on the yearbook. While it was quite stressful, I was able to get it done without too many complications. As people witnessed me running around, they always responded with extreme empathy and concern, always with the assumption that my mother and I had a loving close relationship. People all around me were amazed at "how well I seemed to be holding it together." I never knew quite what to say. Explaining our relationship or explaining how she died was more than a casual conversation could handle. I appeared strong because there wasn't a great sense of sadness, besides I consider my ability to wear the happy, optimistic teacher mask to be quite stellar. It has been a required skill for my survival since early childhood – putting my feelings and my pain aside and convincing others that my life was okay, putting on an act for others, smiling, signing yearbooks, and saying good-bye to the staff and the school that had been a large part of my family's life for the last five years.

I was overwhelmed by the estate work I would now have to do, but it had to get done and I was the only one to do it, so it wasn't like I had a choice in the matter. Besides taking care of what the coroner told me, I had to go to Vegas to look for a will. My grandmother thought she had a copy, but we couldn't find one. My great aunt thought she had one, but she only had a few written directions for a funeral.

As I began to make my travel arrangements, I learned my mother's third ex-husband's name was listed on her mortgage as joint tenant and therefore the house immediately became his. Quite a few of my family members recommended that I should not call him for a couple of weeks until we could get things settled. I didn't think that was fair and felt he had a right to know. He lived in Wisconsin and after I called, he immediately made plans to get to Vegas.

Unbeknownst to me, he and my mother had been in a legal battle for the last four years. When I told him my mother died, he told me that not only the house but everything in it now belonged to him. I knew there was very little in the house I really wanted, but everything? I was the one the police were planning to give the house keys to, so it seemed there was now a race between the two of us to see which one of us could get to the house first to claim anything in it.

My mother had married this man, Jeff, three years after I had left her. I had only met him a couple of times. Apparently, after the marriage, she felt she had been misled and he didn't turn out to be the man she thought. She wanted out, so they divorced after a year. Even as cruel as my mother could be, he still loved her. She knew it and took advantage of him. While my mother and he were married, she owned the house outright with only her name on the mortgage. Several years after the divorce she was having financial difficulties (as she always did every few years, and typically grandma and grandpa would bail her out, but when grandpa died there would be no more bailouts.) With nowhere else to turn, every few years or so she went to Jeff for money and he gave it to her. Jeff got smart fast and learned that she was never going to pay any of this money back, so he finally asked for a deal and my mother was so desperate she agreed. She agreed to put his name on the house. If she ever sold it, he would get half the money and if she died it would become his. When he put his name on the house her expectation was that he was also supposed to help her with the upkeep and maintenance. The demands my mother made were way beyond normal maintenance like having high security, rolling metal screens installed on all the windows – better security windows than I have seen at most banks. She had designs to knock down the garage wall and add new rooms to the house, but Jeff drew the line and said enough was enough and he wanted out. Even he didn't want to deal with her level of crazy on a regular basis. That is where the battle began. He told her she could buy him out of his half of the house or he was going to force her to sell it. She didn't have the money to buy him out. The only person who had that kind of money was my grandmother, but she and my mother hadn't gotten along in years, so Jeff went to my grandmother himself and asked her to buy her daughter's portion, using every ounce of guilt he could try telling her he "didn't want to put her out on the street or make her homeless, but..." Grandmother wouldn't budge. If it meant Joy had to sell the house and live in an apartment then so be it, so the court battle between Jeff and my mother began. It was nothing more than a feeble attempt to delay the impending eviction and considering how important appearances and money were to her, she couldn't face it.

In the meantime, one of her toilets quit working. One of the sons of my great aunt happened to work for a toilet company that happened to be in town doing a trade show, and he had a new toilet installed in her house. Unfortunately, they never spoke again, because there were problems with that toilet over flowing. When the problem ended up flooding the entire main floor, she blamed them personally and never spoke to that family again. The crew that came in to look at it drilled multiple drainage holes in the walls and ripped parts of the ceiling and baseboards off. Although this was a legitimate home improvement issue, by this time Jeff didn't care and had no intention of paying to fix it. My mother was always immaculate in her house cleaning and the appearance of her house. You would think that having huge chunks of her main living space torn up would be something she could not let go without fixing, but she was so stubborn about it being something that Jeff needed to pay for that she refused to fix it. In that respect, my mother got him back after her death because now he was left with a destroyed house that wasn't worth what was still owed on it.

So, I packed up car and drove to Vegas. My first stop was to the police department to collect the keys and my mother's personal possessions. The man who helped me apologized for being impersonal about the conversation, "after all it is Vegas and we have this happen all day long." It was weird to be just another number, but they took me in a room and explained what they do and then brought in her stuff: a few checkbooks, her wallet, a small coin collection, some keys, and all the jewelry they found on her. On the form sitting in front of the officer there was a three-inch red stamp across the form that said, "strong odor." At which point he warned me about the jewelry, since she had been dead for so long by the time she was found the jewelry might still have some of the decomposed skin and a smell. He was right, I could barely open the bag without the wafting smell nearly knocking me over. The smell of death is not something that is easily overcome. We had to sign some legal papers saying I had collected her things, and they sent us on our way.

Pulling into the driveway, the size of the prickly pear cactus in the yard amazed me. When I had lived there, it was a small barrel sized thing, now it was a big as a backyard shed. Its growth was symbolic of the distance that had grown up between my mother and me. Since the police had closed the house, I didn't know what to expect when I walked up to the front door. The door was hidden from view by the cactus. Would there be the yellow crime scene tape like I'd see in all the movies? As I walked around the cactus, I was relieved to not see the large announcement of the yellow tape, but her door was covered with flyers and undelivered mail notices. It had only been three days since I had gotten the midnight call, but it was clear that no one had used the front door to the house in quite some time.

Taking out the keys, I began trying every key in each slot. She had a heavy metal security gate with a bolted lock to get through before the two double locks on the main steal door. There was a tiny bit of trepidation racing through me. Jeff was supposed to be there later that day. What would I do if I couldn't get in? I had tried every key once and wasn't successful at getting all of the locks undone. I took a deep breath and started with the first key again. Luckily, after fiddling with all the locks again, I was able to finally get them all open. I opened the door and was forcibly pushed, stumbling backwards by the tsunami of stench that came pouring out of the house. I had to walk away for a minute or two to prepare myself for what I was about to find. If the smell wafting from the house was that revolting, what was I about to see?

I had been warned at the police station that the smell emanating from the jewelry would also be at the house and would be dramatically worse. In fact, he told me I might want to eat before I went over because I might not be able to eat for the rest of the day. It is a smell that once you have experienced it, you will never forget for the rest of your life. I had been warned about other cases like this, so I had come prepared. I was wearing clothes I planned to throw away at the end of the day and had rubber gloves and a medical mask.

When opening the main door to the house, all I could really see was a small entryway with a wall four feet behind the door. Just in from the front door, I was amazed that the ceiling damage from the flooding toilet had still not been fixed, even though it had been over two years since the last time I was there. I had to walk in around the corner before I could see the rest of the house, but as soon as I turned the corner, I could see everything; the downstairs bathroom, with no door, all the floor molding missing, the living room with animal cages set up in the middle of the floor littered with blankets, food bowls and animal feces (where her dead rabbits had been found) and of course, the bottom of the stairs where she had been found. There was a large black puddle about the size of a large truck tire on the bottom level and more of it on the bottom two steps. I didn't stop to look at it or think about it. I instantly grabbed one of the sheets that had been laid down for the animals and covered the black spot on the floor. All around the house, even in the rooms upstairs, there were large dead flies.

Regardless of the spot and the flies – there was something else that told me my mother had been very sick and not in her right mind - the house was a pig sty. She had always been an obsessive-compulsive clean freak. When I lived with her, I was expected to clean the house to a white glove dust check every weekend of my life. Everything had a place. There was never dust on the furniture or dishes in her sink. There were never bills left on the counter or clothes lying around on the floor. In fact, most of the time her house looked more like a museum than a place where someone actually lived, so when I looked around and saw the mess, I knew she wasn't right. The police had warned me that it was a mess and that they often go in and up-turn things to look for evidence and valuable things, but I knew what I was seeing was not a result of the police. It was something that had taken her months and months to accumulate. There wasn't an inch of the counter that wasn't covered with a dirty dish; there was laundry all over the floor. On the bar, there was a collection of twelve different empty pill bottles. The only thing in the freezer was a huge, almost empty bottle of Vodka, and the only thing in the fridge was a large, overgrown onion, spoiled cottage cheese and a half empty bottle of green olives. Exactly what I remember our fridge being like when she was in her hard-drinking phases.

Upstairs was like walking into a house on an episode of *Hoarders*. I couldn't even walk without stepping on something. There were totes full of books and papers in the hallways, magazines, bills, random papers, clothes, jewelry, dishes and old food everywhere. French fries, drink cups, half eaten hamburgers on her bed, on her nightstand, on the floor -- everywhere. The sheets were off her bed and her bed was half off the bedframe. There were valuable coin collections and jewelry just lying on the floor in the mix of the mess. It was so gross and overwhelming that it was clear the police didn't really spend detailed time really looking for valuables because it would have been impossible to miss some of the obvious stuff lying visible on the floor, but everything seemed to be coated in a layer of dust and bugs and smell. It was like anything you touched was a dirty snot rag from the garbage can and you barely wanted to pinch it with two fingers to pick it up or move it, even with gloves on.

I had less than an hour before the time arranged to meet Jeff. I knew Jeff's name was on the house and it was now legally his, but I still questioned his right to everything else. He could demand the keys and lock me out. Anything that anyone in the family might have wanted from the house without being challenged had to be taken now and had to be small enough to fit into the back of my SUV. There was no way I going to be able to quickly locate anything specifically asked for among the mess, so I just started grabbing things: pictures, art, jewelry, coins. Finding the will suddenly seemed like a daunting task. My great aunt told me it would be under the bed, but with a quick glance I didn't find it there. There were so many papers and so much crap it seemed like finding anything specific was going to be an impossible task.

I had not found the will by the time Jeff showed up. He knew too as soon as he entered the house that my mother had not been well. He was just as disgusted by the sights and smells. He was surprisingly friendly, however. We spent quite a while just talking about things out the driveway where we didn't have to face the horrid reality pouring out from the inside. He didn't want the house. He really wanted someone in the family to just buy him out of his share of the house: $75,000. I didn't have that kind of money, nor could I find it and although grandma had it, she wasn't going to give it to me to buy a wreck of a house that had no value. I didn't know if there was money anywhere in my mother's estate, but if there was, I knew it wouldn't be enough to pay Jeff off. My mother had taken out a second mortgage and still owed more than $100,000. When Jeff and my mother had originally entered into their legal deal, in the mid 1990's they had the house appraised. It appraised for $340,000, but then the world fell apart. 9/11 happened and the stock market crashed, then there was the failure of all the big banks and mortgage companies. The housing market in Vegas took a dive, one of the worst dives in the country. I had a distant step-cousin who worked in real estate in Vegas come in to appraise the house. Considering all the damage from the toilet and the complications from a dead body being there for so long, he didn't think the house could sell for more than $80,000. Leaving Jeff in the hole by a significant amount. There was nothing I could do to help him, so in the end, he had been just as screwed by my mother as the rest of us had been. I felt sorry for him. He now had to take over the mortgage for a house that would do nothing more than suck money out of him.

He didn't think the car was part of the house and agreed that I could take it. He wanted to keep all the furniture in case he wanted to live at the house or rent it out, but he did agree that I could get the piano and a curio and any small mementos that I wanted. I wasn't really prepared in this quick trip to take the car or piano, so this would mean I would have to return to Vegas at a different time, which was unfortunate because I never wanted to go back to that house again.

After we finished talking, Jeff set to work trying to make the car run, while I went through the house again, trying to find the will – which I did - right under the bed where I was told it would be. It was just buried under so much junk and nastiness it was hard to see through everything. Handwritten on the very first page it said to not let Jeff into the house without making him first get court ordered permission. Too late. Even in death she was trying to make this man's life as difficult as possible, as a result, I was glad I called him and was upfront with him from the start. Considering how much he was financially screwed, he ended up being pretty fair and kind. My mother just never understood how fairness and kindness worked.

My mother's will was a handwritten, jumbled mess. She had written things in it, then crossed them out and rewritten it umpteen times. She was trying to control every last thing. She had named my great aunt as the executor of her estate and she had named her ex-boss the receiver of all her government death benefits. So, as her only living heir, the only thing I was left with was the headache of dealing with all of this and whatever Jeff piteously allowed me to take. She had designated who got every individual piece of jewelry (not me). After the itemized stuff she bequeathed to specific people, the rest of her things were to be sold and the money was to go to an animal shelter. But she laid out exactly how the shelter was to spend the money. "It must be used to buy *{this kind}* of doctor with *{this much experience}* to work specifically in *{this room}* with *{these types}* of animals." If they didn't use it exactly as she said, they were not to have it given to them at all.

Half of her itemized belongings she mentioned in the will she no longer even owned. The other half now belonged to Jeff. If there was anything left of any value it would have been used to pay off her enormous debts.

Since the will did not deem me as the executor, I immediately photocopied it and sent it off to my Great Aunt Cheryl – the named executor. It never occurred to me that I could have lied and said I never found it. Just like I couldn't imagine not telling Jeff in a timely manner, regardless of what my mother accused me of, my brain just doesn't work in that kind of manipulative manner. I didn't see a reason to lie. It didn't really matter what the will said since most of it inaccurately assumed she owned stuff she did not. The irony was when I talked to my great aunt (the mother of the toilet bowl salesman) she told me about the toilet fiasco and how she hadn't spoken to my mother since. This made it clear to me that I was the only person left in the family my mother actually had any contact with in the last four years. Everyone else had cut her out, yet I was the one left completely out her will. She left nothing to me.

One of the first things I learned was that as a government worker her whole life, she should have had a large retirement package and that package should pay for all the costs of her burial. It turns out she left the money from that retirement package to her ex-boss – who, I learned upon talking with him, had a falling out with her four years ago as well and hadn't spoken to her since. There was even a page written to him in the will berating him and accusing him of being a turncoat and a liar. Apparently, he had reported her for doing something wrong at work, which forced her retirement. The forced retirement probably had to do with all the papers we found all over the house regarding friends and family members personal information that she used her position in the government to obtain, but had no business having, yet did. She had lists of social security numbers, employment records, details on housing purchases and prices, car purchases, legal filings, arrest records, warrants, you name it, on almost every person she knew. He probably came to the house and saw these things, reported her and had her fired. Yet, he was the man she left her money to. I had never even met this man.

I was still on speaking terms with my mother and all of these other people who hadn't spoken to her in years were the ones she left everything to. Whatever.

I called Ted, the ex-boss. He said he would meet me at the funeral home to make the financial arrangements, but he never showed up. He wanted to check into all the legal implications and his tax liabilities before he got himself involved which I found ironic since they had worked for the Internal Revenue Service. Wouldn't he already know? I understand the need to check into legalities, but the clock was ticking. It was Saturday afternoon on Memorial Day weekend. If I didn't get things resolved quickly, I would have to sit in town until Tuesday to get things done. My husband was home caring for four young kids. I couldn't just sit doing nothing in Vegas for two more days. As a result, just as I had thought, I had to foot the whole bill for the cremation and urn up front, on my own.

The funeral directors took me in the room to make decisions and sign paperwork. One of the first things I had to do was select an urn. There were many beautiful urns, but one thing I have never understood is why we create such beautiful and expensive things just to stick them in the ground and never see them again. I guess I can understand wanting to put someone you love into a beautiful thing, but why are they that expensive? A person can be buried in a utility urn that only costs twenty dollars, but that somehow seemed disrespectful. The cheapest thing in the room was cardboard box that would grow into a tree and it cost $125. On a shelf next to me was an urn that was everything my mother liked. It was purple, gold, gaudy and over $800. She always liked whatever was the most expensive thing. In her will she left specific instructions about which clothes she should be buried in and what kind of casket should be bought. Yes, it would have been ridiculously expensive, but those wishes were irrelevant now. There I was trying to come to terms with what was the best thing to do. I had to decide what was the best way to pay final respects to someone who, in the end, had no respect for me. I compromised and picked a nice hardwood box for around $300. I couldn't help but think as I paid the bill that when you die it is important to have treated well the person who will have to make your arrangements because when you are dead you can't control anything and in the end your wishes won't matter. The person left in charge can do anything they want, and therefore might not do anything you want. I don't think I screwed my mother over, but I know I didn't pick the urn she would have picked, but I was paying for it with my own money. Unlike her, I am a decent money manager and knew I couldn't afford $800, and I didn't think there was a need to go into debt for someone who never treated me well.

Looking back, other than needing to pick up her possessions and keys from the police station, I didn't really need to be the one that actually went to the house, but for some reason I felt it was my job. It was what I had to do. I was the only one who had lived in that house with her besides Jeff. I was the only one who was still on speaking terms with her. I was the only legal living next of kin. It was my job to do as I knew it always would be and I had done it and by doing it alone I think I spared the family many bad sights, bad smells, bad memories and bad family politics.

Everything about my relationship with my mother had always been bad so this was just one more bad thing and I did my best to protect everyone else from it.

Next, I had to go home and prepare the funeral – a whole new familial political mess. Anyone who has ever planned a funeral can understand this experience, but I wasn't really prepared. I had never even helped plan a funeral before. It was like I was handed a grenade, and with every decision I had to make sure I didn't pull the pin.

When I came home and reported back about my experiences in Vegas, Lydia decided we needed to have a family pow-wow to corroborate the family story. It had already been decided that since we didn't definitively have an identified cause of death yet, that we were going to tell people that it just appeared that she had an accident and fell down the stairs. Because they were afraid of how she died and people asking questions, they didn't want to put an obituary in the paper, which was fine with me. In general, I am philosophically opposed to obituaries. If someone knows you enough to care about your death, they will be in the loop to know you died. Obituaries are for social stalkers; people who want to be seen. If you haven't talked to someone in twenty years, why do you feel the need to show up to their funeral? Or if you never knew the person who died at all, only knew their other relations, why do you need to go to the funeral? The funeral is for and about the person who died, if you didn't know them, I don't understand why you would go. I didn't really care about hurrying to get an obituary out and we still hadn't finalized any plans, but so many people started to ask about when they could expect to see one. To solve that, the family decided there would not be an obituary in her home town, only where she lived in Vegas and no information about the actual interment would be listed. Anyone who wanted to pay their respects could send a donation to the local no-kill animal shelter. It was decided that the actual burial would only be announced by word of mouth. It was further decided that Lydia was going to be the family spokesperson to inform the appropriate family members and friends. The only thing we had to do now was to wait for the remains to show up. Lydia tried to tell me to not make any official plans until I had actually received the remains, but I just really wanted this whole mess to be behind me.

I planned for the funeral to be four weeks after I had returned from Vegas to allow plenty of time for the remains to be sent to me, but it almost wasn't enough. It is amazing to me that someone can die in a hospital on a Monday and the family can have a funeral by that Saturday, but we had to wait for what felt like forever. Because of the circumstances of her death, we had to wait for an autopsy, then the body could be shipped to the mortuary. The mortuary had to wait for clearance papers from the state in order to perform the cremation. Then the ashes could finally be shipped to me. Because I was already concerned about the timeline this was happening in, I paid extra money to have the remains shipped with guaranteed overnight delivery. I told the mortuary they were to call me when the remains were shipped so I could know exactly when to expect them. The thought of remains showing up to the house and being left on the front door step for package thieves was a little disconcerting.

Every time I called the mortuary, I got different answers regarding the point at which my mother's affairs were being taken care of. During one of my first calls, they said that her papers were cleared, and cremation would be soon. A few days later, on my next call they said that the papers hadn't even come in yet. During my next call a few days after that, I was told that my mother would be cremated on a Monday. On the next call, I was told maybe sometime between Monday and Wednesday. The LVPD only held my mother's body for five days, but it took thirteen days for the mortuary to get around to cremating it. The answer I was given as to why it wasn't done sooner was "because Chris had over 25 bodies a day to cremate." How long does someone have to work at a mortuary before he forgets he is talking about people and not just numbers? I realize body count is just business numbers for the mortuary, but a human being should never be just be a number for anything. It took another two days after the cremation for the remains to be shipped, and they had shipped the remains without calling to tell me like I had asked, nor did they ship overnight delivery as I had paid for. My mother's ashes were sent through the registered priority mail system, which at the time took anywhere from 2-9 days with no guaranteed time of delivery, so there was no anticipated time of arrival. After many infuriating calls, I learned that once a package has entered the USPS priority mail system there is nothing that can be done to fix the error – even if they are shipping the remains of a person. Because I anticipated overnight shipping, when I originally learned it had been shipped on a Saturday, I began finalizing the arrangements for funeral services for the following Friday of that next week, six days later. The drive from Las Vegas to Salt Lake City only takes eight hours at most, so five days should have been plenty of time for delivery.

By Thursday evening the remains had still not arrived and services for the next day had to be postponed. When the urn finally arrived Friday morning, it was not the urn I ordered. I ordered the vertical rectangle box and received the square box. Granted that really isn't a huge difference, but to me the vertical box was a little nicer. I didn't know much about urns and couldn't imagine that once a person had been placed inside that it could be changed, so I felt pretty stuck.

All the mix-ups and re-planning of the funeral absolutely drove my blood pressure and anxiety through the roof. Even in her death, it seemed everything about having to deal with this was made to be as difficult as possible just to irritate me. But the day to put her to rest finally came. It was a beautiful day. The perfect temperature and clear blue skies. Everything went off without a hitch. We didn't have a memorial service at a funeral home. There wasn't much people wanted to celebrate or remember, so we only had a graveside service. Besides my husband and kids, there were about ten other people who came. It was the smallest turn out to any graveside service I have ever attended, with only a few small floral arrangements. I had created a small paper program with her picture. I gave a short recap of her life and tried hard to focus on the positive. Her grave site was dedicated, and my exceptionally talented husband played the bagpipes. Afterwards, we went back to my grandmother's care facility where we used a small room and shared a meal. Everyone seemed to get along and there were no family fights. As the day started to come to a close, the different factions of the family came up to me to say what a good job they thought I did – that I had taken care of things in a respectful way. With the bitterness that had always surrounded everything to do with my mother, I think they were surprised that the whole family had experienced a day focused on my mother without a single ounce of bitterness expressed by anyone. In the end, everyone seemed to be happy with how everything turned out.

When I woke up the next day it felt like a weight had been lifted off my shoulders. My mother had always been a difficult part of my life - a part of my life that I had always wondered how it would end, and now it was over.

There are still strange pangs of emotions when I drive through Las Vegas or attend family parties in which people refer to me as "Joy's daughter," but finally there were no longer any family tensions or negative things hanging over my head. Through the whole experience, I never shed a tear. I was finally free.

CHAPTER 3

When people are asked to evaluate their mental health, they are often given a list of ten life changing events. If you have many of these life changing events happen at one time it can often lead to depression. Things like moving, marrying, divorcing, getting a new job, having a baby, having a serious medical event, etc. Therefore, it was no surprise that less than two months after the birth of my first child, I was in a dark state of depression and suicide was the only thing on my mind.

Just five months earlier, in May, I was at the happiest point I had ever been in my marriage and career. I had been married and living in California for six years and was pregnant with my first child. I was teaching at a school I loved and building great relationships with the students and teachers around me, having just been asked to speak at my students' graduation. I was a leader on my campus and in different professional organizations off campus. Life was good.

I was looking forward to taking a little bit of maternity leave and going back to work by the end of October. However, by October, I was an unemployed single mother living back home with my parents in Utah. My life had unexpectedly fallen into utter despair almost overnight, and I never saw it coming. By October, the only thing I could think about was taking my own life. I wanted no part of this cruel world and ending it was the only thing on my mind every waking moment. Fear of pain and fear of who would raise my six-week-old son was the only thing that kept me actually waking up each morning. Everything I had worked so hard for so I wouldn't end up with the life that now lay ahead of me had fallen apart and I could barely understand why.

In July, my husband and I returned home from our baby shower in Utah with my family and friends. Most of our friends had been there, all except for Mike and Joanne. Joanne was also pregnant but had just lost her baby. It was very understandable why they wouldn't want to attend a baby shower for someone else. Even my old high school sweetheart and his wife were there. Laughs and presents were exchanged by all and we returned to California.

One night back home in California, my husband and I were sitting watching an episode of *Friends* – not a show I enjoyed. I found the frequent back forth between Rachel and Ross annoying. I just wanted them to admit their love and commit to each other. Relationships didn't have to be that hard. I can't remember the specifics of the episode, but I do remember Rachel and Ross were discussing "just being friends." Based on an overly see-through plot structure, which gave away the idea that those characters could never be 'just friends,' I talked back to the T.V. with a comment like, "Of course you can't be 'just friends' with someone you keep sleeping with."

My husband, Richard, responded, "Why not? Aren't you still friends with Stephen?"

Stephen was my high school sweetheart. "Yes, but that is different."

"How? How is it any different from Ross and Rachel or me and Scarlett?" From the bitterness in his voice, I could tell he was referring to the fact that we had been invited to his high school sweetheart Scarlett's wedding reception the year before, but we didn't go.

"Easy," I said. "Not only do we not continue to sleep together, but unlike how Scarlett left you, Stephen didn't break up with me, we just drifted apart. I didn't pine over him for years, like you did for Scarlett and I'm not still in love with him." It was meant as a flippant, joking remark. Scarlett, a high school freshman at the time she had dated Richard, broke up with him, a senior, once he graduated and started college. She wanted to play the field in high school and not be tied down to an *older man*. I knew he had pined over her for years before we met and had a soft spot in his heart for her. Who doesn't have a soft spot for the first person you really fall in love with? Since Richard and I had been together eight years, six of them married, I didn't think anything about my comment. I was just teasing him – or so I thought.

Maybe it was his guilty conscious that responded when it heard "still in love," or "continue to sleep together," but he stood up stormed across the room and said point blank in a matter-of-fact way, "Exactly, I was trying to give you a second chance, but I can see nothing has changed. I do still love her and she loves me and we want to be together. I want a divorce."

Huh? It didn't even register in my brain. What? We were just sitting there watching a funny episode on television. What just happened? I was stupefied. His comment came from so far out in left field, I couldn't even react as his words flew right over my head.

Stammering out a whisper I responded, "What do you mean second chance? I don't even know what you are talking about."

"I decided I wanted to leave you before you got pregnant. When I found out you were pregnant, I decided I would try to give our relationship a second chance. My parents stayed together only because they had children together and they are miserable, and I don't want to be like that. Nothing has changed between us and nothing has gotten better while you are pregnant, so I'm leaving."

As what he was saying finally starts to register, I gradually find my voice, "What? I didn't even know you felt that way. I didn't even know you were unhappy. How can I be better or fix things, if I didn't even know anything was wrong? That's not fair. I'm pregnant." A woman changes when she is pregnant. Hormones change. Desires change. Temperament changes. Sure, I had been more moody, emotional and needy. I was seven months pregnant.

"Yeah, and that is why I gave you a second chance."

Still, I was lost in a sea of confusion because we'd had a stable relationship. We never fought. We never argued. He'd never done anything to make me think he was unhappy or was living some kind of double life separate from me, I stammered, "What the hell? A second chance at what?"

"Treating me better."

"Treating you better? What are you talking about? How do I not treat you well?" My mind couldn't grasp his words. Not only did I have a full time job to pull my own financial weight, but I cooked him dinner every night, did all the grocery shopping, cleaned the house, always remembered nice presents for special occasions, supported all his hobbies, allowed his friends to hang out at the house whenever they wanted, never put restrictions on how he spent his time, and we never ever fought. Never once had he complained about the way I had treated him before.

He turns away from me and pulls a calendar out of his briefcase. "Look at the X's on this calendar."

"Yeah, okay. What are those?" There were seven X's – one a month since January.

"That's is how many times we have had sex in the last seven months."

"What?"

The realization that his view of our entire relationship boiled down to how often we had sex and he'd never mentioned it and was now why he wanted a divorce, set my blood to boiling. Shaking, I almost couldn't get the words out fast enough or loud enough, "I am seven months pregnant and you have done nothing to make this pregnancy a happy, pleasant experience and you're telling me I was supposed to treat you better by having sex more often? I have been tired and sick, and yet I have continued to hold down a full-time job, while maintaining the household cooking, shopping, cleaning, all because you don't come home until late. How many nights have you come home in the last few months and found me crying because I was so tired, and you weren't there? Or I was crying because you showed no excitement over this child at all? You didn't come to the ultrasound appointment; you haven't wanted to touch my belly or discuss baby names or wanted to plan for the nursery. You have treated me like I had a contagious disease, avoiding me and not coming home at night. I am having my first child with the man I love. It was supposed to be the happiest and most joyful time of my life, yet I have been alone and miserable, and you are judging me because I didn't have more sex?"

"If you are so in love with me, then why don't you have sex with me?"

"Are you kidding me right now? Did you just hear anything I just said? I am seven months pregnant!" Even without being pregnant though, sex just wasn't a big deal to me. I didn't want it, didn't need it and I didn't miss it. He had never said anything about wanting or needing it more. He never tried to approach me, and I had never rebuked him or turned him away, so I wasn't really aware that he was feeling like our sexual relationship was a problem. Since he didn't seem to want it either, I thought we were on the same page. Clearly, I was wrong.

Yelling, screaming and blaming went on for at least another hour. Little by little the details of his current relationship with Scarlett emerged. Apparently, he had never let his relationship with Scarlett go. He would take off work and drive the two hours one way to meet her for lunch or at least it started out as lunch, but it was much more than that now. This had gone on throughout our entire marriage, and I never knew. Apparently, as she got closer to her impending marriage, she reached out to him as more than a friend, for a sort of final fling. Only it turned out to be not so final, so even though she was recently married, they had developed a rather steady physical relationship as well over the last year. She apparently was giving him everything I did not. While I was sleeping, pregnant with his child, he was in the next room having phone sex with her.

It was like I was Ralph in the Simpson's episode where Lisa yells at Ralph on Valentine's Day, then Bart shows her the video and says, "You can actually see when his heart breaks." My heart was being torn into shreds. Learning about their physical relationship was my tipping point, and I told him to get out. He didn't protest at all. He went upstairs, put together a bag, came back downstairs and walked out the door without even turning to look at me as he walked out. Fourth of July weekend – two weeks before our 6th anniversary.

He was the only family I had in California and pretty much my only friend as well. I had no one to turn to and nowhere to go. I had no one close by to come over and comfort me. My closest friend lived more than 150 miles away. I was alone. If felt like I had been dropped on an island in the middle of the ocean. We had never so much as even slightly raised our voices to each other before. At no time in our marriage had either of us hung up the phone on one another, stormed out of the house or for that matter even stormed out of a room in anger with one another. We'd never had even a slight argument, and this seemed so extreme and out of the blue. I didn't want to call anyone because maybe this was really just our first bump in our relationship and we could work it out. Besides, I tried to tell myself, after actually walking out and living without me for a few days, he'd regret it and come back, right? I was his pregnant wife after all. There is no point in alarming anyone. We can work through this and no one ever needs to know.

My head was swimming. I couldn't get through a single coherent thought. My instant reaction to this betrayal and clear rejection was one simple idea that kept returning to my head: suicide. I knew it was wrong, but it was like the medicine cabinet and the razors were calling my name. I had to work hard to stay calm, to focus and clear my head, so I began to write:

> "*How can he do this to me? How can he do this to his son? I wish he could feel every ounce of pain I feel. Oh, how my wrists are burning to be cut! It feels like I am alone on an inflatable inner tube with a hole in it, in the middle of the ocean, afraid of the sharks circling around me as I am baked by the sun from above, starving, while I wait to die as the air slowly leaks out of my tube. The only thing keeping me writing is the child I have growing inside me. It is the only thing keeping me alive. I only have to wait twelve more weeks until the baby is born before I can place him in his arms and die.*
>
> *I could go buy a gun. They say that the only reason men are more successful at suicide is because of the method they choose to accomplish it. I wish there wasn't a waiting period, but that is probably exactly why there is one. The faster death happens, the less pain there would be. I just don't want to feel the pain.*
>
> *How can I kill myself without pain? But by the time the baby is born, the waiting period for a gun would be over. I can make it twelve weeks.*
>
> *Over and over again, my life has come to no purpose. Nothing positive has come from it. The world is not a better place because I am in it. I have nowhere to go and no one to turn to. My life is nothing more than shame and defeat. There is no desire to go on. What's the point?*
>
> *The only reason to write this now is so that when my son grows up he will know why I made the choices I made. Some people can never understand why I would consider this decision, but I have battled my whole life for the desire to want to live. I don't have the strength to hold myself up alone. I have lived all but the last few months of my life never knowing my biological mother, living instead, as the daughter of an alcoholic, adoptive single mother. Richard doesn't want his son to relive his life? Well, I don't want my son to relive mine. It seems I was born only to suffer. Everything imposed upon me, nothing has ever been my choice. I have barely survived. It doesn't matter if I live to be a mother, Richard says he has plans to live with Scarlett, so if I died they baby would still have a family and a less complicated one without me in it. Without me my son will have more advantage than I ever had or could ever give him as a single parent.*

Has Richard even thought about what this is going to do to his life? Where is he going to live until the house sells? It could be months. After the house sells and I have custody and he's paying child support/alimony does he think he could afford to live in the Bay Area by himself? He couldn't. He would have to quit his job, move, and find a new job. Is he prepared to do that? He can't handle that much effort and change. He'll never be able to really do it.

I hope he tells his family the truth. I hope to God he doesn't create a picture of me being this horrible wife that made him suffer. In his heart, he would know that wasn't true. I hope he takes responsibility for his own feelings. He is being very selfish and isn't thinking about the responsibility he has for the child he is bringing into the world. What a good father - to choose not to be a part of his life -- to choose child support over him before he is ever born. To walk out over sex, without even giving me a chance. It's like I am a sixteen-year-old who had unprotected sex and as soon as the guy found out I was pregnant, bolted just so he could get more sex somewhere else.

Now I have no one. I worked so hard in my life to be in the right place when I finally decided to have a child and now this. I am exactly in the place I didn't want to be. Completely alone – and I can't leave this house. I have to stay here because this is the only place I have medical coverage and there is no way I could afford to have a baby without it. I am stuck. The next few months of being alone every night will be a living hell. I am powerless. It's like being in a pitch-dark cave surrounded by heavy smoke. You can't breathe, and you can't see enough to find your way out.

I really just want to die.

If I can survive this, I can't stay here. There is nothing for me here without Richard. I can't live on my own in the Bay Area either, and there are no friends or family for me to turn to here. There is nothing for me anywhere else either, but at least I can afford to live if I go home. If I can survive this, I have no choice but to go home.

I wonder how that will make Richard feel, to know I will live in another state and he will only see his son a few times a year if he is lucky. How would he feel knowing his son wouldn't have a father? If he is so concerned about the quality of his son's life if he were to grow up in a house with us together, how much better does he think it would be to grow up in a house with no father? Until he is five or six, our son couldn't travel on a plane alone. That would mean the only time he would see his son for the most formative years of his life -- would be when he came to visit and how often could that realistically be? By the time the child was old enough to visit him, he wouldn't know who Richard was. Imagine how traumatizing that would be. I used to get shipped off to my father every summer. Does he know what that does to friendships for a small kid -- they don't get to do anything with their close school friends. Then you have to go to your summertime friends and try to force yourself into their school year cliques -- meanwhile back home, your friends are growing further apart from you because they have gotten closer to each other over the summer through experiences you haven't shared. Richard has never lived being shipped from home to home. He hasn't had step-sibling relationships forced on him then ripped away. He hasn't had to go intrude into someone else's home and room three months of every year - sleeping on someone else's bed, playing with someone else's toys because there is only so much that can be packed in a suitcase. He hasn't had to deal with all the awkward, uncomfortable times at graduations, weddings and holidays when each parent is vying for attention and wants something their way. I have. I lived it.

What you teach your child is the only legacy you will have that will live on after you are gone. To live your life and know that you have made a positive difference in the life your child is the most important job you will ever have as a human being. You can tell your children what you believe to be right and moral, but children learn more from example than from words.

I wish he would listen to my experience! It feels like I have been bound and gagged and I am mumbling through the duct tape on my mouth.

Why can't he see this?"

That was just part of the first night, and it didn't get easier. I spent most of the next few months completely un-functional – a crying heap of flesh. Days would pass, and I would never leave the house – never leave my bed, unless physical needs necessitated it. Sometimes Richard would come back to the house and sometimes he wouldn't. When he did come over, it was never because he wanted to be with me. It was only because he 'worried' that I had no one else to call if I went into labor. He knew there was no one there for me and felt guilty. School was out for the summer and I had nothing to fill my day, to give me purpose and take my mind off the impending doom, so I would spend all day at home wallowing in my misery while he got up and went to work and didn't even stop to think about the consequences of his choices.

I had no one to talk to, so when the temptations to end it all got too strong, the only thing I could do was write:

"I have an incredibly strong desires to go through the house destroying everything. The only thing holding me back is knowing that financially

speaking, if I can survive this, I will need the things in this house when I am alone.

Spending the afternoon listening to the garage door open next door and each time hoping it will be him. Hoping he will come home to say he's sorry, he loves me, and he wants to work this out. With everything he doesn't do, it becomes clearer to me just how much he doesn't love me and how truly far apart we were. It hurts. I bet while he is at work that barely a fleeting thought of me has crossed his mind, yet he is the only thing I can think about 24 hours a day.

I don't really know why I would torture myself this way, but I want to understand, so this morning I went to the spare closet, found his old box, and went through his box of old letters from Scarlett. They were insightful. I realized I have no idea who I am married to. It explains why when we got married the only thing he could say in his vows was "I love you. You are my best friend." No matter how much time has passed, he still considers her to be his best friend, not me. I am nothing. His wedding vows to me were just lies he was telling himself to convince himself he was doing the right thing. The letters made me understand that he never did love me. It makes me wonder why he ever went to Utah, and why he ever proposed. It makes sense why he never discussed marrying me with anyone before he proposed. He did not really want to ask me. He knew he could be easily talked out of it. He settled for me since he could not have her. The one moment that has meant so much to me in our relationship had nothing to do with me: we had known each for a summer while on tour and then one day at the end of the tour I told him our relationship was over and it was time for me to move on and then later that day I found him in a corner, curled up in ball, crying, listening to Styx "Don't Let It End." He wasn't sad about me. My wanting to leave him was just reminding him of her leaving all over again. That was his break-up song for her too. It was not special or specific to me, and to think I bought into that sight as a pivotal moment in our lives!

Why is it when you are depressed every song seems like it speaks directly to you? I got in the car today to run errands and I thought maybe, just maybe, he had planned for me to hear the song cued up in the CD player, track five from a Dire Straits album:

> *"Baby I see this world has made you sad*
> *Some people can be bad*
> *The things they do, the things they say*
> *But baby I'll wipe away those bitter tears*
> *I'll chase away those restless fears*

That turn your blue skies into grey
Why worry, there should be laughter after the pain
There should be sunshine after rain
These things have always been the same
So why worry now"

I played it over and over and cried the entire time, wishing from every fiber in my body that was what he was trying to say to me.

Later he came to house to take me to a doctor's checkup, when we got in the car together the CD started on track six and we just kept listening. After a few songs he pulled out the CD case and picked a new CD. We never listened to track five. It was evident it had no special meaning intended for me. However, it was clear he was listening to the lyrics as intently as me because as soon as they sang:

"I'm tired of being in love and being all alone
When you're so far away from me
I'm tired of making out on the telephone
because you're so far away from me."

It was like he couldn't take the CD out of the player fast enough. He knows he is ruining my life and causing me pain – enough that he pays close attention to the music selections he picks because music and lyrics have been a foundational way for us to express ourselves to each for years. I know he reads the lyrics into his feelings.

More than anything I wish I could see even a little bit of fight in him. A little bit of fear. A little bit of wanting me. He says he has been in this big indecisive mess because a little bit of him does not want to leave me, but other than him saying that there has been no evidence to really show it. Saying he is indecisive means nothing. He is being indecisive not because he loves me but because leaving me is too risky for him. He is waiting for Scarlett to leave her husband first, and he doesn't want to end up alone if she doesn't. Yea, I am the consolation prize if he stays. I feel so loved."

When you are going through a divorce every little behavior, look and action from the other person is analyzed with intense scrutiny. A look or a simple item left on the counter may have never meant anything before, but suddenly every little thing has a meaning. I had known for a long time that we had album labeled Whitesnake in our CD collection. I had never had a desire to listen it. I hate that kind of music. However, one day after he had used the car, I found the CD in the passenger seat after he'd left. Whitesnake really wasn't his kind of music either. I had never put the pieces together until then and I knew immediately it was not really a Whitensake album. Whitesnake isn't really the kind of music for someone who lives his whole life communicating though lyrics to listen to in the middle of a divorce. I knew he would want the sappy, overly emotional love songs that represented all his repressed feelings. So when I opened the case, it all became clear. He had labeled it Whitesnake because he knew I would never listen to it, so I was not likely to ever open it, but right there on the inside cover was the real track list:

1. You Are the One	by Mike and the Mechanics
2. One More Night	by Phil Collins
3. In Your Eyes	by Peter Gabriel
4. Remember the Feeling	by Chicago
5. That was Yesterday	by Foreigner
6. I know You're Out There Somewhere	by The Moody Blues
7. These Dreams	by Heart
8. Hold On My Heart	by Genesis
9. Blue Eyes	by Elton John
10. Find A Way to My Heart	by Phil Collins
11. Your Wildest Dreams	by The Moody Blues
12. Can't Turn Back the Years	by Phil Collins

It was like the plastic case in my hands was a knife ripping open my heart. This CD had been in our collection for months.

The masochist I am, I listened to the first seven tracks. It told me more about his feelings than he ever had ever actually told me himself. Each song caused a part of my heart to wrinkle and wither to nothingness. It was one of the most painful things I have ever consciously chosen to do to myself. I know he never intended for me to listen to it, but as he was making it, how could he think the act of making it would not eventually lead to something that would hurt me? As he recorded every song, he should have been thinking about what the mere act of recording it was doing to our relationship. Creating that CD with the meaning he had in his heart, alone, was an act of adultery.

It says a great deal about him that he actually took the time to gather all these songs together in one place, so he could pine over her, and then kept it there in front of me in our house for months. It made me sick. I had to wonder when he made it. I could remember it being in the CD collection for a while, but just how long it was there I couldn't remember. Then I wondered, "Did she got a copy of it too?" Was this how they sent messages to each other - through the lyrics of the music? Were they reliving their cheesy, high school romance?

Knowing he was leaving and he didn't love me and allowing him in my house to check on me created immense internal conflict. Do I even let him in? Do I try to convince him not to leave? How do I treat him when he comes? Do I try to make up for lost time? Do I try to have sex with him now? How can I have sex with a man who plans to leave me? But if I have sex with him, maybe he won't leave me? Is there any other way to the save the marriage? I can't have sex with someone whose heart is somewhere else. What do I ask or not ask him to do? Do I ask him to do the dishes or do I treat him like a house guest? Do I leave him downstairs by himself when I go upstairs to sleep, or do I make him leave? Can I trust him in to be in the house unsupervised? Is there anything we can do besides sit in awkward silence and stare blankly at the television?

Anything I said or did felt useless because I knew nothing I did mattered to him. It was like trying to drain all of an alcoholics' beer or crushing a smoker's cigarettes. You can never empty the supply because they will just go out and buy more. Anything I did for him, he was oblivious to because he didn't care what I did. He could come over to a clean house, where I made him dinner and cleaned up after and it wouldn't even register to him that I was going out of my way to be generous; he wouldn't appreciate it. That level of care was what I had done for him for years. It was just a normal expectation.

In an effort to save things, I found a marriage counseling weekend retreat for couples with troubled marriages. He didn't want to go. He didn't see the point, but I guess his guilt over how this was crushing me cajoled him into going. I still had hope that I could convince him to stay. Of all the days we spent together after he said he was leaving; these were the worst we'd experienced together so far. There is nothing more painful than looking inside yourself and facing the truth.

Ironically, there was a wedding going on in the building when we arrived. My heart slowly imploded when I saw the bride and groom cuddling each other as they walked out of the reception room. All I could think was that a year from that moment, it could be him and Scarlett walking out of their reception. Just seeing the happy couple, in contrast to being days away from the end of those shattered dreams of living happily ever after, all I wanted to do was cry, but I didn't want him to see that such a simple thing could hurt that much, so I quickly turned away.

I had always thought we were real with each other. We were always honest. I thought we knew everything about each other and that I didn't have to hide anything from him. I could just be me and that was okay. I thought he was my best friend and my best support system. I liked what I thought was us. It shattered my reality to learn that everything wasn't what I thought it was.

One of the focus points at the retreat was that the spouse who did wrong needed to not continue to berate themselves over it. They needed to learn to forgive themselves, and the way they were encouraged to forgive themselves was to make things right with the spouse they had hurt. However, as we began to discuss this idea, he wouldn't acknowledge that he had hurt me. He didn't think he had done anything wrong that needed forgiving. He thought he was the one who had been hurt by choosing me. His mistake was not lying and cheating on me but choosing me to begin with and the way to forgive himself was to move on, away from me.

I felt like a car skidding out of control on the ice. Bare knuckling the steering wheel and praying to come out of the skid safely on the other side. I wished...I wished...I wished I felt loved. I wished I felt optimistic. I wished a lot of things, but after feeling like my life was just spinning and spinning and spinning uncontrollably on the ice, I couldn't even wish anymore. I was spent. I felt like a piece of trash; a vegetable that had been shut up in the fridge for so many months it couldn't be recognized anymore, so awful and smelly that someone has to put on plastic gloves and hold their nose to take it out to the dump. There was no coming back from this.

To find out that your life wasn't what you thought it was, that you have been living a lie, that your existence causes someone else pain, that you have never once been loved by your life partner, that you have always been nothing to them and that your child is nothing more than a mistake to them, that everything that you had worked for in your life was crumpling around you -- the only way to describe it is painful, like someone cut a hole in my body and took out my heart while I was still conscious and breathing, then sat there and laughed at me while they were doing it because I was the fool who just sat there and let it happen.

As my due date was getting closer, and since this was my first child, I thought it would be a good idea for me to take the prenatal classes at the hospital. Richard felt it was his duty to attend with me since he expected to be there when I gave birth. In retrospect, I did not learn anything I could not have read in a book. The pain I had to endure for each class definitely wasn't worth it and in many ways was worse and more long-lasting than the actual physical pain of birth. Richard not only robbed me of what should have been the happiest time of my life, but he drove a knife into my heart while he did it.

Every class was the same. Since we were coming from different places, we would go to the class in different cars. He was always late, but that was nothing new. He was always late for everything, I didn't want to sit out on the sidewalk with the pillows by myself - advertising I was alone, so I sat in the car until I absolutely had to get out and go into class without being noticeably late. Every class, I was left wondering if maybe this was the day he had decided to really leave me. Each day I watched as couple after couple drove up together; each new couple tearing at my heart.

In class I saw all these couples happy and excited, smiling, whispering and holding hands. When Richard would come in we hardly acknowledge each other's presence. Even though I knew he was physically sitting next to me, he was not emotionally there for me. Anyone can be there physically. I needed someone to be there emotionally. I was doing this all on my own even with him sitting right next to me.

We'd get on the floor to relax and all the guys were holding their hands out and helping their ladies get down on the floor. The couples were all touching each other, leaning back on one another or a head in a lap or some other kind of touch. I had no help. He wouldn't touch me. I fumbled to the floor by myself and we sat so far apart you could fit a stroller between us. The instructor turned off the lights because it was supposed to be more calming without the harsh florescent lights. During the relaxation exercise the instructor would say, "Imagine. Imagine someone's strong loving hands rubbing your back in a heart. We move in the shape of a heart to show our love...Your baby...Your baby..." Exactly, MY baby, not our baby. We were supposed to have our eyes closed, but as I looked around all the men were rubbing their partner's back, while Richard just sat their arms folded across his chest, wrapped up in his own little world. Every week I would cry through the entire exercise and he didn't even notice.

At some point in every class, the pressure would finally build up too high and I would break down and run out of the class. He never followed me out. I would wait down the hall to see if he would follow, but he never did, and I would just drive myself home. I can only hope that the other couples in the class just thought I got sick a lot. Later he told me his interest in the class had more to do with Scarlett than me, because she had already had a baby and he wanted to know what she had gone through. During the whole "rub the back" exercise, he was imagining caressing her while ignoring me – the actual one pregnant with his child sitting right next to him.

Was it really so hard to actually care about me? To give me a chance? His best friend once told me that years ago Richard had once told him his girlfriends were nothing more than sperm receptacles – no different from the sock he would masturbate in. I cannot believe a man would say that about anyone, let alone someone he called girlfriend (or wife) and supposedly loved, but I guess that is all I have been to him too – nothing more than a dirty sock.

One night after cooking and serving him dinner, I was standing doing the dishes and with each dish I picked up my anger towards him grew. I was almost forty weeks pregnant. The baby could come at any moment. Why was I doing dishes at ten o'clock at night while he sat and watched television? Clearly, he had no love, thought or even concern for me. I knew why I was the one doing the dishes and it was demented. I did it, so I wouldn't have to sit next to him, so I didn't have tell him it was something *he* should be doing for his forty-week pregnant wife. He should have been my knight in shining armor. But when I needed him the most, he just sat there like a lump staring at the television. Besides someone had to do them and he never did, so I guess it was unreasonable that I would expect him to start now? It was my dream he would not ask me if I needed help, he would just step in and take the dishes out of my hands and tell me to sit down. I had trusted that he would be there to care for me when I needed him, but under these circumstances, if he asked if I needed help now I would never admit it. My stubbornness would never allow him to help me just because he felt pity for me. I needed him more than ever, but I wouldn't ask for or accept his help ever again!

Every time he asked me, "How are you feeling?" I had to keep myself in check. At forty weeks pregnant, with a husband who was leaving me, I was a train wreck. However, under those circumstances I would not tell him anything about how I felt unless I had to go to the hospital. I wouldn't answer him. It did not mean I was fine. I just didn't want sympathy or support from someone who did not love me, and I was not going to allow someone who had made it so obvious they didn't care about me to feel better about themselves by allowing them to take care of me. What forty-week pregnant women feels great all the time? Truly, I was always feeling crappy. I had gained over forty pounds and could no longer touch my toes. I had to pee all the time and going upstairs made me run out of breath, but he didn't seem to notice, and he certainly didn't do anything to help me be or feel any more comfortable.

Then one day I woke up at four in the morning in wrenching pain, so Richard took me to the hospital. It was time. During the day, Richard would come in and out of the room. He'd watch sports on the TV. (I hate sports!) I guess the birthing class prepared me well because my experience was exactly like the birthing class. Richard was physically at the hospital, but he was hardly ever in the room and when he was there he was useless to me. After only very minor complications my son, Tom, was born around six o'clock that night. Even though my parents lived in Utah and drove the whole way to California, they only missed the birth by an hour. My parents stayed at the hospital for an hour or so, and as soon as they left, so did Richard. While the baby and I were in the hospital Richard and my parents would come visit for an hour or so each day. I was essentially alone with a newborn baby that I had no idea what I was doing with.

My parents stayed at my house for a couple of days. While they were in town, Richard stayed at the house to help them out since they had never been to our house before. They thought everything looked like it was going well between Richard and me. My entire life they have always thought everything looked like it was going well, even when my entire world had been crumbling around me. They thought if they left, it might be better for us. Little did they know - they were the glue holding everything together. We had to play nice when there was company around. Two days after I got home from the hospital, my parents left and the reality of the hell I had been living in returned with a vengeance. Two days after my parents left, Richard went back to work. After only a week, I was home alone with a newborn infant and no one to help, no one to check on me or visit, or even to talk to. I had never had siblings to care for. I had never really babysat for anyone. I had never even really held a baby before my own and suddenly I was a week into motherhood and I was essentially completely alone.

I never sent out birth announcements. No one except for our immediate families knew about the impending divorce. What was I supposed to do? "Joyfully announcing the birth of our son and by the way we are getting a divorce?" Sending out a cheery announcement just seemed so contrary to everything that was happening in my life.

Richard and I only lived together for two weeks after Tom came home. The pressure was intense. I tried hard to be nice, but I just could not take the emotional indignity any longer. Sure, Richard would come home at night, but he was not there. He would hold the baby for a little while, pass him back to me and then fall asleep on the couch. He didn't help with diapers or middle of the night feedings or meals for us or laundry or shopping or anything. He still expected me to provide all the meals and clean up after him when he was done – after all it wasn't really his house anymore. He wasn't there to help me. He was there to play with his son – a new novelty toy. He didn't provide support or relief or make any attempt to build our relationship, so to me there was no point in him being there. All his presence did was make it more difficult to get through the day while making me even more angry and tense. We would lash out at each other and he would leave. I tried to shield Tom from the screaming, but I couldn't, and every night would end with me crying to sleep holding Tom in my arms. One night when Richard stormed out after an argument, I put the baby in the car and followed him. I didn't know where he was staying or where he went after he left me. I found out soon enough when he drove two hours straight to Scarlett's house. He was driving four hours round trip each day, just to rest his head on her pillows? Clearly, she had kicked her husband out too. It was my breaking point. I decided that night that I would start making the arrangements to move back home.

I went to a lawyer and formally filed the paperwork for a divorce and took papers to Richard to ask for legal permission to move to another state with Tom. Richard didn't even pause for a second before putting his name on the paper to let me leave the state. He even volunteered to drive the moving truck back to Utah. He wouldn't sign the divorce papers though. While I initially held out hope that it might be because he wasn't really sure if he wanted a divorce, I later learned the truth. Scarlett had been working out the details of her divorce for months and she had told Richard that all of the details of the divorce had to be approved by her before he could sign, and that is how it would be for the next 18 years. Richard was never allowed to talk to me or make decisions without a script and approval from her.

It only took me a few weeks to get all the details finalized. After packing my things, he came back and accused me of stealing his things. He went through every single box I packed and realized, in fact, that I had not taken a thing that wasn't agreed upon first. While I had not "stolen" anything, I really had to resist the urge to destroy everything else I left behind in the house. I wanted to scratch every CD in his stupid, precious collection. I could not believe he – the cheater, the adulterer - had the nerve to accuse me of being untrustworthy.

I had given up my first professional job – one that I loved - and put my house on the market. When Tom was six weeks old, we boarded a plane, and I returned home to Utah. I moved back in with my father and step-mother. Finally, after six weeks with a newborn alone, I finally had someone to help me, but my nights still ended the same. I held my son in my arms and cried myself to sleep praying no one could hear. Even though I moved back in with my dad and his wife, it was still just me staying up every time Tom woke up in the night. No one could hear him but me. My relationship with my dad and his wife had never been the best. My step-mother always treated me as an outsider, so it was hard enough to ask them to allow me to move back in. Most of my life I had been very self-sufficient, so unless there was help that was willingly offered, I couldn't bring myself to ask for more, so every night, it was just me.

After moving to Utah, I thought things would be better: calmer, quieter, with less anger, and more people I could call on for help. Things were better for Tom. Grandparents to "ooh and ahh" over him and spoil him with cuddles, but emotionally nothing was better for me. Even though I was home, surrounded by friends and family, I did not feel I could talk to anyone. I could not be honest about my feelings because no one around me understood. I did not call any of my friends to tell them I was divorced and living at home. After all, the last time I saw everyone was at my baby shower when everything was hunky-dory less than three months ago. How could anyone understand how things could go so sour so quickly? Explaining my failure to friends who believed marriage was "for all time and all eternity," was not something I could find the courage to do. For them, three months sailed by, but for me time had passed like I was trying to swim across an ocean of molasses with a hundred-pound weight tied to my foot. Each day was eternally long, and I was just trying not to drown while the weight pulled me down.

Leaving California meant facing the reality our marriage was over. This nightmare had been going on for months and I still don't think I believed it was happening, until I was home. I lost it. I did not want to live. I could not see the point. Divorce feels like you are someone who has never been on a roller coaster and you are terrified to get on, but you are shoved into the seat as the employees force the lap bar down to hold you in. You are racked with fear as each click of the track goes by dragging you to the impending moment when the car will hurdle out of control over the edge. You can see the edge coming and with every tug of the car pulling you closer, and the sound of the ratchet echoing the pound of your heartbeat, your fear begins to mount. You have no control and you have no idea what to expect and right as you reach the top of the arc you think you are going to die. Then the coaster starts to fall. You hang on tight, close your eyes and scream your lungs out. You twist and turn, lifting you out of your seat as race along the track. Then it's over. No matter how much screaming you did, there was nothing you could do to make the car stop. But finally, your body slams forward against the lap bar, then everything instantly slams backwards as you whiplash to a jarring stop, at the end of the ride, right back in your original starting place. There is no getting off in the middle of the ride, you just have to wait the ride out, but I didn't want to wait. I wanted to jump out of the car and I didn't care where the car was or what was underneath me. If I jumped out the car, there was no way the ride could technically be over. If I jumped out the car, the ride ended on my terms.

Raising Tom alone seemed like a living nightmare and I didn't think I could handle it. Every waking moment all I could think about was killing myself. I actually started a living trust and got a life insurance policy set up, so he would be taken care of when I died, not knowing the policy would become invalid if I killed myself. With everything I saw and did, I thought about how I could use that object or that moment to kill myself. Driving a car was a difficult task, because the thought of running off the road came so easily. I would let go of the wheel and drift before correcting at the last minute. I had essentially stopped eating – only enough to not look suspicious to others, even though my weight was dropping quickly. Nothing anyone could say would make me feel any kind of hope. I was ashamed to become a single mother. No one would ever want to love me again. I knew the misery I had as a child and I believed Tom was destined to relive it – only he would really never have enough of a relationship with his father to know who his father was.

Every morning I woke up, I was amazed I had survived another day and I didn't know how I made it because every waking thought was about death. I knew if I didn't reach out for help soon that one day I wouldn't make it and I would be gone. I couldn't go to my parents. They didn't understand depression. Every time I had reached out for help from them in the past, they made it clear they felt depression didn't exist and was something to be ashamed of. "Depression isn't a real thing. People don't get depressed in our family." My father had told me once when I asked for help shortly after leaving my mother. Okay, so then what do you call it when your every waking thought is about how to end your life? I knew I was in trouble and I knew I had to do something, so eight weeks after my son was born, two weeks after returning to Utah, I went to ask a doctor for help. It seems ironic that someone who only thought about death would actually reach out for help. If assisted suicide were legal that would have been the help I asked for, but it's not. It is extremely hard to explain to people who have never experienced depression the back-and-forth tug and pull between the ideas of life and death that occur simultaneously – wanting nothing more than to die, but at the same time, asking for help. I just wanted the pain to go away. The doctor had barely walked in the room before I broke down in tears and within the hour, after being deemed a danger to myself, I found myself being checked into the psych ward.

Welcome home!

CHAPTER 4

Being checked into a psych ward really wasn't home. I had never been in a mental hospital before, but depression and suicidal thoughts were not new, but to sink to a level that required hospitalization meant my *regular* depression was on serious steroids. I was co-morbid (meaning occurring together). I had my *regular* depression added to a severe case of post-partum depression – on their own either one can make a person suicidal. A woman who has never experienced depression or had any traumatic life experiences can have post-partum depression. The mere physical and hormonal changes triggered by post pregnancy can cause it. Take my normal post pregnancy self, drop even more weight than normal - extremely fast, add a few horrific life changing experiences and my poor body chemistry didn't know which end was up. Experienced together, it was the closest to causing my own death I have been – which is really saying something since suicidal thoughts have always rumbled around in the back of my head.

A short while after arriving and settling in the doctor walked in. "How are you doing this morning, Elizabeth?" the doctor asked.

"Fine." I mean what do you answer when the doctor asks you how you are doing when you just finished checking in at a mental health facility? If I was fine, I wouldn't be here.

"I am not so sure 'fine' is the right answer."

"I am still alive."

"Okay. That's fair. Well, in order to get to the bottom of why you are here, we should probably talk and take a look at a few things. Are you prepared to talk this morning?"

"Sure."

"Great. My first question this morning – is this the first time you have ever considered suicide?"

"No."

"How many other times have you thought about killing yourself?'"

"Lots of times."

"Really?" Long pause as he scribbles notes in his notebook. "When was the first time?"

"I was thirteen."

"What was going on when you were thirteen? Why don't you tell me about that?"

The first time the thought of suicide crossed my mind was a clear blue skied, spring Sunday when I was living in Las Vegas. I had told my mother I was going to church and I left the house to walk to the chapel. Dressed in my best Sunday dress, I made my way moodily down the sidewalk. It was the day after the worst blow up my mother and I had ever had. As I was kicking rocks and slogging my way down the street, I found a rusty razor blade laying on the sidewalk. I picked it up and rubbed the flat edge between my fingers, then laid it flat on my wrist and pushed down until my skin wrapped around the edges of the blade and bulged up through the hole in the middle as the sharp edges began to tear the skin around it before I pulled it away leaving a rectangular indentation on my wrist. It was a novel game. Just how far could I push the razor into my wrist before it hurt? It was my own little game of truth and dare. I continued walking down the street, this time playing intentionally with the sharp edge against my skin seeing just how far I could push before it would bleed. It was when I saw the red inky blood form a drop on my skin that the consequences of what I could do with this razor began to sink in. What would it be like to die? How much would it hurt? How much would I care that it hurt? Would anyone if care if I died? If I did it right there, right then, how long would it take someone to notice? Slitting your wrists on the sidewalk of a neighborhood street in broad daylight seemed a little ridiculous, but death – causing my own death was suddenly a new, palpable and pleasing thought. I never made it to church that Sunday. I just walked around with the razor and pondered my life.

The disagreement my mother and I had the last two days was ridiculous, but she wouldn't let it go. Friday night, we were following our normal routine. I was lying on my back on the floor, and she had a table lamp on the floor turned on right next to my head. Her glass of vodka was on the coffee table, and her favorite television show was on – Miami Vice or Magnum P.I.. While I listened to the television, she would hover over my face for at least the length of one show, possibly more and dig her acrylic nails into my face digging at every pore on my face for any white or black oozing treasure she could find. She seemed to find a sick pleasure in squeezing into my face and watching the tiny trails of the white ooze from my acne build onto her fingernails.

She was deep in concentration on the spot on the side of my nose when the first knock on the door rang out. By the time she had gotten up and made it to the door, whoever was on the other side had knocked insistently many more times as if they were direly impatient for someone to open the door. I got up to follow because we never had visitors and I was curious who would be knocking so insistently. She looked out the peep hole while flailing her arms at me to shush and back away. Whoever it was, she clearly had no intention of answering it. There were no lower-level front windows visible to the door or street from our house, so they could have no idea we had gone to the door and were watching through the peephole. We waited silently in the entryway waiting for the knockers to leave, but the people on the other side of the door just stayed there, knocking every so often. After a few minutes, she looked out the peep hole again, and this time her composure seemed to melt away. The fear of making a sound they might hear left her and she grabbed me by the arm and started screaming, "You little slut. Who the hell are these degenerate boys you have brought to our house? Is that bastard the group home boy?" (What? To know of him, she would have had to have been reading my dairy because I never talked to my mother about anyone I knew - especially not boys. It wouldn't be surprising though, only the year before I had come home from church one night to find her sitting on the couch with my open diary in hand.) "You think you are so cute? You whore! Bringing these troublemakers to our house. I'll show you." She went to the phone and called the police and told them there was a gang of teenagers trying to break into our house. While she was on the phone, I took the chance to look through the peephole myself. There were four boys probably 16 or 17 years old dressed mostly in black standing awkwardly and looking around nervously. They looked kind of scared themselves, not menacing. To me they looked like kids whose car might have broken down that found the first house with a light on they could find but were scared of what would happen when the door opened anyway. Regardless, I didn't recognize who they were. I was in eighth grade. I didn't know any boys who were old enough to drive. Moments later I could hear sirens closing the distance to our house and began to get frightened for everyone – me and the boys. I had run back to the couch and the next thing I knew the red, blue and white lights were shining through the windows in our vaulted ceiling and bouncing off all the walls while policemen outside started screaming for us to let them in. When my mother opened the door four men with large two-handed S.W.A.T. team looking guns came running into the house. While one stayed with us, the rest ran through to the backyard and searched the perimeter of the house. They quickly came back and said they couldn't see anyone and the other patrol car they had was searching the neighborhood and they hadn't encountered anyone either. They asked my mom some questions, said there was no immediate danger and left.

Even though the police had repeatedly assured my mother that we were safe, I don't think she believed them. The minute the police left the house, she rushed me like a front lineman, tackling me to the ground, blindly flailing her arms through the air in an attempt to hit me screaming at me the whole time that I was a slut and a whore and I would get pregnant by 16 just like my slut of-a-birthmother and this was all my fault and I was a liar because she knew I knew the boys at the door, so I made her look like a fool to the cops. One of the boys must have been my tramp of a boyfriend and I must have warned him the police were coming when I looked out the peep hole, so they could run away.

It went on and on until she was so tired, she couldn't lift her arms anymore – luckily for me her adrenaline burned out quickly. When she rolled off of me and collapsed on the couch, I scampered up the stairs and hid in my room until she slammed open the door the next morning and told me to get ready because we were going to the mall – the other thing we did like a ritual every Saturday, because we didn't have an air conditioner and it was too hot to stay in the house.

I began to get ready. I was finished with breakfast and did my hair, but I still hadn't gotten dressed, so I was back in my room again when she burst in, bouncing the door off the back wall as she slammed open the door, again.

All I saw was her imposing black outline blocking out the light from the hallway as she bellowed, "Before we leave, you had better get your chores done, whore!" then she turned, grabbed the door and began to slam it behind her as she tried to walk out.

It was my job to do all the dishes, garbage, laundry, dusting and vacuuming of the whole house every Saturday. Those chores had been my Saturday routine for the last three years, ever since her second divorce. "I can't be expected to work and do everything else around here, so you better pick up the slack," she had said. The only problem was I never saw the "everything else" she was referring to. While I went around the house dusting and vacuuming, she would be sitting on the couch talking to her friends on the phone, drinking her vodka and staring at the television. While I was left home to do laundry, she was off to the beauty salon to get her hair and nails done. Cooking seemed to be against her religion, so if it wasn't cereal or food that came in a tin that I could heat in the oven, I didn't eat. Luckily for me our entire yard was hard clay dirt, otherwise I would have been expected to mow the lawn as well. I wasn't "picking up slack". I was doing everything except for the car maintenance and writing checks to pay the bills, so it wasn't like I needed a reminder, but her rude tone and name calling coupled with the reminder, started to set off my anger. I didn't even know who those boys were, and I was tired of being accused of things I didn't do and knew nothing about, so I rolled my eyes as I grabbed the door she was trying to slam and pushed my way passed her into the hall to make a point I would start the chores that very moment.

Before I had gotten out of reach, she gripped the hair on the back of my head. My head whipped back, and I felt her foot connect with the back of my knees as she shoved me forward. Losing my balance, I tumbled forward and down the flight of stairs. Towering at the top of the stairs in her purple satin robe with pink curlers in her hair, she was throwing the swatch of my hair that she had just ripped out of my head at me as she screamed, "Who the hell do you think you are? This is my house! These are my rules and don't you dare look at me that way! After what you did last night, I can't believe you have the balls to look me in the face. I can't look at you, get the hell out of my house."

This wasn't the first time I had been thrown out and I knew better than to be told twice. Even though I was still in my pajamas and had no shoes, I ran out of there as quick as I could and slammed the door behind me. We had a short two-foot brick wall that separated our yard from our neighbors, and I just sat there kicking rocks and playing in the dust while I waited for her to calm down and my sentence of exile to be over. It usually took about a half hour or so before she would wander out and give me some other order to follow immediately. I didn't expect her to run right out, but she knew I was in my pajamas with no shoes and I knew she would be more concerned with how that looked to neighbors than actually worrying about me, so I thought she would let me in sooner rather than later, but time seemed to drag on longer than usual when suddenly the garage door started to open. She was already trying to reverse the car out of the garage before the door had even really cleared the height of the car. As she pulled out of the driveway, she glanced over her shoulder at me, pointed the garage door opener at me while she clicked it, waiting to make sure it closed all the way without me trying to run underneath it to get inside. Then she turned back around and drove away. I sat there awhile thinking she would drive around the block and come back. I waited... and waited. Eventually, I started to get bored and hungry. I had probably been outside at least an hour or so by now, and I didn't want to sit out front in my pajamas all day, so I thought I would try to go to a friend's house. A friend she didn't know about because most people I knew would have been off limits according to my mother's rules of the kinds of people who I was allowed to be friends with. In order to be an allowable friend, they had to be a female of the same age and same religion who had parents married to each other who had lived in their house for more than four years. These were the only "trustworthy and reliable" people – except there was no one who lived anywhere near us that fit those requirements. As a result, I didn't have any close friends because I could never have anyone one over, nor could I go over to anyone else's house. But I still had friends, just none she knew about. After walking a block or so, I wound my way through the maze of nearby apartment buildings to my friend Stephanie's apartment. We had gotten to know each other since we walked the same way home from school every day. Every day after I left her at her place, I would continue on another block or so to my house, making sure to be home to call my mother at work from our house phone within twenty minutes of the bell from school so she knew I was home, otherwise if I didn't make the deadline there would be hell to pay when she got home. My parents had worked my whole life, so I had been a latch key child my whole life. Ever since first grade, I had been expected to get myself to school on time and get home within twenty minutes of the bell ringing after school. That had been the routine for eight years. There were no acceptable reasons to not be home on time, and recently she had taken to calling me every half hour or so, just to make sure I really still was at home. It was like being confined to prison.

I felt relieved when Stephanie answered the door and let me in without a lot of questions. Luckily, her mom wasn't home because she had to work. Stephanie let me borrow some clothes and we made sandwiches and hung out watching movies until her mom got back from work later in the afternoon. I didn't want to leave, and after dinner my friend eventually told her mom why I was there. Her mom started in on me, "You need to go back. Your mother will miss you. My daughter ran away once and I was at my wit's end."

"This is different. I didn't run away, and she won't miss me."

"Every mother will freak out if her baby is gone and she doesn't know where she is. Trust me; she misses you. You need to go back."

"I really don't want to go back."

"Darlin', I can't be responsible for you and since you don't want to go, I can't just send you out the door. I need to drive you home, so I know you make it there. Trust me, this is the best thing to do. I know your mother's heart is hurting. Even if she told you to get out, she regrets it now. I know. Come on, let me take you home. I can't let you stay here and I am not going to let you leave just so you can go somewhere else."

After listening to her insistence and heart felt pleading for a while, Stephanie's mom started to make me believe that my mother might really care and be worried. This is the longest I had ever been gone without my mother knowing where I was. Every other time I had been kicked out; I had never left the property. Besides, what choice did I have? I had been at her house all day. It was getting dark. I couldn't really expect to stay any longer. I was afraid to go back, so even though it was only a block away, I let her drive me home. We pulled up to the driveway, and Stephanie's mom had come around the car to walk with me up to the door and had been trying to assure me I was doing the right thing when my mother came staggering out of the house reeking with the stench of alcohol and screamed, "What the fuck are you doing back here?"

Yep. That was the loving, motherly reception I expected. Exactly why I didn't want to go back. All the proof I needed to know that my mother really didn't care about me the way Stephanie's mother said she would. She hadn't missed me. She wasn't remorseful for her part in why I had been gone. It actually seemed liked she was angry I had come back. Stephanie's mom stood there, stunned. After a moment she stammered, "Mrs. Wexler..." But my mother cut her off, "What goes on between me and my daughter is none of your damn business. Get the hell off of my property before I call the cops." Then she grabbed me by my arm and pulled me into the house after her, leaving Stephanie's mom just standing there, silent.

Back in the house, my mother shoved me down on the couch and promptly called the police to let them know that I had come home. She had called them to report that I had run away – not that she had kicked me out. I just sat there waiting for the inevitable wrath to come just like it had the night before. She yelled and screamed about how this looked to everyone. "I just can't imagine what the neighbors think of me! What that lady thinks of me! How dare you bring that shame on our family! What happens in this house is nobody's business but mine! You had no right to leave this property! You had no right to bring that lady into our family business! Who do you think you are? Did you run away because you were afraid of facing the consequences for the shit you pulled last night? You deserve to have the police haul you away for all your little lying deceitfulness. You liar! Every single part of this is your fault. You brought this all on yourself. You'll get no sympathy from me. You little whore! Get the hell out of my sight."

As I have said before, experience has taught me not to wait for a second time to be told. I immediately started heading for my bedroom. When I had made it ten feet away, she called out: "Who do you think you are? How dare you walk away from me without saying goodnight! You need to tell me you love me. Show some gratitude for the woman who puts a roof over your head and food in your belly. You are so damn ungrateful!"

Loud enough for her to hear I mumbled out, "Goodnight," then followed under my breath with, "mommy dearest."

"Excuse me? What the hell did you just say?"

"Good-night. I love you."

"That's more like it."

The next morning, I tried to wake up and sneak out to church before she awoke. Church was the one thing she let me do by myself ever since I had been baptized the year before. She had grown up in 'The Church' and she and my father had actually been married in the LDS temple for "time and all eternity." Eternity only seemed to last four years, and she hadn't been back to church since. I liked going to church. I liked to feel like I belonged in the family atmosphere and I could have friends there. I went every Sunday, if for no other reason than to get out of the house and away from her.

I was just finishing cleaning up my cereal, and was heading for the door when she yelled, "Good you need to go to Church to repent for your sins and learn some

Christian values – like respecting your mother." She was standing at the counter pouring her first glass of vodka for the day as I walked out the door.

Making my way through the neighborhood to the chapel, I started to evaluate my situation. I knew I just couldn't live with her anymore. I was literally frightened for my life. I knew one day she would be too drunk and lose control and she would kill me, and there would be nothing or no one to stop her. As I walked and found the razor on the ground, it was like I was being sent a message from heaven - why not just beat her to it and end the miserable suffering now? I had tried to so many times to reach out for help, to explain to people what it was like to live with her day in and day out, but no one ever believed me. Everyone thought I was exaggerating or being overdramatic. When adults invariably talked to my mother about my accusations, she always had a way of turning the story around to make her look like the saintly put-upon parent of the child from the exorcist.

I had been asking to live with my father almost since the first day I knew my parents were divorcing. I wasn't given a say in who I wanted to live with. The last time I had tried to convince my mother to let me live with my father (the year before), my uncle-in-law called and started crying telling me about life with his single mom. Telling me how much my mother needed me and how sad I would be if I left, and how it would break my mother's heart. Everyone who knew I wanted to live with my father always told me the same things. No one seemed to care how much living with my mother was breaking me. She was the only one that mattered. The problem is just like Stephanie's mom, everyone was operating under the assumption that my mother was a normal, sweet, loving mother. They closed their eyes to all the evidence to the contrary even when it was right in front of them.

The whole family had been together just four months earlier when we had all traveled from our different parts of the country to stay at my grandma's house for Christmas. We were less than a mile from my father's home, but I wasn't allowed to see him or even tell him I was in town, even though I hadn't seen him in two years.

One day while we were there, my mother and I were in the basement alone. At twelve years old, I was sitting on the floor, and she was doing my hair because I could never do it *well enough* for her liking and she "wasn't going to be seen with a daughter who was not presentable enough." It seemed like she was always angry when she did my hair. It was as if she were resentful she had to take time away from her busy, important life to make sure I looked good enough to be seen with her. I could feel this resentment because she was never gentle about doing it. She always ripped the comb through the snarls, ripping out knots of hair. There were never attempts to work through the knot or save the hair or concern for what it felt like to me. She would just rip them out, and in order to get the braids perfect she would pull the hair as tight as she could. If I cried out or squirmed, I would get hit, and even when I tried hard to sit still, I could never sit still enough for her liking. Every hair session with her included her hitting me with her plastic comb or brush– across the head, across the back, across the arm – anywhere she could make contact, getting harder and harder until she thought I was still enough. Flinching, jumping or squirming away from a hit only resulted in more hits. On this day, in the middle of a twisting squirm after she had yanked down on my hair, I remember seeing my grandmother peeking through the door as my mother was in mid-swing of her fourth or fifth hit and my grandmother just silently watched until it was over and did nothing. She just stood in the doorway like a creepy stalker peeking around the edge to watch the whole punishing, hair-fixing ordeal.

A few months after that trip, I had even reached out to Child Protective Services myself -begging for some kind of intervention. I had a friend in class who had been taken away from his parents and been placed in a group home. He helped me find the name of someone I could talk to. The group home facilitators headquarters was just a few blocks from our house, so one afternoon after school I went home and called my mother, so she would think I was home, then left again to go see them. Even though they let me in to see them, they seemed put out and in a rush. I didn't feel like they were actually listening to anything I said. They asked me if I had any evidence of abuse.

"What is considered evidence?" I asked.

This wasn't exactly the first time Child Protective Services (CPS) had been a part of my life. Five years earlier, in third grade, after receiving a beating so bad I was covered in bruises all over up and down my back side and couldn't sit down at school the next day, the teacher confronted my parents about the bruises. My parents made up some excuse about me accidentally slipping down some concrete stairs, and when the teacher called CPS and my parents were called, I received a follow up beating worse than the first because I had "tried to make them look bad." I don't know what my parents told the CPS worker when she called, but no one ever came to talk to me. I had evidence all over my body then, but no one came to look.

Because of talking to my friend, I knew they would want evidence, so I had started collecting what seemed like evidence to me. It seemed my mother was always grabbing at my hair to shove me around, usually resulting in large wads being torn out, so I had started to save them. I had the letter that started in my handwriting and then changed to hers - mid-paper, that she had forced me to recopy telling my father that I didn't think he loved me anymore because he wasn't paying child support. (He stopped paying child support because she hadn't let me see him in over two years.) I had stories of all the times she had kicked me out and stories of the times she had beaten me.

"I'm sorry, but none of that counts. Unless you have visible evidence of abuse, we can't help you."

"So just because I don't have any bruises *right now*, you can't help? The daily mental abuse means nothing."

"It's hard to prove mental abuse, so unless you have something physical, I can't help."

"This hair? These letters."

"All of that could be fake. You could have cut your hair, and anyone could have written those letters."

"They are in her handwriting."

"Doesn't mean they aren't fake."

What? That didn't even make sense. It was hopeless. I had to wait until I was beaten again before anyone would believe me. But what if next time was the time she killed me? Or what if the next time, I just decided to kill myself?

I was tired of everyone taking my mother's side. Tired of all the adults who refused to see and admit the truth. I was tired of being told no. Holding that razor blade in my hand that day, I knew it was her or me. I had to find a way to get away, so instead of going to church, I walked to the 7-Eleven on the corner and called my father, collect. It was the first time I had heard his voice in long time. I told him about everything that had happened the last few days and he was shocked. "She kicked you out?"

"Yeah. That's not the first time. She has been doing that for years."

"Are you kidding me? Why haven't you told me this before?"

"I don't know. We haven't really had a chance to talk without her around and that isn't something I really want to talk about." The phone just sat in my hands. He had nothing to say and the silence began to build. "Dad," I started with trepidation, "you know that letter you got from me?"

"The one that said, 'I don't think you care about me.'"

"Yeah, that one. I didn't write that. She wrote what she wanted and forced me to copy it."

"Hum...that is good to know."

My voice started to catch, by the end of my pleas, I was sobbing. "Dad, you have to get me out of here. I can't live with her anymore. Something bad is going to happen if I don't get out of here, and you can't tell her. If you ask her or tell her, she will stop you. She won't let me go and I can't stay here anymore."

"Well, I don't know what to say. This is a shock and is kind of taking me by surprise. That is quite a lot to ask for. I can't make you any promises. That is something I am going to have to look into. Can you give me time to check into it? Can you call me back in a week."

"Yeah. I can do that."

Even though he hadn't answered yes, the mere possibility of being saved from the belly of the beast allowed me to go back home and live to face the monster another day.

Four months later, I stuffed a backpack with everything important to me and as many clothes as I could and went off to summer school. Even though I was straight A student, my mother signed me up for summer school, so I would have something productive to do with my time during the summer and used it as an excuse for why I wouldn't be able to see my father during that summer. An hour later, my father met me at the school, we drove straight to the sheriff's office to deliver the legal papers to be served upon my mother to give notice that I would no longer live with her. My father drove to the Nevada state line as fast as legally possible, so there was no reason to stop us because once we crossed into a new state, my mother no longer had the reasonable assumption of legal custody.

After arriving at my father's house in Utah, I had to go into hiding for a few weeks until the legal issues between the adults were settled. No one knew I there. I was encouraged to stay in the basement as much as possible, so I wouldn't go in front of any windows and all of the curtains had to remain closed. I was living my own little prisoner of war captivity. We couldn't take the risk that my mother or someone she could hire would come and kidnap me and take me back.

Ironically, to her dying day she accused my father of abducting me. He was the responsible adult and therefore my leaving her was his fault. To me, I consciously chose to leave and found a way to make it happen. After many tries, it was the first time I was able to successfully run away from her and there was never a day of regret.

CHAPTER 5

"Wow, Elizabeth! That was quite a story," the doctor said as he finished writing in his notebook and looked up.

Great! Even the doctor thinks I am being a drama queen.

"It seems there was a lot going on between you and your mother," he continued.

"Isn't there always stuff going on between a mother and daughter?" I asked.

"Well, no. Not always."

"Okay. Always is a strong word, but it wouldn't be a stereotypical trope if there weren't problems for many mothers and daughters."

"Or maybe people just overexaggerate all the time?"

Was that a challenge? Did the doctor really think I was exaggerating my story just for him? "Maybe, but I am *not* exaggerating," I said.

"Hum," he mumbled with a tone of unbelieving judgement. "Then, maybe you should tell me a little more about your mom and dad."

Feeling a little flippant after the doctor's comments, I gingerly respond, "Which mom and dad?"

I watch the flash of confusion cross his expression before he recovers. Taken aback, his words stumble out, "Well, uh, whichever mom and dad you want to tell me about, I guess."

The way he said it made it sound like he was expecting me to start taking about imaginary moms and dads in my head that whisper things to me in my dreams – like I must be schizophrenic to think I had more than just one mom and dad.

"Fine. I will tell you about *all* of them."

When I was four my life was perfect. My mother and father we married to each other and we lived in big split-level home with an apple tree out front and horses (not ours) out back on the mountain bench overlooking the valley where we lived. One day I was out riding my tricycle around the sidewalks in my cul-de-sac alone, which was strange because I was never allowed outside without an adult nearby, when I hit a rock and tipped over scraping my knee. Blood trickling down my knee, I wandered into the house sniffling, looking for someone to kiss it and make it better when I heard arguing coming from my parent's bedroom. When I pushed open the door, they both went quiet and turned to look at me. After and uncomfortable period of silence while we all stared at each other, my mother barked, "Go back outside right now!"

"But, But..."

"You heard me."

"But, mommy. I scraped my knee."

Between gritted teeth, she paused between each word as she yelled, "GO...OUT...SIDE!"

I backed out of the room closing the door as I went, but I still didn't go outside. I stood there on the other side of the door and listened. It stayed silent for a moment or two as they waited for what they thought was an appropriate amount of time.

"When did you plan to tell *her*?" my dad said.

"I don't know. I hadn't thought about it. She isn't my concern right now," replied my mother.

"Well, she ought to be. This isn't fair to her."

"Who said life is fair? She'll get over it. She'll be fine."

I knew they were talking about me, but I had no idea what they were talking about. Get over what?

"Are you going to let me see her?"

"Maybe, I don't know right now. We are moving to Arizona before the end of the year."

"Just like that? You can't just leave me like that."

"Watch me. I can, and I will. We are over, Robert, face it.

My little brain tried so hard to make sense of what I was hearing. Over? Moving? Where is Arizona? What? Nothing about the conversation sounded good, and I didn't want to hear anymore. This time I ran outside and slammed the door behind me. I went to the curb and sat down and began to cry. What was going on?

A moment later my father sat down beside me. "You were standing outside the door, weren't you?"

I nodded.

"Do you understand what you heard?"

"No. I just heard mom say that I wouldn't be able to see you because she was taking me to Arizona."

"Yes. Apparently, that is true."

"Why? I don't want to go."

At that point my father explained to me what divorce was. He explained how mommy and daddy weren't going to be married anymore and how we wouldn't be living together anymore. He told me he would always love me and always be there for me but explained nothing was going to be the same anymore, and he was right.

The next morning my mother and I moved out and moved into an apartment in another city fifty miles away. At first, I would see my dad every few days or so, but the time between visits started to get longer and longer. My mother would frequently leave me at her friend's house who had children my age while she went out. Then one day when she came to pick me up, she had someone with her – another man. She introduced him as her *nice friend* and said he would be spending more time with us. It seemed like we had only left my father a few weeks or so ago, and now this new man was always coming over to our house. (I was too young to understand at the time, but my mother had cheated on my father and left him for this other man.)

It wasn't too long before my mother married this other man and he moved into our apartment. I don't ever remember getting in trouble when I lived with my mom and dad, but this new dad, David, was very different from my old dad. My old dad was a P.E. teacher. He wore shorts and a t-shirt and loved to joke around and have fun and play games. David worked for the government. He always wore a three-piece suit. He believed children should be seen and not heard. David never played games with me. He'd send me to my room and tell me not to come out, to find something to play by myself. Now, I was always being yelled at by David or my mom to be quiet and go away. I hated my new life. I began to stomp around the house and throw my toys around at the walls. A few months had gone by and I was not *getting over* this change in my life like my mother said I would.

Then one day, I was called into the kitchen for a family talk. "Elizabeth," my mother began, "David and I have talked, and we think that since David is going to be your father now, you need to stop using his name and start calling him dad."

"No, he isn't my dad. I already have a dad."

"Yes, but David is your new father."

"I don't want a new father."

"That isn't the point, Elizabeth. David is your new father and you need to respect him and call him what he wants to be called."

"But he's NOT my dad. He is not *my* family, so I don't *want* to call him dad," I knew my tone was already over the limit of acceptability, and it was going to lead to trouble, but they were already doing everything they could to push my dad out of my life and in my opinion having to call David dad was like admitting I would be leaving my dad behind forever and I couldn't do that.

Then they went on to explain how family doesn't have to mean you are all blood related. I didn't understand what they were saying. I didn't understand the term "blood related." People just didn't decide who they wanted their family to be or so I thought.

"Actually," my mother said, "that is exactly what people do."

She then went on to tell me that she had chosen me to be her daughter – that she had not given birth to me, but that my birthmother didn't want me and had given me away, so that she could take me home and become my mother.

Again, my poor little mind was racing. "Huh? What does that mean? You aren't really my mother?" She tried to reach her hand towards my shoulder, and I jerked it away and began to back up. "You aren't my mother?" I stammered again in disbelief. "I..." I couldn't finish my sentence as I ran to my room, slammed my door, and hid in the back of my closet and sobbed.

They left me there for a long time before she came in. "Just because I didn't give birth to you doesn't mean that I love you any less than if I had. I chose you that makes you more special than anyone else. Come on, Elizabeth. Come out of the closet."

"I don't believe you. You don't love me, and I don't have to listen to you because you aren't my mother," I snapped.

"Have it your way," she said casually as she turned and walked out of the room.

I don't think she liked what I said, and it wasn't going to be the last time she heard it. Anytime things got really bad and I thought I was being treated exceptionally unfair, I would always pull out the "you're not my real mother anyway" card, but soon after that fateful day we packed up our things and the three of us moved to Arizona.

From then on, it always seemed like I was always getting in trouble for one thing or another. I couldn't do anything right to please either of them. I didn't make my bed the right way. I didn't put my things away in the right place. I didn't load the dishwasher correctly. I didn't unload the dishwasher correctly. I didn't sweep well enough. I didn't fold the towels the right way. I didn't comb my hair well enough. I didn't dress myself in appropriately matching clothes. I riled up the dog too much. I didn't want to finish my dinner. I ate things out of the pantry that I didn't know were off limits. I left my stuff in the living room. I wouldn't stay in my room all night once I was sent to bed. I wouldn't practice for dance class enough. I didn't read long enough. I didn't bring them something they asked for fast enough. I didn't get perfect marks on my papers at school.

It didn't matter what I did because nothing I did was right, and every time I got in trouble I was spanked and had to stand with my nose in the corner for an extended period of time, and I don't mean five or ten minutes. I mean, a first grader trying hard to stand still staring into the corner for 40 or 50 minutes at a time, sometimes multiple times a day. After months of staring into the corner, one day I broke down and told them how much I hated them and yelled, "I am going to run away!" I was hoping my daring declaration would frighten my parents because they would be sad I was gone, but it didn't even phase my mother. She picked me up, sat me on the bed, then proceeded to get my little travel suitcase out and put some clothes in it. I sat there in dismay that my tantrum hadn't scared her, but in fact she seemed to be supporting it. She picked me and the suitcase up and carried us out to the front porch. She dropped me down and threw the suitcase at me.

"Fine, then leave," she said as she turned and walked into the house and slammed the door, locking it behind her. The passion-orange rays of the setting sun fell quickly behind the roof tops as I resignedly picked up my little lavender paisley suitcase and began to walk. For some reason, I decided to walk right down the middle of the street – either out of pure defiance or the hope that someone would see me and take pity on me. I was hoping that someone would question why a little girl was walking so forlornly down the middle of the street trailing a travel suitcase, but not even a single car drove down the road. No one noticed me. I didn't know anyone who lived on our whole street, not a single neighbor or kids, so there was no one I was hoping to really see me anyway. The housing development was more geared to the older, retired set that flocked to Arizona for the sun. If there were any kids that did live by me, I never saw them outside playing and even if I had it wouldn't have mattered because I never would have been allowed to play with them.

I didn't know where to go, so I just kept walking. I'd gotten a good distance away – seventeen or eighteen houses, before our car drove up beside me and I was yanked inside. I had the pleasure of another spanking and more staring at the sponging patterns from an inch away in the corner of my room the rest of the night because I had the gall to actually walk away when I was dropped outside and told to leave. Punished for doing what I was told. It was a battle I would never win. Nothing I did was right. Even though we only lived in that house for two years, I still think I could redraw the entire fantasy world out I created out of the sponge designs in the corner.

CHAPTER 6

"Wait?"

Yep. I knew this reaction was coming. It always did. From that whole story, he had really only heard one part. That part that always gets people's attention.

"You are adopted?" he questioned.

Yep. That always gets everyone's attention. This is the part where the doctor says all the problems I had with my adoptive mother were because I must have an attachment disorder. All the problems in the family stemmed from my impairments not because the woman who raised me had mental health problems because all adoption agencies go through lengthy selection processes and it is common knowledge that being adopted potentially predisposes adoptees to all kinds of attachment problems.

Even though his research was not respected in the psychological community, in 1978 David Kirschner coined the term Adopted Child Syndrome. His studies suggested that adopted children were more likely to have behavioral problems related to bonding and attachment, and were more likely to lie, steal, react violently and defy authority. My mother used to cite this research religiously when talking to other adults to explain why I was such a difficult child, and why nothing I said about her should be believed. Nothing about my behavior was her fault. It was my fault because I came to her that way. She would talk about how she was such a great sacrificial martyr who should be pitied because she took in such a difficult child who made her life so hard. The reality even Kirschner admitted was that these characteristics only relate to a small number of adopted children; however, it is commonly accepted that children who are not adopted until after they are six months of age or who have spent long periods of time in an orphanage will likely develop Reactive Attachment Disorder (RAD). Children and adults with RAD tend to be averse to touch and physical affection. They tend to have control issues, anger problems and difficulty showing care and affection for others. Technically, I have never been formally diagnosed with any psychological problem other than depression, but when looking at the case studies of other adults with RAD, it probably applies to me. The only person I will really allow to hug me is my husband. I don't offer hugs or even handshakes to anyone, even my own children. Saying I have control issues is a severe understatement. But I only spent nine days under state care before being given to my new family. If I developed RAD, it wasn't because of circumstances surrounding my adoption. It was the unstable, unloving environment I was raised in. If RAD was something that I actually did have, the time out scenario described in the last chapter, is the exact opposite of how a child with RAD (or honestly, any child) should be disciplined. Spending hours of time alone in the corner would only serve to reinforce the idea that I was alone and unloved and deepen my sense of resentment and detachment. Being alone is exactly what a person with RAD can't handle, so it is ironic that my mother would blame the adoption and not her poor parenting choices for my behavior.

So, when the doctor finally learns that I am adopted, I know that means we have just added hours of time to our discussions. I know the questions coming next. The first question is always: "How did you learn you were adopted?" As predicted, the follow up questions were, "How did you feel about being adopted? Did you know your birthparents?"

"Uh...that is hard to answer. I didn't know my birth parents growing up, but I do now."

"Hum," the doctor answers as he starts to scribble more notes into his notebook. "Well, first things first. Tell me about how you felt being adopted and how your parents came to adopt you."

I heard my birth mother held me once. She was able to look at her creation, her tiny infant, staring up at her through the trusting, pure, untouched eyes of newborn innocence. Was it hard for her to let me go? What was going through her mind at that very moment? Was it a heart wrenching moment she would never forget or a moment as mundane as getting dressed before starting another day? Something that just had to be done. How can anyone spend nine months with her own flesh and blood developing inside, then gaze into her tiny innocent eyes and let her go?

For some children knowing they were adopted is no big deal. They are being raised by people who are thankful to have them and truly love them. Even though the adopted child may question their heritage and identity, they still feel a sense of security in their place in the family where they are being raised. However, for other adopted children, for whatever reason, they are raised in environments where they are not secure in their parent's love, and then the questioning of the circumstances regarding how they ended up where they are becomes a bigger fixation in their life. This was me.

Being adopted made me different. It wasn't a piece of information about me that irrelevantly just hung out in the background like how many times a day I blink or what my blood pressure was. It wasn't information that would force me to go out of my way to become aware of it – like counting how many times I blink or going to the doctor to test my blood pressure. Being adopted was a piece of information that stared back at me every time I looked at the woman raising me. I did not look like the people around me. I did not behave like the people around me. For most of my life being adopted was just as obvious to outsiders as if I had had a disability requiring me to use a wheelchair. It felt like people were always staring at me and always wanted to talk about it. It's like being an amputee. You live with a profound sense of loss. The adopted family is like a prosthesis. It tries to fill the gap for what is missing, but you are still very aware of what isn't there. You feel the phantom pains. You know what is supposed to be there - the story of you and how you came to be - but isn't there. There is always that horrible moment in the doctor's office when they ask about what medical conditions other family members have had and you can't answer, or the horrible grade school project that requires you research your family history, only you know it isn't really your family's history.

Everyone wants to know who they are and where they came from. For most people these questions can be easily answered. What is my culture? Do I share the same talents and abilities as my family members? Are my interests a result of nature or nurture? Do I look like other people in my family? Will I have the same medical problems as other people in my family? All these questions are parts of an individual identity that people raised with their biological family can learn the answers to with a simple conversation at the dinner table, but for a child of adoption the lack of answers to these questions creates a hole that is always waiting to be filled. More than anything you just want to know what the story is that led your birthparents to giving you up.

Every child regardless of whether or not they were adopted wants to know, more than anything else, that they are loved. If an adopted child doesn't feel love from the family they are placed with, the sting of adoption can hurt even more, because it can feel like being rejected twice. My birthmother didn't love me, my adoptive mother doesn't love me. No one loves me.

A birthmother signs her rights away for a variety of personal reasons. Most do it trusting that her child will be loved and cared for in her new home because if a couple is seeking to adopt, they must really want that child. The birthmother must believe that an unborn child's life is important and this other family can give this child a better life, give the child more than she could, that giving the child up for adoption is the best thing to do, right? Otherwise, why not keep it? Why not abort? Adoption must mean faith in something better, right? That was what I kept telling myself.

I am sure if my birthparents or the agency that handled my adoption knew what was going to befall me in my future neither one would have given me to my new family, but alas no one can predict the future. Because of the nature of her illness, she was able to hide it until after her second divorce. Most mental illnesses don't present until someone is in their later twenties. I was adopted when Joy was twenty-seven. The other facet of the mental illness she had, narcissistic personality disorder (NPD), is the ability to put on a mask for the public that makes it appear as if the sick person were really the best person in the world which hides the horrific nature of the reality of living with them on a daily basis behind closed doors.

Joy's reality was a difficult one. She was a war baby. Her father, Fred, came from a Polish immigrant family that had come to the United States and settled in New York, but during the great depression Fred needed to find a job and joined the Civilian Conservation Corps (CCC). The CCC brought Fred to Utah to work on many projects up and down the Wasatch Front. One day he met Yvonne, who came from a large LDS family. After finishing his time with the CCC, Fred settled in Utah to be near Yvonne, but a short time later Fred was drafted into World War 2. The weekend before having to ship overseas, Fred went AWOL for the weekend. He met Yvonne in Nevada and the two got married. Nine months later my mother was born, but Joy wouldn't meet her father for another two years when he was finally able to come home from the war.

Those first few years were difficult for Yvonne raising a child alone, but she had help. Her own mother had given birth only a year earlier. Yvonne's sister and my mother were raised together. Yvonne spent a lot of time at her parent's house those first two years. It would be odd to have your sister and your own daughter be essentially the same age, but that was how it was. As a result, Cheryl, Yvonne's sister, and my mother were close friends most of their lives until, as it inevitably happened, the abrasiveness of my mother's personality made it too difficult for Cheryl and she eventually had to cut my mother out her life. (The great toilet bowl incident.) And rumor had it that Yvonne's father was a very harsh man known for inappropriately touching young girls. So, the home Joy lived in for the first two years with a missing father and predatory grandfather was not the safest environment for her, and when Fred got home from the war, things didn't miraculously get better.

Fred also had a reputation for being a stern, harsh man who loved his beer and laid down the law in his family and what he said went. For him, it was reality, not a stereotype, to be sitting cleaning a shotgun when boys came to pick my mother up for a date, and if my mother and the boy parked too long out front upon arriving back home after the date, he would use the barrel of the shotgun to knock on the car window so she would come inside. Consequently, my mother didn't have many second dates.

Utah in the 1960's wasn't terribly different from living in Utah now in the respect that most young women believe that if they aren't married by twenty-one years of age, they are old has-beens with little prospect of marriage in the future. At twenty years old my mother was not married and had no fish on the line. Subsequently, Fred took it upon himself to find a husband for her. He didn't go looking too far because there was a nice respectable boy who sometimes stayed with his sister's family who lived across the street.

Robert was seven years older than my mother, and during the summers he would come to live with his sister because he was still young and both of his parents had already passed away. His parents had immigrated with their families from Switzerland when they were both young children. His dad died of cancer from exposure to mustard gas during World War 1 when Robert was only seven years old. Robert was the youngest of seven children and raising that many children alone took a toll on Robert's mother. She died shortly after Robert graduated from high school. Robert was a weekend warrior in the National Guard and a recent graduate from BYU with a teaching certificate – every stable thing a father-in-law could want.

Soon Joy and Robert were paired up together and in a little over a year, the two were married. Not long after they were married, they received the news that Joy was pregnant with a baby boy. They shared the euphoric news with everyone in the family. Everyone was ecstatic, but when the day finally came, it was not the joyous event everyone had been waiting for. There were complications during delivery and Joy had to be rushed into an operating room. When she would retell the story of what happened that day, she would say she watched the whole thing. She felt herself floating over her body, looking down and watching what the doctors were doing to her. Sadly, their son was stillborn, and even after the delivery Joy was losing too much blood. In order to save her, the doctors decided to perform a complete hysterectomy while she was on the table. When Joy awoke, she was despondent. When the doctors came in to discuss what happened on the table, Joy retold them the story herself. They were dumbfounded. She was put under with such heavy medication that there was no way she could retell that information without having been awake (or without having an out of body experience), which was her belief of what happened.

She had gone into the hospital to become a mother and instead came away without a child and completely barren. Her dreams of family and motherhood were crushed. This is an experience that is hard for any woman, but Joy had been raised LDS. She had been taught that the entire purpose of her life was to become a mother, and to lose the ability to perform what you believe is your only sacred duty in life shattered her.

Joy spiraled into a severe depression and it was only a year or so later when Robert suggested they entertain the idea of adoption that Joy started to pull back out of it when she found she could find another way to be a mother. The process of becoming an adoptive parent is not for the faint of heart. It is a long, arduous, expensive, heart wrenching process. They saved up the over $7,000 in fees and registered with the Children's Aide Society. From there they had to write their autobiographies and submit to random house checks and background checks and the exceptionally long waiting period. If parents are willing to adopt a child with medical problems or an older child, the wait might be shorter; since these children are harder to place there might actually be these kinds of children available. However, there are hundreds of couples who are desperate to have children and cannot, and most of them would prefer to adopt a healthy, newborn baby. The problem is there are not enough babies to go to all the families that want them, especially if they want healthy babies that sort of match their racial profile. Many families can't wait that long and will choose to adopt children from a different ethnicity or country just to have baby.

To be selected by a birthmother, or agency or however a family is selected to receive a newborn baby that shares similar ethnic traits is almost equivalent to winning the lottery. After the heart wrenching process of letting the adoption agency into every facet of your life as they take thousands of dollars, complete interviews, require autobiographies, recommendations, home inspections and everything else, most families would be thankful after waiting for two long years to finally receive the call that says, "We realize that you wanted a baby boy, but we think have found the perfect match for you, Mrs. Lewis, with a baby girl instead. Would you like to come down and see her?"

You'd think the potential new parents would break every conceivable speed record known to man to get to the adoption agency to see the child, only that isn't what happened when Joy Lewis finally got the call after two years of waiting. After being told about finding a baby girl, Joy said, "My husband is coaching a game tonight, so I don't know if we will be able to come down right away. Can we come tomorrow?"

"Okay, just be sure to bring a new outfit in case you decide to take her home."

In case? After waiting for two years, why would there be an "in case"? It makes it sound like I was a new car ordered in from a different lot. If Mrs. Lewis doesn't like this year's model, she'll wait until a new one comes out? How does anyone know if the car and the driver are a perfect match until after they have gone for a test drive? Who are these people to think they know what a perfect match is anyway? All the agency really knows about me is that I come from European decent and appear to be healthy. I was a healthy, European, newborn, girl - that makes me a perfect match? Really?

Needless to say, nine days after I was born, I was given to Joy and Robert to take home to complete their family.

When I was growing up, Joy had always told me that my mother was a 16-year-old slut who was forced to give up her child because she didn't want me because she couldn't face the shame of being such a young unwed mother, and that was all I was ever told. No one knew anything about my father or either of their medical histories.

Shortly after my 18th birthday, I went to the office where my parents had adopted me. I asked for any information they could provide me. They said that until I was twenty-one, they could only provide me with non-identifying information, and after I was twenty-one they could only provide information if my birth parents had requested it. At the time, I didn't much care how much or how little they could provide, I just wanted anything I could find. When the woman brought an envelope out from the backroom, she said, "all of this information was provided to your parents when they adopted you."

"Okay. Thanks." I said as I turned and ran out of the building ripping open the envelope. To me the most shocking piece of information was the age of my parents. Both my mother and father had been 19. Joy had supposedly known this all my life and she had lied to me. Maybe in her mind there isn't a big difference between 16 and 19, but the difference in societal judgement on girls who get pregnant at those two different ages is gigantic. When you are older and out of high school people tend to look the other way. Getting pregnant in high school, you are ostracized and called every name in the book and for whatever reason Joy picked a fictional tale she could hold over my head the whole time I was growing up, "You don't want to be a slut like your mother," she would say.

But if Joy really did know my birth mothers real age, what else might she have known at the time about my parents that she lied to me about?

The non-identifying information didn't really provide any earth-shattering surprises. I learned my heritage was French/German/Scottish/English – not the Swiss/Polish culture I had been raised with. I learned I was born in Salt Lake City, not more than fifty miles away from where I was living at the time, so it was entirely possible my parents still lived in the area and one day we might have walked right past each other and would have never known. It made all those times someone had said, "I saw someone who looked just like you the other day," be someone I might have actually been related to. I learned both of my birth parents had been baptized LDS. There was information about hair color, eye color, height and weight and it was all pretty generic.

When I shared this information with my adoptive father, Robert, he got mad, which I thought was an odd reaction, especially if they had been told this information when I was first given to them. The piece of information he fixated on was the height of my birthfather. Robert was 6'4" and his height had essentially been the defining characteristic of his life, since he went on to play college basketball, win a national title, and become a high school basketball coach later in life. Being tall was important to him. Robert hardly ever raised his voice at home – ever, so I was stunned when he learned that my birthfather was only 5'9" he loudly barked, "They told me your father was tall. 5'9" isn't tall!"

Okay. I guess in a profession where everyone around you is over six feet tall, 5'9" isn't tall, but in my little 5'5" world my birthfather still would have been tall to me. It was bothersome that Robert seemed to feel betrayed by this information, like he had been denied the tall, slender, athletic child he had dreamed of all because of this height statistic. So, if he had known my father wasn't over six feet tall the day they had the chance to take me home, would he have said no? His reaction made me think so. I wasn't tall and athletic. I was a disappointment.

CHAPTER 7

When I turned twenty-one I was able to start looking for even more information about my birth parents. The adoption agency was no further help though because my records had been sealed. This was 1993 and the internet was something that the general public was just starting to use on a somewhat regular basis, so I turned to the internet for research. Keep in mind that Google didn't exist back then, and searches didn't usually come back with a million hits every time. While it was still better than going to the library, the internet in 1993 was nowhere near as visual and user friendly as it is today.

I went to every birth parent search registry I could find to put in my information. There are tons of sites where the adoptee puts in their information and a birth mother or father can put in their information and if the information matches, the registry will contact you and connect the two of you together. I went to site after site, filling out form after form, but months went by and I never got confirmation of a match. With only non-identifying information, the day and hospital I was born in, I didn't think there was any way I would ever find my parents.

After months of waiting for a match, I figured my search had come to end. There were no age requirements for birth mothers to wait for, so I figured if she had wanted to find me, she would have already put her name in at the registries, so if she was there the matches would have been instantaneous. After months of no matches, I figured I was out of luck and it was time to move on with my life, after all I was about to get married, move to California and start a family of my own.

Five years later, I was standing in front of my class when my cell phone rang. I don't know why I chose to answer it. Answering a call in class, is not something I would normally do, but having my phone ring in class was so odd and seeing it had a Nevada area code, I thought it was an emergency related to my adoptive mother.

"Is this Elizabeth?"

"Yes."

"Elizabeth, this is the Nevada Adoption Registry." Immediately my head began to swim, and I fumbled down into my chair. My students saw my reaction and were suddenly silent and worried.

"Elizabeth, we think we have found a match. We think we have located your birth mother." It had been five years. I had completely forgotten about signing up with this specific registry. I had moved to a new state and changed my address and phone number multiple times by then. How could they have found me?

"Uh, okay," I stammered. "What does this mean?"

"It means that the information you entered into our system matches the same information that was put into the system by a birth mother looking for her child."

"Okay," was all I could get to come out of my mouth. I didn't know what else to say. There was a moment or two of silence before the woman continued.

"Well, I have reached out to you today to confirm the information and to see if you are still interested in meeting your birth mother. If everything matches up, then I will provide her with your phone number, so she can reach out to you later. Is that okay with you?"

"Um... yes. I guess so. When would I expect to hear from her?"

"Maybe later today, if that is okay with you?"

"Uh... sure. Fine."

"Great. Let me just confirm a few things, then I will let you go."

When I hung up the phone, I lost the small amount of composure I had been maintaining and broke into tears right there in front of my students.

"Is everything okay, Mrs. Costas?"

I nodded my head up and down.

"So those are tears of joy."

I nodded my head up and down. We all just kind of sat there for a moment until I could find the voice to explain what had just happened. Then, I went down the hall to the faculty room and explained to my peers what had just happened and explained there was no way I would be able to keep my mind focused the rest of the day and I needed someone to take my classes, so I could go home. Everyone was willing to help me out and I went home as fast as I could, calling my husband and father on the way. I made Richard take the rest of the day off from work to be there when she called because I didn't want to be home alone when I took the call.

I didn't know what to expect. All those reunion shows on the daytime television talk shows show people always running to each other and hugging and crying and everyone is always so happy. That can't happen over the phone. Waiting at home for the phone to ring, I was more filled with fear than joyful anticipation. I always kind of thought once I found out where my birth mother lived, I would walk up to the house and pretend to be a census taker and just ask tons of questions and then just walk away. I just wanted to know what they looked like, know their favorite things to do, favorite things to eat, medical things I needed to be aware of. My family life had always been a mess up to this point, I really didn't want to become part of another dysfunctional family, but I didn't know what my mother was hoping to get out of this relationship either. I was scared.

The first ring of the phone hadn't even finished ringing before I picked up the phone.

"Elizabeth?" Her voice sounded old and scratchy, someone who has lived a difficult life. People always mistook my voice for being a guy's voice on the phone. Is this what I sound like?

"Yes"

"I think I am you mother."

"Yeah, the registry thinks they found a match."

"Yep."

"I bet you have a lot of questions." Understatement of the year!

"Um, yeah."

"Where do you want to start?"

"How did you find me?"

It was now 1999 and the internet had exploded. Everyone had a personal computer, and everyone was dialing in to connect to the web. Apparently, she had told a friend about me and the friend encouraged her to get online and put her information into a few registries, and when she did, one instantly called her back. She had been shocked and overjoyed it was so easy to do.

I explained how I had put my information in years earlier and had given up so this was taking me completely by surprise, so to excuse me if I wasn't quite reacting like she had expected. Neither one of us had a kind of "Oh, my God! I'm so happy! I'm bawling!" kind of moment. It was all just so matter of fact. From there she went on to tell the whole story of how I was put up for adoption and the reality was nothing like I had imagined all those years.

I had known a few church girls to get pregnant during their teen years, most of them kept the babies. I only knew one who gave hers up for adoption and it was because her dad was the bishop, so when she got pregnant they shipped her away and tried to hide the pregnancy from all the neighbors, but that young girl loved that child and resented what her family made her do. There was a famous LDS church musician, Michael McLean, who at the time had some famous songs about giving a child up for adoption and they were always so loving and peaceful with lines like, "from God's arms, to my arms, to yours." I imagined a beautiful young girl in love who was kind of naive and sheltered, so she didn't really understand how birth control worked. She loved the baby growing inside her, but knew she couldn't offer the baby a good, stable life, so put her child up for adoption with every good intention for the child's happiness. She would have come from a loving and supportive family, and all was pink ribbons, butterflies and roses. After all, both of my parents were baptized church members, so this little fictional church family – not unlike the Bishop's daughter who lived next door, was the fantasy world I had built up in my head. The truth was something I could never have imagined in thousand years. The truth was a more realistic scenario, but it wasn't a scenario that had ever crossed my mind, so I don't think I was prepared for her story.

Her story started out in Idaho. She was a farm girl in a very small town – a population less than 3,000. She had dreamed of getting out of there her whole life. One weekend, before she had graduated high school, she had gone down to the big city (Salt Lake) with some girlfriends to have fun. She loved it so much, she decided to stay and finish high school there. Long story, short: she met my father. My father was a wild man. A high school dropout who promised to give her all the adventure she longed for. He was a member of the Sundowners Motorcycle club. Black leather, motorcycles, heavy drinking, drug running, drug smoking, extortion and every other evil known to man. A far cry from the church going butterflies and pink ribbons of my imagination, and a far cry from her quiet, rural Idaho farm girl life.

Life with Spider, my birth father, promised all the excitement she was after. She became his named "property." To be considered property within a motorcycle club was not insulting; it was an honor, she had to work hard to earn it, but it came with a very heavy price. He was the final say in everything in her life. He decided where and when she went anywhere and who she was allowed to speak to or be with. She was to be seen and not heard and was to be at his beck and call whenever he wanted, but the drugs, alcohol and sex flowed freely. It was the early seventies. The era of free love and the booming hippie culture.

They took a picture together in front of a motorcycle shortly after my mother had found out she was pregnant. I had accidently left the picture open on my computer screen and left the room one day when my adopted father saw it. After looking at the screen he called me into the room, "When did you take this picture of you sitting on a motorcycle?"

"Well, dad," I explained, "that is actually a picture of my birth parents. The one you thought was me is actually my father!"

The story, as my birthmother tells it, was that Spider never wanted a baby the whole time and sometimes he would hit her or kick her hoping to spur a spontaneous abortion. He tried to convince her to give me up for adoption and they had talked to the Children's Aide Society (CAS), but she had decided she didn't want to give me up, but after my mother was wheeled away into the delivery room he called CAS and someone brought over the paperwork. People in Spider's family had known she was pregnant and that she had gone into labor, so as people started to arrive at the hospital Spider told everyone that the baby had been stillborn and that it was too difficult to accept visitors at the time. The next day, the agency worker came back to pick me up. Spider drugged my mother, forged the signatures and handed me over. By the time she had fully recovered from the drugs her legal right to me had been signed away and I was gone. He threatened to kill her if she told anyone about what he had done. She knew her place as his property and knew she could not contradict him. The death threat was not idol, she knew he had participated in other gang killings, so angry as she was to have been so deceived, she didn't feel there was anything she could do about it without putting her own life in jeopardy.

Six months later, the agency worker came back to Spider and my mother's house to make sure that adoption was what she really wanted – that she hadn't regretted it or felt she made a mistake. The final adoption would not be legal for another six months, and Hilary, my mother, could change her mind if she wanted, but Spider wouldn't let the agency worker in the house and held a gun to Vickey's back side while she told the worker through the opening in the door that she was okay with the decision and to never come back.

It took a year, but Hilary and my father stayed together only long enough for her to find a way out of the relationship without putting her life in jeopardy since he threatened her life every time she tried to leave. Four years after she left him, Hilary married and had another daughter. When that daughter was sixteen, she gave birth to a baby girl and when that little girl was sixteen, she gave birth to a baby boy. Hilary eventually divorced her first husband and years later married someone else and lived happily ever after. In order to support her family in-between the two marriages, she had become a long-haul truck driver. When I had been born, she hadn't been very religious, but she had since found God and said she had thought about me with love and regret every day of her life, and that was her story.

With Hilary's help I was able to find my birthfather as well. She remembered his dad's name and suggested it was a unique enough name that if I found one in Utah, it was probably him – Klinn. That is one advantage to the strange names people have in Utah; it makes them easier to find. I easily found my grandfather's name and called to introduced myself, which was hard for him to believe since his son had told everyone I had died at birth. He called his son to verify my story and they shared a moment where Spider confessed the truth. It ended up that Spider's sister called me back to invite me to a family get together where everyone could meet. Spider's family had always been in Utah and while the rest of his family was very religious, my father was not. He had never really left the motorcycle club culture and had never really lived any kind of stable, respectable life, moving from one job and one house to another, addicted to drugs and alcohol. He never married but did have a son with another woman. My half-brother was a good twenty years younger than me. The son lived with his mother but was eventually taken away by Child Protective Services because she was also a drug addict. The boy was put into the foster care system and everyone in the family had lost contact with him. Due to the alcohol and drugs my father had taken most of his life, his health was horrible, and he died before his fiftieth birthday from heart complications about a year after I met him.

Hilary was still working as a truck driver when we first made contact, so although she was living in Wisconsin at the time, she found a way to manipulate her truck route to come see me. We have actually met up a few times now, and both times she has had to come to me. She had retired and moved to Florida but was recently diagnosed with stage four liver failure and sold her house to buy a fifth wheel to travel to the country. My half-sister really wanted much more of a relationship with me, but it was difficult for me to maintain and this last year she died of an unintentional drug overdose.

Hilary and I keep tabs on each other regularly through Facebook, but we don't really talk or have a mother/daughter relationship. It is just like following an old classmate from high school when you just kind of like one of their posts every so often, but never much more than that. While Hilary may wish for more, I give about as much as I am comfortable handling, which really isn't much.

Finding out I was adopted, my parent's divorce, mother's remarriage and moving to a new state all happened by the time I was five years old. It was a tumultuous time in my life that never really returned to any kind of normalcy until I left Joy seven years later.

CHAPTER 8

"Elizabeth, while all of that is great, you didn't really address how you feel about it. How do feel about being adopted?"

Yeah. I was trying to avoid an actual answer to that question. Wasn't the implied answer obvious enough? I should have known the doctor would try to corner me on that one.

"I know I should be grateful. I didn't grow up in the home of drug addicted father who was committed to a life of crime. His only other child was taken by Child and Family Services. My mother got pregnant with me at 18. My half-sister was pregnant at 16, and her daughter got pregnant at 16. None of my real parents or siblings got a college education. Being adopted allowed me to eventually have a 'better' life. I have a college degree. I wouldn't have achieved all I have in my life without the experiences I have lived through, but if you want to know how I feel about it - I am bitter and resentful. At least my half- sister grew up in a happy, functional, loving home. My half-sister grew up with a sense of safety and security. No, she didn't have money or a nice house or a good education, but she was loved, and she was happy - two things, I never had."

"Really, Elizabeth? You were *never* happy?"

"No. I honestly cannot remember a happy moment living with my mother. Maybe there were times, but I don't remember them now."

"I think you only remember what you want to remember."

"Maybe, but abuse is pretty hard to forget and has a way of overshadowing everything else."

"Abuse?" There he goes, writing little notes in his notebook again. "You feel you were abused growing up?"

"Oh, Doctor!" I snicker in my head. "The doubt and judgement dripping from your question, implying yet again that I am nothing more than an exaggerating drama queen. It is those kinds attitudes and assumptions from people that have brought me to be here right now. People never believe my story. People look at me and assume I led some kind of privileged life. Why am I even talking to you? Do you even care about the truth? Everyone assumes my trauma is about the adoption, yet in reality the role it played was miniscule. I haven't even begun to scratch the surface of my life. Maybe you ought to bring in a recliner, doc. We are going to be here awhile." Of course, I don't actually say any of that. What actually comes out is a flippant, "Yes," as he glances up with the recognition that I feel insulted. "The woman who raised me was a narcissistic, alcoholic, child abuser," I finish once I have his full attention.

More writing in the little notebook. "Narcissistic?" he questions with impunity like only a mental health professional could possibly understand the implications of the word.

Since true narcissism is so rare and occurs in men way more often, I don't think he believes me. He thinks I am using the word in a more common way, but I am not. "Yes. Narcissistic," I reply.

"Really?" Again, his question is dripping with doubt. "Tell me more about that."

Why didn't the adoption agency see it? Why didn't other people in my family see it? My mother, the woman who adopted and raised me, was Joan Crawford. My mother didn't have fame or wealth, but she did have the alcoholism and narcissistic personality disorder (NPD). And that is the problem with NPD, unless you live day to day behind the curtain with the wizard, you have no idea what [s/he] is really like. It is easy for the wizard to manipulate others to create a larger-than-life miracle worker persona that has all others believing in the myth of their greatness, when in reality, behind the curtain there is a sad, sick little man (or woman) trying to hide from their fears and insecurities. I was the one whose visit behind the curtain with my mother lasted longer than anyone else's, but not because I wanted it to.

I was nine years old and my mother had just left her second husband when the movie *Mommie Dearest* came out. Interviewer Elizabeth Day, who wrote for the Guardian, called the movie, "a blistering autobiography that portrayed Joan Crawford as a sadistic perfectionist, an alcoholic prone to unpredictable squalls of maternal fury who would punish the mildest misdemeanors with disproportionate force."

Yep. That is the best defining explanation of the woman who raised me. Even at nine, when I sat in that darkened theater, I was mesmerized by seeing my life recreated on the large screen in front of me. I knew I was Christina and I knew my mother was Joan. Scene after scene in that movie was almost an exact replica of my life – conversations or arguments I'd had with my mother – word for word played out in front of me, like my life had been filmed with a candid camera and was now replaying before me on the screen. It was unsettling.

Feeling a little dazed and discombobulated walking out of the theater, I had walked past the first set of garbage cans without throwing away my soda cup. Bringing me back into the world of the living, my mother said, "Go throw your garbage away." It was a simple request. There was no malice in her voice. It was just one of a thousand directions she gave me every day. Still kind of wrapped up in my thoughts of the movie and realizing it was my life, I jokingly responded with an amiable, "Yes, mommy dearest" as I headed towards the trash.

I hadn't even made it more than a half step away from her, when she harshly grabbed my elbow and yanked me around to face her, slapping me across the face with her other hand. "You will never call me that again. Do you understand me?" she hissed between her lips. I guess the movie had struck too close to home for her as well, since she didn't see my off-handed remark as a joke but as a direct insult.

I just stared at her. She had just hit me in front of everyone, and all I had done was tried to make a light-hearted moment out of an intensely emotional show. Sure, I knew my little quip had truth and meaning behind it, and maybe I *was* testing her to see if she understood all the same comparisons to our life that I had, but at its heart my comment was just a joke. Yet, she had just proven my point. Slapping me and calling me out in front of everyone just solidified her as Joan. The tenseness between us was palpable as others exiting the theater fearfully glanced at us sideways as they walked in a wide circle around us, careful not to draw my mother's attention to themselves.

I resentfully watched them all walk silently by. In my mind I repeated with contempt, "Yes, mommy dearest." But this time, I knew better than to say that aloud. Filled with indignation towards her for the embarrassment I felt as people continued to walk by and stare, I didn't say anything. I just stared back at her.

Her eyes narrowed to tiny slits, shooting daggers towards me as she grabbed both of my shoulders and shook, "*Do* you understand me?"

"Yes, I understand." I growled back at her softly with an equally obstinate glare.

"Good. Let's go," she said as she grabbed me by the arm and drug me out of the theater behind her as I stumbled every few feet trying to keep up.

It wasn't the last time I ever called her "mommy dearest" though. Just like the "you are not my mother" phrase I would fling at her in anger, I now had another weaponized phrase I could throw: "Yes, mommy dearest."

Every Mother's Day there is a cable channel that will air the show in a non-stop marathon, and every Mother's Day I wonder what is going through that program directors mind because that is not a happy, feel-good movie. One time, a couple of years back, I decided to re-watch it, to see if all the things I remembered about it were true. At the time, I wasn't aware it had garnered a cult like following. I remember thinking it was just like my life, but the movie had become some kind of joke – a meme to bad motherhood. People treated it similar to the *Rocky Horror*

Picture Show, bringing their own hangers and powder to the theater and shouting back at the screen. People watch the movie and see the abuses as over the top exaggeration and laugh. Even Christina Crawford said in her next book that she didn't like the way the directors had made the movie about Joan, not about the struggle Christina was trying to overcome and said it was a lost opportunity to discuss the ideas of child abuse. The true meaning of the movie is lost on most people who watch it. It is just like the reality of living with someone with NPD, it doesn't matter how much you tell your story, no one believes you. No one believes the story can be that bad.

The real Christina Crawford had the same problem. There was a difference of opinion of what reality Christina actually lived. The first two adopted children in the house, Christina and Chris reported abuse, but the last two who came along eight years later, Cathy and Cindy thought their mother was wonderful. Yet, some Hollywood stars reported that they were worried about the safety of the Crawford children, and some said they were too afraid of Crawford's backlash to do anything, while others said they never saw a problem.

Physical abuse is hard to deny or ignore, but mental abuse is a whole different ballgame – hard to prove, and for young children, it is hard for them to know there is something totally different from their world experience, for them to even understand that what is happening to them is wrong.

When I sat down to watch the movie again as an adult, I was stunned. I expected to see it for the cult classic it had become. I expected to see it in a different light with all of the experience of adulthood. I expected it to be an overblown melodramatic exploitation of abuse, but it wasn't. Scene by scene, it was still like watching my life on film. There was nothing campy about it. It was my life. The very opening scene where Joan gets white gloves and runs her fingers over the baseboards and gets mad at the maids for not cleaning the house well enough and then getting down on the floor and doing it herself, I lived it - only I was the maid getting reprimanded for my work.

Almost as early as I can remember, first or second grade, I was tasked to clean my room every Saturday morning, and my mother would come in with a literal white glove and inspect the job I had done. My room constantly had to look like a photographer from *Better Homes and Garden*s could come in at any moment and take a picture.

There were never toys, stuffed animals, coloring books, clothes or school projects or anything left out in my room. I was allowed one or two collectible knick-knacks on the shelves, and during inspection, she would pick up every one of them to make sure I had moved them when I dusted. She would check the molding around the top of the closet and the baseboards behind the door, and the lines from the vacuum had better be perfectly aligned. Haphazard vacuum lines on the floor were atrocious. If had missed even one single spot, or hadn't lined up the vacuum correctly, she would yell and scream, pick up things up and throw them across the room, rip covers off my bed, empty out my closet and tell me to do it all again, and I would be grounded to my room for the rest of the day.

By the time I was in third grade the bathroom had been added to my chores and by fifth grade the kitchen as well. The hand towels had to be perfectly folded into thirds and hung exactly equal over the towel rack, there couldn't be streak marks on the glass, and she would pull off the toilet nut covers to make sure I had cleaned the base of the toilet.

I am not quite sure how my mother did it, but she somehow found more things to clean anytime anyone came over to visit which thankfully wasn't that often, but when they did, I dreaded the last few days before they arrived. The only thing we did was clean and scrub, and I knew it meant endless hours of being yelled at for not being able to remember everything she wanted me to about how things were supposed to be cleaned or where certain things she didn't want people to see were hidden. (Depending on who was visiting certain gifts, paintings or knick-knacks had to be hidden, so as not to incur family fights about who she was getting those things from.)

A scene or so later in the movie, we see Joan and Christina at a birthday party and there is a squabble over a grass stain on Christina's dress. She was wearing the exact kind of dress with the exact kind of hairstyle my mother always used to put me in for important events. I was a tomboy and always wanted to play soccer, climb trees, or dig in the sandbox which is hard to do when you are dressed in frilly little lace dresses, with white knee-high socks and patent leather shoes. I was always being told to sit still and act like a lady when all I wanted to do was run and play. A grass stain would not have been possible, but if I so much as dropped a crumb on those dresses there was hell to pay.

My entire life my appearance was always seen as a reflection of my mother, and I had to look picture perfect all the time. When I brought home my school pictures in second grade, I got in horrible trouble because there was a wrinkle in the fabric on my chest, so the picture wasn't perfect. I had to do extra chores for a month to work off the cost of the pictures, since she wasn't going to "pay for such a disgrace."

A scene or so later in the movie we see Christina in the bathroom, playing with her mother's make-up and brushes as any little girl is bound to want to do and Joan comes in, livid to see her daughter playing with her things and angry that her daughter is always trying to get attention (even though she isn't) and furiously cuts off Christina's hair. I knew better than to touch anything my mother had in the bathroom because she would warn me about it when she would do my hair. But even on normal days, the way Joan rips through Christina's hair as she is brushing it, is the same way my mother would rip through mine on a regular basis, and on more than one occasion it would result in a similar hair chopping of anger.

Every morning my mother would call me into her bathroom and begin to fix my hair. She usually did it the same way with very little variation: a ponytail on each side or a braid on each side. With my stupid frilly gunny sack dresses and my double braids, I always felt like I looked like the bully, Nellie Oleson on *Little House on the Prairie*.

I hated it. I would try to stand as still as possible to make it easy for her. If we were fifteen minutes in and not done yet, I would begin to develop sweaty palms and I would begin to shake and shiver. I would beg and plead with her to let me go and sit down and this would only anger her more and increase her resolve in forcing me to stand up straight. After being hit in the head by the hard-plastic brush a few times, I would eventually pass out, and when I would come to, she would be yelling at me to get up and accusing me of faking it. If I could control my passing out in order to avoid being hit in the head with a brush, believe me I would have. Standing at the bathroom counter while she pulled and tugged at my hair to braid it, the only thing I could move was my eyes. I would look at her make-up and jewelry lying all around the counter and she would say, "The things in this bathroom belong to me, and if I ever catch you using any of my things there will be hell to pay. Do you understand that?" Oh, I understood. It was hell just to try to stand there perfectly still every morning without getting hit by the brush. If just trying to stand there could be painful, what pain would be involved if I actively broke the rules?

I didn't have to use her things or touch her make-up to get in trouble though. Once when I was in fifth grade, I bought some lip gloss on my way home from school. When my mother saw it on me, she just about lost her mind.

"You look like a whore. What the hell do you have on your face?"

"Huh?"

"Your lips. What do you have on your lips?"

"Just some lip gloss."

"Lip gloss is for whores. Where did you get it?"

"I bought it from the store on the way home from school."

"Where did you get the money?"

"It was mine."

"Yeah, I don't believe you. Let me see it."

I handed her the gloss.

"Go wipe that crap off your face. You are not getting this back. You are too young to wear make-up. You look like a tramp. You are just inviting trouble to come your way. Is that what you want to be, a tramp?"

Whining, I replied, "But...all the girls at school have some. They carry it in their backpacks."

"I don't give a shit what the other girls do. They are not my daughters. Just because they all jump over a cliff are you going to follow them? Go wash your face!"

"But I bought it with my own money. It's mine."

"I don't care whose money you bought it with. This doesn't belong to you anymore. In my house, you will do what I say. This is not a democracy. You have no say in the matter. You will never touch this or anything like it ever again. No gloss, no lipstick, no blush, no mascara, no eyeshadow, no jewelry – nothing. You are a little girl and you are going to look like a little girl. I'll be damned if I have my daughter grow up to be a whore. Now go wash your face off, and don't ever let me catch you with crap on your face again."

And that was the way it was for the rest of my time in her house. Throughout junior high all the girls (heck, even the boys) were experimenting with make-up, hair color, earrings and jewelry, but not me. After all it was the early eighties. Gaudy eye make-up, wrists and necks covered with bracelets and necklaces was the trend, but not for me.

And in fifth grade, one day she was pulling her way through my hair with her little black plastic comb. "I'm sick of this," she screamed as she threw the comb across the room. "I am sick and tired of spending twenty minutes every morning combing through those rat's nests and snarls you call hair." Without a comb or brush in her hand fear ran through me. What would she do now? I knew better than to move until she was done, so I stood there frozen.

She rummaged through the drawer and took out a pair of scissors and started cutting. Other than a trim, I had only ever had long straight hair that went half-way down my back and that morning she chopped it all off on a whim. I didn't pull away, because who knew what kind of horrid mistake could happen if I did, so I just stood as still as I could and stared into the mirror and watched the tears roll down my face as giant stands of hair fell to the floor. By the time she was done I looked like a boy with a bowl cut. It was so short I couldn't do anything with it. In the era of long, luscious, Farrah Fawcett hair feathering, I looked like a boy. I have never in my life allowed my hair to be cut that short ever again.

A few scenes later in the movie Christina has been served a raw steak for dinner and she doesn't want to eat it. Who can blame her? It was raw, but as a result, the steak is served to her over and over again for every meal as her only meal for days and she still refuses to eat it. This is a battle that Christina eventually wins. I don't know if today's generation of kids understand the experience of being served the same meal over and over, but for parents who were raised by Depression era parents this was a common way to deal with children who would balk at such a valuable resource as food.

This idea of not liking or even being unable to finish what was served and having it be served to me over and over again until the plate was finally cleared was a common experience for me. I wouldn't consider myself a picky eater, or even a delicate eater. Compared to the experience of raising my own children, I'd say I was dream, but nevertheless there was frequently a battle over an unfinished plate. If something was put on your plate by you or someone else you were expected to eat every last bite, regardless of how you liked it or how much you had eaten already.

One time in about fourth grade I remember going to a restaurant with Joy and David and ordering something with fries. I remember thinking after the first bite that I knew there was going to be trouble because the fries were disgusting. Giant, cold, mushy, undercooked steak fries. It was essentially like eating a cold, raw potato. As everyone else began to finish up, my mother noticed the large pile of fries still on my dish. "You need to finish those fries. We aren't going anywhere until every last fry on that plate is gone."

"But, mom!"

"Don't you 'but, mom' me young lady, eat!" Twenty minutes later, I was still sitting there trying to make the fries disappear. It gets to a point when all I have to do is look at the plate, I don't even have to put the food in my mouth, and I begin to feel myself regurgitating. I try closing my eyes and holding my nose while I eat, so I didn't have to taste them. "Don't be so melodramatic, Elizabeth. Just eat!"

I wasn't trying to be melodramatic. I was literally just trying to not throw up at the table. Nothing was helping until I had a brilliant idea. One by one, I start to pick the fries up and pretend to put them in my mouth and chew while I palmed the fry and then threw it under the table. No one seemed to notice, so I thought my plan worked. Ten minutes later the plate was empty and my step-father got up to pay the bill.

I sat there silently praying that as he walked back to the table he wouldn't look down and see what I had done. My feet didn't go all the way down to the floor, so I tried to slink down in my chair, so my shoes could cover the pile on the floor. As he started coming towards us, I could see the anger begin to build on his face, and I knew I had been caught. He didn't even sit back down. He stood at the edge of the table and began a tirade right there loud enough for everyone in the restaurant to hear. All eyes in the restaurant turned to stare at me. Turning beet red, I tried to slide even further down in my chair, lowering my head in shame. "Since you are half-way to the floor already, get under there and pick up every last one of those fries. How dare you be so disrespectful to the people who work here. They are not paid to clean up after disobedient children who make such a mess. Pick up every single thing you find under that table, not just the fries. Everything!" he screamed.

The waitress came over to try and calm my father down and stop the scene from occurring. "It's okay, sir. It really is no big deal. We can get it. We are used to having kids here."

"It is a big deal. I will not have my daughter behaving this way. She will pick up every single thing and then she will apologize to you and your manager."

"Really, sir. It's no big deal."

"Hurry up, Elizabeth. Get up here. What do you have to say to this woman?" I crawled out from under the table and tried to kind of hide behind my father's leg in embarrassment, but he pushed me around to the front.

"I am sorry for making such a mess."

"And?"

"And I will never do it again, I promise."

The waitress stood there looking at me with a face full of empathy and compassion. She didn't even know what to say. My father piped up, "now, please go get your manager so she can apologize to him for causing a scene." The waitress held my eyes for an extra few seconds before she turned to go. I knew she felt bad for me, but we both knew there was nothing she could do.

As the manager approached, he began, "What can I help you with, sir."

"Nothing, but my daughter has something to say to you." I had tried to scoot back around his leg again, and this time he pushed me even further out front.

"I am sorry for making a mess and causing a scene, sir. I promise it will never happen again."

To me, my father said, "You are damn right it won't because I will never bring you here again." To the manager he said, "I am sorry for the problem and inconvenience we caused you here tonight. Your service was impeccable. I just have a daughter who doesn't know how to behave. Thank-you for a pleasant evening." He shoved his hand between my shoulder blades to start me walking to the door as he turned to help my mother out of her chair.

"Well, I am glad everything worked out," the manager stammered with a small air of confusion. "Thank you for coming," he said as he watched us walk out of the restaurant.

As soon as we were outside, my mother hit me upside the head.

"What the hell is your problem? What were you thinking? Did you think we wouldn't find out? They were just french fries for God's sake? How hard was that? You made us look like fools in there and I don't appreciate it. We will never take you out somewhere nice like this ever again. You can't be treated to nice things. You ungrateful brat," she finished off by opening the car door and slapping me on the head again as she shoved me in.

As we drove away, I looked back at the restaurant and could see the manager and waitress staring out the window after us still trying to figure out what just happened. I was just happy that they didn't make me finish eating the fries after they were on the floor because that wasn't out of the realm of possibility.

The scene the movie is most famous for, the one that is considered the most farcical, was also a scene I actually lived through. "No more wire hangers!" Joan screamed at her daughter while hitting her over the head with the same said hangers. I don't think my mother was drunk, and she didn't come off as the same raving lunatic as Joan because it was just a regular Saturday outburst of one more thing I not done correctly.

During one of the Saturday inspections sometime around third grade, long before the movie even came out, she opened my closet to inspect the way I had put away my laundry. Apparently, I had not done it well because some of my clothes were hanging crookedly on wire hangers. She ripped a hanger out of the closet and ripped the shirt off the hanger, threw the hanger at my face and started in, "I am sick and tired of you not being able to take care of your things properly. You can't even hang up a shirt!" shaking the shirt in my face before throwing that at me too. She grabbed at another shirt, "Why the hell is this just draped over the hanger? Look at this!" she growled as her voice started to rise and she started throwing shirt after shirt. "All these clothes just shoved in here! No wonder you always look like a wrinkled, rumpled mess." She was pulling off everything that was on a hanger and fifty percent of the time throwing things at me and the other fifty percent of the time throwing things to the other side of my room. "When you use wire hangers and don't hang your clothes properly it leaves indentations in the shoulder. Can't you see that? Don't you have any common sense? Are you blind? Where did you even get these wire hangers? Never mind. I don't care. Get these out of here. I don't want to ever see another wire hanger in your closet ever again. Why the hell do I even buy you nice things? You don't even deserve half of what is in here. I should probably just throw half of this stuff away since you don't know how to take care of it." She went around the room and picked up an armful of the clothes I liked to wear the most, which isn't saying much because I was never allowed to pick out my own clothes and I hated what she picked most of the time, but she took her handful of clothes and stormed out of the room yelling after her, "now clean this mess up and hang those things up like they should have been in the first place! I will be back in twenty minutes and it better be done correctly or you will do it over again until you get it right" She left me standing there in a room that looked like a tornado had just blown through it. My closet was full of empty wire hangers hanging on the rod since every piece of clothing I owned was strewn to the four corners of my room. She didn't bring me other hangers or explain where I was supposed to put the clothes now. Shocked, I plopped down on my bed and stared at the mess. I didn't understand what I was supposed to do. I waited for what seemed like forever to see if she would bring me something different because I wasn't going to point out to her that I didn't have anything else to hang my clothes on, so finally, without direction, I eventually started stumbling around my room to pick things up and put my room back together, hanging all the clothes on the same wire hangers everything had been on before.

In the movie, Christina was sent off to boarding school and at the school she got caught in a romantic moment with a boy which resulted in a call home to her mother which then resulted in her mother coming to the school and causing a scene and pulling Christina from the school. When they return to the house there is a reporter waiting and Joan tells the reporter Christina was expelled. For the first time, Christina stands up for herself and tells the reporter her mother is lying and Joan, not being able to tolerate the blatant contradiction and defiance in front of the press, physically attacks Christina and tries to literally choke her to death before Joan is pulled off of Christina.

As I think about this scene and Joan's firm denial (almost delusional belief) that she wasn't lying about Christina's expulsion, it reminds me so much of the lies my mother would tell people about me all the time. She was always telling people I was the disrespectful brat that was always getting into trouble. She would blame my behavior on the adoption, telling people that the agency warned her that my parents had done drugs and as a result I could have difficulties as I grew up. All of my problems were the result of my birth parents, and people should feel sorry for her for being saddled with this difficult and rebellious child. In looking back on the movie now, rather than seeing herself in Joan, and seeing Joan as the horror that society saw her as, my mother probably felt sympathy for Joan for having to raise such a willful child. Mind you, as portrayed, I don't see Christina as willful at all. I see her as a cornered animal that needed to defend herself, just like I wasn't the horrid child my mother made me out to be.

We weren't wealthy enough to afford a boarding school, but as a young child I didn't really know that, but there was a boarding school not far from our house. There was a drab grey two-story school building set back half an acre from the street surrounded by a giant ivy-covered wall. The only way to see it was through the giant iron gate blocking the driveway. It looked like a prison. Sometimes Joy would drive me past the school and threaten, "If you don't straighten up and fly right, I am going to drop you off here one day and this will be your new home." As much as running away was a regular thought process for me, this place seemed so gloomy and depressing that the threat of having to go there actually frightened me. In the actual book, *Mommie Dearest*, there was way more detail about what life for her at the boarding school was like. It explained how her mother would call the headmistress and expect reports about her behavior and how her mother would often not provide her the appropriate kinds or amounts of clothing in order to get by at school.

Again, my life was the same. When it came to school, my mother was extremely controlling. At the end of first grade there was a parent teacher conference to inform parents about how prepared their students were to go to the next grade. While all of my academics were advanced for my grade, I tended to be a little too social and had difficulties sitting in my chair properly. (I would lean back in my chair and sometimes I would go too far and tip over.) Because I hadn't received perfectly glowing remarks, at the start of second grade, my mother made 3x5 index cards regarding my behavior at school. Each card had one question, and a spot for each day of the week for the morning and the afternoon. The questions ranged from all kinds of things like: Did Elizabeth tilt her chair at school today? Did Elizabeth keep her feet on the floor? Did Elizabeth return from recess on time? Did Elizabeth walk quietly in line? Did Elizabeth keep her hands to herself all day? Did Elizabeth play well with others? Is Elizabeth's desk neatly organized? Did Elizabeth write her name on all her papers? Did Elizabeth turn all her work in on time? Did Elizabeth listen to the teacher at all times? Did Elizabeth stay focused on her work at all times? Was Elizabeth polite to you and her classmates? Each question had a ranking scale of one to five, with five being the best. I had to take new cards to school every Monday and I had to bring them home every Friday. I was embarrassed to have to give these cards to the teacher every week and have little conferences about my scores on Friday's before I went home. The other kids always looked at me and wondered what those cards were about and what kind of trouble I must have been in. I always felt bad for the teacher too, having to do all this extra work just for me. The problem was that the teacher had no idea what happened to me if the cards came home with anything less than a five for every single question. Nothing less than perfect was acceptable to my parents. If a card ever came home with anything less than a perfect five, I was spanked and sent to my room. The more bad marks there were - the more time spent spanking and the more time I spent isolated in my room. As a teacher, I can imagine it would be impossible for any child to get perfect marks on those questions every single hour of every single day in second grade. Even though I knew the consequences, it didn't matter how hard I tried, I never came home on Friday having fives on every single question all week long. I hated going home on Fridays because I always knew the night would end with a spanking. Educators tend to be smarter now, they know the research supports the idea that when academic reports go home on a Friday, incidence of abuse goes up.

At the mid-year parent teacher conference, even the teacher commented that she didn't understand what the purpose of the cards were because I was one of the best students in the class and she didn't see why my parents felt I needed them. My parents countered that I was probably one of the better students in the class precisely because of the cards and that they didn't trust me to behave as well without them, so the cards were still sent every week.

Since teachers were on break during lunch hour, my parents even had the janitor checking up on me. He was supposed to report to the teacher, who would then make notes on the 3 x 5 cards. He was supposed to tell my parents if I threw away my lunch at school and whether or not I drank my milk or tried to trade my lunch with someone else – all of which were cardinal sins to my parents. I don't remember the school having any kind of school provided lunch, all I remember was taking a sack lunch to school every day, and I absolutely detested sack lunches and anything found inside them that came from my house. Other kids always had cool things to eat in their lunches, but I never did. Other kids had Pringles, Cheetos, Twinkies, Oreos, pretzels, grapes, and peanut butter and jelly sandwiches, but I never did. I always had smelly, greasy, warm ham, turkey or bologna sandwiches with a side of carrots or celery.

Even though I had recognized my life on the screen the first time I saw the movie, I was too young to realize it was also prophetic. When the movie had first come out in theaters, I hadn't really discovered boys yet, so when I saw the movie then, the scene where Joan is driving Christina home after having caused a scene and removing Christina from the boarding school, I didn't realize it was projecting my future. In that scene, while they are driving home, Christina makes a snide comment in reference to her mother's alcoholism by pointing out the closest liquor store to which Joan responds, "I should have known you'd know where to find boys and the booze." Even though I would never have much experience with either of these, it was just the type of accusation my mother would fling at me for years to come.

When I was in sixth grade the all the students who had received straight A's all year were rewarded with a roller skating party. I had never been to a roller-skating rink before and I was so excited because my mother was actually going to let me go. When she drove me to the rink and parked, I was a little taken aback because I thought I was just going to be dropped off, so right off my excitement dropped a level as she walked into the rink with me. She said I wasn't going to be there that long and it was too much driving to go home and come back, so she was just going to stay. After we got inside, she went to a table around the edge of the rink and sat down. I went to the counter to ask for skates and was met by a group of my friends. We all put our skates on and started to fumble our way out to the rink. I was relieved that most of my friends were just as inexperienced on roller skates as I was. We were holding on to each other or the edge of the rink for dear life! Little by little we started to get the hang of it and venture out in pairs until we felt confident enough to go solo. After a song or two and a couple of laps around the rink most of us were doing moderately well. We were having a good time laughing, making fun of each other when we crashed or fell. And like all skating rinks do, after a couple songs, it was time for a special skate. They made everyone clear the rink and announced it was "girl's choice." The lights dimmed; the song got slower, and after looking around the rink, we understood. It was the girl's choice to pick who they would skate around the rink with which meant it was time for a bathroom break, of course! My friends and I skated off to the bathroom to avoid the whole thing. It was great. We came out just as the song was ending and thought we could get back to the normal group skate, but we were wrong. The DJ jokingly announced, "Well girls, that was kind of lame. Only a couple of you were brave enough to get out there. Let's see of the boys can do a better job. Let's go boys! Get out there and find a partner to skate." Again, the lights went down, and the song was slow. Now we all stood around awkwardly because we really couldn't run to the bathroom again, so one by one my friends started to pair off, when a boy named Albert skated up to me and asked me to skate with him.

"Okay," I said as I reached out and took his hand. I didn't think anything of it. All my friends had been asked before me and we were just the last ones left and were just following behind the group. We were tugging and pulling each other along and making fun of who was skating with who, after all this whole *couples* thing was hilariously awkward to all of us. We came around the curve to the first straightaway and there was my mother standing at the edge of the rink beckoning me over to the side.

I apologized to Albert, leaving him skating alone in the middle and skating over to the edge to talk to her. "You little slut! How dare you!" She had made no effort to lower her voice. In fact, it seemed she almost screamed it to make sure she was heard over the music.

"What?" There was no mistaking what I had heard her call me, but I was just in shock.

"You are leaving right now!" she growled.

"Huh?" It still wasn't registering in my head what she had said and what she had meant, "We just got here! It hasn't even been forty-five minutes."

"I don't care, you little hussy! Go put your shoes on. Now!"

"Why?"

"It doesn't matter why. Because I said so! That's why! So, go!"

By now, my friends could tell something was wrong and they were staring at us. I shrugged at Albert to let him know I wouldn't be coming back out on the rink. I stepped on to the neon flecked carpet and began to make my way to the counter. By now my friends had stopped skating and were gathered at the side watching. Albert caught up with me while I was unlacing my skates. "What's up? What are you doing?"

"My mother is making me leave."

"Why? You just got here. We have another whole hour to skate."

"Yeah, I know. I don't know why we're leaving."

"Well, that's too bad. We were having fun."

"Yeah. I know." I mumble as I glare at my mother from a lowered glance.

"Well, sorry you have to go. We won't have as much fun without you."

Now my mother was at my side, looming over me, glaring. A nonverbal challenge, clearly telling me I was not to speak to Albert again. "Thanks," I mumbled, subtly trying to convey my apologies and embarrassment with all the meaning I could get from one word.

Albert could look between us and feel the tension, so he got up to leave, "See you Monday. Bye."

I had barely started my reply, "B -," before the sudden force of my mother yanking me up by the arm cut of my word as she started dragging me toward the counter to drop off the skates. The whole time she never let go of my arm, like she was afraid I was going to run away. Albert and my friends had all gathered to watch from a distance because they didn't understand why my mother suddenly seemed so angry.

"What?" I grumbled back at her as I dropped the skates on the counter.

"You little slut. How dare you!" she repeated as her voice began to rise loud enough for people around us to hear.

Trying to save what little dignity and respect I could in front on my friends, "Dare I what? I wasn't doing anything," I snapped back at her.

I should have known there was no way to save myself by now. She doubled down. Stopping in her tracks, with her signature move she yanked me around like a ragdoll with one hand and slapped me across the face with the other. Now it wasn't just my friends watching, everyone in the rink zeroed in on us, staring. Tears of anger and embarrassment began to well up in my eyes, as I now tried to pull us both away towards the exit door.

"Don't you dare to talk to me with that tone of voice, you little whore," she said as she followed behind me hitting me again on the back of the head with her free hand. Once we were outside and the door to the rink slammed closed behind us, I thought she would let go, but she continued to drag me to the car, opening the door and shoving me inside. Getting in on her side she began, "How dare you make me look bad in front of other people!" hitting me between each sentence, "Who do you think you are?" hit. "Slut!" hit. "How dare you hold hands and skate with a boy." Hit. "You are in sixth grade." Hit. "You are eleven years old." Hit. "You shouldn't even be talking to boys." Hit. "If I so much as ever see you talk to another boy again, I will beat you within an inch of your life." Hit. "Do you understand me, you little whore?" Hit. "Do you want to end up pregnant just like your mother?" Hit. "Well, you are well on your way, you little whore." Hit.

She started the car and we drove home in silence. From then on, any time we went anywhere like the grocery store or the mall and I might happen to run into a male classmate from school, if he said "Hi" to me in passing, I would pretend I didn't know them because regardless of whether I responded or not, just because a boy spoke to me she would always turn and call me a whore.

There was another scene with Joan and one of her husband's, who was the owner of the Pepsi cooperation. It was another scene I would see play out over and over again in my mother's life. Joan had just come in and given Al's apartment a major makeover, going so far as to tear down walls. Al tries to make her live within her means, but Joan just responds, "The real world expects us to live a certain way." Joan felt she deserved certain niceties in life regardless of whether or not she had the money for them or had actually worked for them. She felt she had to look a certain way and have her home a certain way to maintain her reputation, and my mother was no different. I don't know what Joy expected of my first father, but a school teacher lifestyle was not good enough for her. My father was always content to coach and teach, which pretty much means he resigned himself to a life of semi-poverty. My mother would never admit that was why she left him, but deep down, it was probably the one of the biggest reasons – being lured away by a man who made more money with a management position in a government job. With Joy's second husband, he was the one to leave her, and it was because she constantly wanted more. Nothing was ever good enough for her. She was driving the family deeper and deeper in debt, and he wasn't willing to go there. When he left, he left us with absolutely nothing. It forced my mother to crawl back to her parents and beg for help. They weren't going to abandon her and leave her to raise a child on her own, so they helped, but she kept coming back to them year after year with bigger and bigger requests for more and more money until they could no longer afford to help her either. Then she found her third husband, who only stayed married to her for a year because he quickly learned his entire roll in their relationship centered around money as well. Every relationship she had was about what was in it for her and how much bigger and better it was for her than the last one. It never mattered how tight the finances got, she always had her hair dyed and nails manicured. She always had the latest name brand clothes and perfectly matching accessories. She always traveled places with her friends and went out to dinner regularly – even if she could barely afford to pay the mortgage. Appearances were the priority and always had to be maintained.

The part I never understood in the movie was when Christina goes to accept an award for her mother who is about to die, and she looks right into the camera when she knows her mother is watching and with a complete lack of sarcasm says to her mother, "I always loved you." Every part of that movie was something I had seen or experienced myself – except for that. Having essentially lived through the same abuse, I don't know how Christina could feel that way. That is the most unbelievable, most campy part of the movie to me. I don't know how she could walk away from that relationship with any love in her heart. I have had to work hard in my life to come to a place of forgiveness for my mother, but that has never led to me to love. At first, I thought the producers must have put that part in because they couldn't have an entirely negative movie or people wouldn't like it. Then I thought maybe the producers put it in because, much like the rest of society, they held this unspoken expectation that all children and parents, deep down, must actually love each other. However, when Christina did interviews after the movie, she did talk about how she loved her mother. Granted the movie and the book only showed small snap shots of the Crawford's lives, so maybe there were other things events that allowed a love to blossom between the two women, but that is definitely a part where our experiences were different.

CHAPTER 9

"That is an interesting comparison. You have interesting stories."

"Yeah and they aren't even my best ones. Most people don't believe me when I tell them about how my life was so similar to the movie, after all it is just a campy, overexaggerated, exposé. No one believes me when I tell them I lived it, but my reality was even worse than that because my mother wasn't a rich and famous movie star."

"Well, to most people who see the movie those scenes do seem like an extreme exaggeration."

"Only they're not. I lived them."

"You don't need to be defensive, Elizabeth. I believe you."

"Really?" This time the doubt and the judgement were dripping from my words. I knew the truth. I had told this story a thousand times before; no one ever believed me. They always accused me of blowing things out of proportion.

"Maybe we should stop here for today. I think we should both take some time the think about all the things you have shared."

"I don't really need to think about it. That's kind of the problem. I have been thinking about it for years."

"Well, we will take a break for now and I will get you started on some medication, and we can talk some more tomorrow. How does that sound?"

"Whatever you say." It's clear he thinks the rest of the stories are going to be more of the same, and it's clear he doesn't even believe the ones I have already told him, so what's point? He's right, we should end the session.

I spent the night, just as depressed and miserable as when I'd walked through the doors earlier, but I missed my baby. The hospital brought in a breast pump, so I could at least try to make an effort to get as much milk as possible out before I sent medications coursing through my body. Choosing to be medicated also meant choosing to stop breastfeeding since I wasn't going to risk Tom being exposed to unnecessary medications. Even at this point, I was still trying to make decisions to ensure that my baby would have the best life I could give him. I knew I couldn't stay in the hospital for long and have him be cared for the way I wanted. I had to find a way to get my head in a better place.

The next morning, the doctor was back in the room.

"Good morning, Elizabeth. How are you feeling this morning?"

"Better, I guess."

"You guess?"

"Yeah." Does he think this place works miracles? Does he think just telling someone my life story will suddenly make it all better? I have only been here less than 24 hours. Things aren't going to get miraculously better in 24 hours. My husband is still leaving me, and my life still sucks. Tom is the only good thing in my life.

"Well, let's see if we can't get that answer better than a guess."

"Yeah, okay," I said, resigned to being locked up another day.

"Yesterday, when you were telling me about your life, you were kind of jumping all over the board."

"Uh-huh."

"Well, those younger years in your life play quite a significant role. In fact, the great Greek philosopher Aristotle once said, "Give me a child until he is seven and I will show you the man."

"Except I am a woman, but okay." The doctor didn't even crack a smile at my lame attempt at a joke. Here I thought he would be impressed that I *could* still joke, but I guess not.

"Well, I would still like to know more about you - your 'better stories' as you implied. Tell me a little more about those."

"Hum, maybe he actually was listening and actually did believe me," I thought before I began again.

One of my first memories was being told by my mother and father that adopted me about the divorce when I was four years old. Soon after, my mother married a man named David and we moved to Arizona. We only lived in Arizona for five years before they divorced, and my mother and I moved to Maryland. Looking back, I question the relationship my mother and David had. Was he really just as evil and narcissistic as she was or was he just the executioner of her evil deeds? It really wasn't until I was much older that I was able to understand the relationship between the two of them. David *had* been my mother's executioner and when he left us things turned more difficult in a variety of ways. Leaving us financially destitute increased her general level of anger and anxiety towards everyone, especially me, but when he left, the prolonged beatings ended. With David my mother would control her *anger until Daddy got home* and then would turn me over to him for long drawn-out punishments. Once he was gone, she became the disciplinarian. She didn't have the physical strength to hold me down, and there was no one else to wait for to get home, so there were more frequent physical outbursts and her own ways of inflicting pain, but there was nothing compared to campaigns David waged against me. For years, I not only hated him, I was deathly afraid of him. Five years after their divorce, when I was a sophomore in high school and living with my adoptive father, out of the blue, David called and wanted to speak to me over the phone. I was so afraid of him that not only was the concept of a simple phone conversation out of the question, but I ran and hid under the basement stairs. I was fifteen years old and hid like I was toddler. It took my father, Robert, a long time to coax me back out. It wasn't until I had my own sophomore aged children, that I could appreciate just how extremely odd that behavior was, but it speaks to how much fear he inflicted in my life. Robert convinced me to meet David for dinner and Robert would go with me (my mother's two ex-husband's and me – awkward), but about a year later Davis flew in from California for this dinner date and I went. During the dinner, I realized that many of the stories my mother had told me about both of these men were lies. Knowing the lies she told other people about me, I really should have known better, but I was young. It wasn't until the three of us sat down together and each told our versions of the divorce stories that I learned how things really went down.

I didn't realize until that night that the timeline of when my mother divorced my father and married David implied that she had been having an affair with him which David admitted. Robert explained how my mother refused to accept her responsibility for the divorce and she refused to tell her family about it. She had already divorced my father and moved in with David, so months had gone by when one night Robert had taken another woman out on a date and had run into his ex-in-laws at the restaurant. My grandfather approached my father at the table, accused him of stepping out on his daughter and almost laid my father out cold before my dad could get the words out to tell Fred to go find his daughter and ask her about the divorce.

When David and my mom divorced, he had just been coming out on the other side of a very serious battle with cancer. She had told me that the reason for the divorce was that he had a brush with death and realized he wasn't living the life he wanted with her and decided to leave us. After he left, our lifestyle dramatically changed, and we were left in abject poverty. We had gone from living in a four-bedroom, two bath house, where I had my own room and bed, to a studio apartment where I shared a mattress on the floor with my mother. She had told me that he had emptied every dime out of our bank accounts and left us with nothing.

His version of the divorce was very different. For one thing, he didn't like the way she treated me. He was being told how and when to punish me, and she would hold it against him if he didn't do exactly as she said. He said that the cost of cancer treatments had depleted a large part of our money, but that my mother didn't care and still expected to live the same lifestyle. He reminded me of certain vacations we had taken shortly after he had gotten sick and explained how the entire vacation was funded on credit because we had no money. He also explained that my mother refused to accept or face the financial difficulties and that it was actually her decision to walk out because he refused to live a lifestyle he knew he couldn't afford. He talked about how heartbroken and devastated he was to have been left right as he was living through his cancer nightmare. He talked about the cruelty of her choosing to leave him at the most difficult time of his life. He told me about calling Robert and begging him to try and get custody of me because he knew life with my mother was toxic, and it was David, who Robert went to for advice on how to get me out of there when I finally called to beg for help. It was this whole other reality that I had never known, yet now having grown up and seen how she dealt with me, I knew David was telling the truth. He wasn't a monster. He was just as much a victim of her lies and brutality as the rest of us. We all bonded that night as survivors of her madness, but when I was living through it, that isn't what I saw.

I was five when we arrived in Arizona. We lived in a small community where every house on the street looked very similar to the house next to it and there were only a few feet between each house. There weren't any children in the neighborhood, but there were plenty of older retired couples, and since there weren't any children my age to play with, I spent most of my time indoors trying to find a way to entertain myself usually playing with my dog, my two cats or the lizards I could catch in the backyard.

One thing my parents did to fill my time was enroll me in dance and piano classes, which I did not mind going to. In fact, I loved music and dance. I was always singing and moving around no matter where I was, and I was always getting in trouble for it. My mother was always telling me I sounded hideous and off pitch, and she was always telling me to shut up and sit still. "Children were to be seen and not heard." So even when they were actually paying for lessons for me to get better, I would be yelled at every time I would practice or made a mistake, so I didn't want to practice because I didn't want anyone to watch me or hear me in case I screwed up. Mistakes were not allowed. It always had to be perfect. She would stand behind me while I practiced the piano and would smack me every time I played a wrong note. I would try to avoid practicing whenever she was home, but then if I told her I had practiced at a different time, she didn't believe me. If she didn't see me practice, then I must not have done it and I would get in trouble because, "these were precious lessons" that they were shelling out big bucks for, and if I wasn't practicing it was a waste of time and money.

Even in first grade I had body image problems. Considering dance leotards show off every curve of your body, I felt naked. I hated how it would always ride up in back and my underwear would show. People aren't supposed to see your underwear, that's why it is *under* wear. My mother would drag me around town to run errands and go shopping after my lessons with me still dressed in my tights and leotard, and I hated it. I always felt people were staring at me. I always whined and complained, begging for a skirt to wear over it or for the chance to change my clothes, but she didn't care. I think she drug me around town in my leotard so that other people would look at her and admire her for having a dancing daughter that she was devoted to, but it wasn't long before she stopped taking me to lessons because let's face it, when your kids have all kinds of lessons after school, it's the parents who have to do all the work of driving them around and paying the bills, so the lessons never lasted a long time and the reason for quitting was all blamed on me. As long as the lessons made her look good, I could go, but as soon as she realized the true sacrifice of her time and money, they were over. Later when I begged to take lessons again, I was always denied. She would remind me how I would never practice. No matter how old I was or how much I begged, I would forever be the girl who wouldn't practice.

One particular day, while running errands after lessons, I guess I had been complaining too much, so as a punishment to shut me up David put duct tape over my mouth. We drove to the grocery store and he tried to take me in. He couldn't leave me in the car in Arizona; it would get way too hot, but I didn't want to get out because I was incredibly upset about having people see me being punished, so he grabbed me by the arm to pull me out of the car. I was tugging and pulling against him with one hand, trying not to go in and trying to rip the duct tape off with my other hand. Realizing that he couldn't easily hold both of my hands to ensure I wouldn't rip the tape off, David stopped, turned around, let go, got in the car and drove off leaving me standing alone in the parking lot. Even though it was far away, as soon as his car was out of sight, I took off the duct tape and walked home by myself. It must have looked strange to see a little seven-year-old girl in a leotard and ballet slippers walking down the side of the road by herself in a mostly rural, undeveloped part of town, but no one stopped for me. It wasn't the first time that he would leave me at a store or restaurant, and it would not would it be the last either. When I got home this time, it wasn't just a spanking, it was more of a beating. Apparently, he had driven back to the store to find me, but I had already started walking home, and I had gone a much shorter way, cutting through the desert, so when they couldn't find me, it scared them. And they showed me just how much it scared them with the smacks of the wooden spoon against my back.

The time that David disciplined me that scared me the most though was in third grade. One day, after my parents had left for work, I was walking through the kitchen when something glittery caught my attention out of the corner of my eye. Searching the counter to see what stopped me from going about my business, I saw a ring. It was a beautiful gold and diamond ring. "Wouldn't all my friends think I was cool and grown-up if I had a ring like that to wear in the pageant today. Nobody will miss it." It had been sitting on the kitchen counter for days. I thought to myself as I slipped the oversized ring on my finger, grabbed my lunch and headed out to school.

Since the ring was a little big for my fingers, it was getting in the way of class work, so I took it off and tucked inside my desk. Quickly the teacher guided us from one activity to another, and before I knew it, I was on stage for the third-grade pageant without the beautiful ring. While on stage singing some ridiculous ditty like, "The Mexican Hat Dance," I noticed my mother walking in late. When the show was over school was out for the day, so I gathered up my things from my desk to go home, but the ring was gone. I started to panic. If I couldn't return the ring to the kitchen counter before anyone walked in, they might notice it was gone. My panic didn't last too long, because my mother walked in and promptly questioned, "Are you looking for something?" I mumbled something about a lost pencil. "Oh, I thought you might be looking for the wedding ring you stole from me that I found in your desk." Stunned by the fact that Joy had come into my classroom and gone through my desk, instead of waiting in the audience with the other parents, I just stared at her in disbelief. I shouldn't have been shocked because she always went through my desk at parent teacher conferences, and the cleanliness of my desk was one of those things the teachers were supposed to monitor with my 3 x 5 cards but going through my desk now just seemed so odd. "You cannot deny the evidence young lady, so let's go. Your father will handle this when he gets home!" Her lips barely moved as venom seethed from the sides of her mouth. I lowered my head in silence and shuffled my way to the car behind her. There would be no explaining or reasoning that could get me out of this one. I knew taking the ring was risky, but I had planned to bring it right back home before anyone knew it was gone. I didn't know it was a wedding ring. Borrowing a pretty ring left lying on the kitchen counter shouldn't have been that big a deal, but the threat that "your father will handle it," told me that this wasn't going to end with a simple apology, or even a simple nose in the corner. I knew at the very least a wooden spoon would be involved.

We drove in silence to Taco Bell. She placed an order and we silently drove home. The first sign I had that this was going to be different was David standing at the door waiting for us when we drove up the driveway. I was immediately sent to my room without supper. Down the hall I could hear the thousand decibel explanation of how I had *stolen* her ring, and that I was "a thief - a disrespectful, ungrateful, lying, sack of shit, only out to hurt her and destroy the family."

"Joy, don't you think you are overreacting?"

"Overreacting? She stole my God damn wedding Ring! She did this specifically to hurt me. Get in there and take care of it!"

Confused by Joy's reference to her wedding ring, David said, "That isn't your wedding ring."

"It was the ring from my first marriage, you moron. What difference does it make?"

Kowtowing a little further away, he stammered, "Well, did you get the ring back?"

"That doesn't matter. That little brat had the nerve to steal my ring. What if she had lost it? Do you know how much this is worth? She needs to be punished like there is no tomorrow. She needs to fear for her life. She needs to fear taking anything from me ever again. If she can still sit down tomorrow, you haven't done a good enough job. I want that little brat to suffer for this. Do you understand me?"

"Joy, that seems..."

"I said suffer!" She screamed. "I don't want that brat to be able to sit down for a week, and if you don't go take care of this right now, don't bother coming to bed tonight."

"This is not my job."

"It is too your job. You need to stand up and defend me. You need to show her she can't treat me like this. You're the man of this house, and this is what needs to be done. That little brat needs to pay for what she did, and you are going to make sure she does."

"Joy." I could hear the frustration and anger start to raise in his voice.

"Stop talking about it. Get the hell in there and take care of this and don't come out again until it's done."

Then there was silence. I heard the carpet crush with every step David was taking down the hallway. I cowered in the farthest corner in the room I could find, but it did me no good. There was never any way to escape the spoon. When his shadow loomed in the doorway, I could see the weapon in his hand. He silently motions me to follow. The death sentence had been pronounced before the defendant was even able to speak. I knew from experience that if I didn't go willing and silently to the slaughter, the punishment would be more severe.

I will never forget the date. October 28th, 1980. It was the night of the Regan/Carter presidential debate. I think David was resentful he wasn't able to watch it. He wasn't my father, so why was he forced to do the disciplining? He had his own pent-up frustrations to take out, regardless of what I had done. Being as I had received this wooden spoon sentence many times before, I got prepared. He walked into the empty Sylvester and Tweety wallpapered room we kept vacant until his son from his first marriage came to stay with us and sat down. He silently urged me to assume the position with a simple beckoning curl of his finger. Alone in the room with my stepfather, I pulled my pants off and laid down over his knees. With the first crack of the spoon, I thought I would be in luck. It broke! Only now he seemed even angrier. He shoved me off onto the floor and raged to the kitchen returning with the entire jar of spoons. This was the second sign I should have had of how the evening would go; there were over ten spoons in that jar. Before the night was done every one of them would be broken on my backside. The only thing that made the beating end was the lack of usable weapon. There was a beast unleashed in David that night. Hitting me with his full force might have been his way at getting back at my mother for making him do it – hoping that she would see the result of what she had really asked him to do, but it didn't even phase her. She didn't even come near the end of the house where the spare bedroom was where her precious gift of a daughter was screaming at the top of her lungs and pleading for her life. I thought, "If I scream loud enough maybe someone will hear me and help!" I screamed and screamed...

"No one will hear you, and even if they did, why would anyone care about a lying little brat like you?" Smack! "Are you going to be good?" Smack! "Don't bother answering; it will only be a lie! All you do is lie." Smack! "Do you want me stop?" Pause. "Okay, I'll stop." Smack! "Oh, I didn't stop." Smack! "You lied, and I can lie too." Smack! "You have another thing coming if you think I am going to stop in the near future!" Smack! "You're crying because you think it hurts now, you just wait." Smack! "You little brat! I am sick and tired of you ruining my life." Smack! "I'm tired of listening to her." Smack! "I'm tired of not getting what I want." Smack! "By the time I am through with you, you won't even be able to sit down!" Smack! Smack! Smack!

This went on for well over an hour, when he suddenly stopped and shoved me onto the floor again and told me to go take a bath. "My dinner is cold," he growled as he left me lying on the floor.

Sitting in the tub, I could hear the mumble of the debates on the television and the sound of crunchy tacos. I was drying myself off and preparing to put on my pajamas when my name echoed through the hallway. I meekly poked my head out from behind the bathroom door. He was standing there with a spoon in his hand. It wasn't over. He had just taken a break to eat dinner. The terror continued for what seemed like at least another hour before it finally subsided. This round neither of us said a word. When I finally was permitted to go to bed, I was overcome by the idea that I had just undergone a beating that took so long that it included a dinner break.

David was right; the next day it was difficult to sit down. After sitting on the floor for ten minutes listening to our teacher read *Tom Sawyer*, I needed an excuse to get up and asked the teacher if I could go to the bathroom. I wandered around the school a little bit before I finally made my way into the bathroom, even though they were located right next to my classroom. Besides needing to walk around, I might have been in denial about needing to use the bathroom. Our stalls did not have doors and I was very self-conscious about using them. I hated them, but since I probably would not be let out again if I really had to use the bathroom, I knew I had better go. I had taken way too long, because Mrs. Hallier sent someone in to check on me. I was turned around flushing and pulling up my pants when I heard, "What happened to you?"

Thinking I was in the bathroom alone, I jumped, turning around, I mumbled, "Uh, nothing. I had an accident."

Later that day, Mrs. Hallier asked me to turn around and pull up my shirt. She saw the bruises that were all over my body. About a week went by, then I remember one night I was in my bed reading when David came in, with another spoon. They had gone out and bought a new set. It was clear what was coming, but I didn't even know what I had done to deserve it.

"What have you been telling your teachers?"

"Huh?"

"Do you even know what child abuse is? If you thought you were abused before just wait. Get out of bed. Let's go." He stood there watching me in the doorway as I left my room and went to the Sylvester room. I don't know why punishments had to take place in a different room, but they did. I stripped down out of my nightgown as he went to sit in the chair. After he was settled, I took my place across his lap. Smack! "You are such a liar!" Smack! "When are you ever going to learn to stop telling lies?" Smack. My whole back side was still covered with bruises from the last adventure in this cartoon room. It was hard not to flinch and squirm every time the spoon touched my skin. "What's your problem?" Smack! "Does this hurt?" Smack! "Oh, you poor baby!" Smack! "Maybe you had better learn to keep your mouth shut." Smack! "Who do you think you are?" Smack! "You are not special. Maybe a special pain in the ass." Smack! "You think you are so special you don't deserve to be punished?" Smack! "What kind of stories have you been telling people?" Smack! "I can't believe you." Smack. "What are trying to do? Rip this family apart?" Smack! "I am so sick of this." Smack! "You just don't care about anyone but yourself, do you?" Smack! "I told you last time I was sick of you ruining my life and now look what you have done." Smack! "I will make you pay for this, girl." Smack! Smack! Smack!

Lying in bed that night, running away really didn't seem like such a bad option, until I heard the wolves howling outside my bedroom window. The bruises from the first beating hadn't even healed before the next beating came, but there was nowhere to go and no one to help.

But things seemed to go from bad to worse almost overnight – literally. Third grade ended, and I left to spend summer vacation with my father, Robert, getting to know the new family he had just married into, but I returned in time for school to start and one night I had woken up due to a bad dream. I frequently had dreams of spiders crawling all over me or of me falling from a great height, but then I would wake before I actually hit the ground. Either dream would jerk me wake me, making it difficult to go back to sleep, so would I lay in bed trembling. Sometimes, I just needed the reassurance that everything was okay in order to calm down enough to sleep again but making the decision to go to my parent's room to tell them about a bad dream was almost as scary as the bad dream itself, so I would just lay silently in my bed staring at the ceiling for a long time. Sometimes just lying awake created its own fears – each creak of the house, each scratch of the trees on the house, each animal crying outside my window. This particular night, it was all just too much and I couldn't get back to sleep. My bedroom was on the complete opposite end of the house from my parents, so the distance to travel in the dark felt like the span of the Grand Canyon and was not a distance to be traversed slowly lest any bad guys in the house could see me or catch me. Once the decision was made to go, I threw the covers off and went sprinting across the house to their bedroom, coming to a sliding stop, inches from my parent's bed only to look and not recognize the body in my parent's bed and I began screaming and stumbling backwards. My mother flipped the light on from her side of the bed, and David bolted upright.

This was not the first time I had come running into their room in the middle of the night, but it was the first time I saw David bald. It wasn't until the lights came on that I recognized the rest of his features. This was how I learned that my stepfather had cancer. I knew cancer was bad, but as an eight-year-old that statement had very little meaning for me. My parents had done everything they could to hide the illness from me. I never remember him being in the hospital, or even being sick at home. Part of the reason I didn't know what was going on was because the timing coincided with my summer break. While I was spending the summer with Robert in Utah, Joy and David were going through a medical nightmare. When I came back home, everything about them seemed normal to me, but I was wrong. Very wrong.

It was a difficult enough time adjusting to the idea that my father, Robert, was now married, and my new stepmother had two children of her own and my father was going to be living with them and being their dad every day of their lives. David was a father before marrying my mother, but his son only came to visit us every so often, so I didn't really think of him as family. Now, that would be me, I would be the outsider that came every so often to step into their family life. My dad wasn't my family anymore, he was theirs.

But unbeknownst to me, back home in Arizona, the family I lived with was falling apart. It wasn't too long after the shocking reveal that my stepfather had cancer that I had another stellar shocking reveal. We had gone out to eat at some nice sit-down restaurant, and before the end of the meal my parents had begun to argue over something. I don't really remember what. I didn't pay attention to it. It didn't seem like the argument was any different from the hundreds of others I'd seen them have. I typically just tried to just keep my head down, so I didn't get pulled into the middle of it by one of them asking me to agree with them or support their side. When we'd finished eating, David got up to pay. My mother had a sip or two left of her drink, so we continued to sit at the table as she finished. We were just getting up to join him, when David went outside. It was raining, so we had both assumed he had gone to pull the car up to the door, so we didn't have to go very far in the rain to get in.

We were watching out the window of the foyer, when he just got in the car and drove out of the parking lot and down the street. My mother mumbled, "That bastard."

"Where's he going?" I asked. It was beginning to dawn on me that the tension was a little higher than normal.

"How should I know?"

"He is going to come back for us, right?"

"How should I know?"

"Great." I mumbled as I went to find a seat in the waiting area and plopped down to wait. I don't know if my mother had ever experienced the whole "being left" thing before, so I don't think she knew how to handle it. By this time, it was a somewhat regular occurrence for me. I knew it was raining and we were far from home, so I knew he would back. I just didn't know when. The only thing to do was sit and wait. Sometimes, when they left me at the grocery store, or the mall, or a dance class, or a restaurant or whatever, it would be as simple as a quick drive around the block just to *scare* me. Other times, I would be left for half hour or more. The first few times it had happened I cried, afraid that I really had been abandoned, after all they threatened to ship me off to the boarding school all the time, but after being left a few times, I knew how to play their game. You just waited. Rather than having the effect of making me scared and repentant, I just waited. They always came back, but I had never been left with an adult before, so who knew how this experience could be different. The only thing to do was to wait and find out.

My mother, on the other hand, didn't know how to react and she refused to sit. After a minute or two she began shifting her weight from foot to foot and after another couple of minutes she would open the door and look around outside, then walk back over to me, then walk back and look out the door outside. It was like watching a pot start to boil. First, you see the little tiny movements of displaced water, and little by little the movements start to get bigger and bolder as the bubbles start to get bigger and bigger. I knew when he finally did come back for us that the bubbling water would spill over the top of the pot and all of us were going to get burned.

In the grand scheme of my waiting times, this one really wasn't that bad, but if you aren't used to playing the waiting game, ten minutes can feel like eternity.

"Let's go," my mother growled as she saw the car turn back into the parking lot.

We got into the car and the lid from that boiling pot hit the roof. My mother screamed, "Who in the hell do you think you are? How dare you drive off and leave *ME*!"

"Who in the hell do you think you are? You're no princess sweetheart. You think you're so special. You're no better than anyone else," David retorted

"Screw You!" And then it was silent for the rest of the drive home, but I could cut the humid tension in the air with a knife. The angry heat steaming up from my mother was almost a visible ripple in the air. As we started pulling into the garage she growled, "If you think this conversation is over, you've got another thing coming."

"Oh, yes it is sweetheart. You are lucky I came back because I am so done with you," David snarled as he slammed the car door getting out.

"Yeah, well I am not done with you," my mother snarled as we walked in the house.

The sparks were really flying this time. Kind of as a way to remind them that I was still a witness to this conversation, I followed my mother's comment with, "Great. Here we go again," as I plopped down on the couch ready to watch the fireworks.

"Not this time, Elizabeth. Your mother and I are getting a divorce!"

I laughed a little as I said, "Okay." I mean, I didn't believe him. They fought like this all the time. That was why we had a big sign over our fireplace that said, "Compromise." Besides, divorces were things decided behind closed doors. His comment had to be a sarcastic zinger for attention, right?

"Oh, you think this is funny, do you?"

Sobering up quickly, I replied, "Um, no?"

"Good, because I am leaving," and with that I watched as my stepfather separated all of his clothes and went to the spare bedroom, the opposite end of the house from my mother and slammed the door. In my mind, moving down the hall to the spare bedroom didn't really count as leaving, so I figured I was right. And while it wasn't a part of their fighting I had ever seen before; I still wrote it off as no big deal. The rest of the evening my mother and I went around the house working through our nightly routines in complete silence, keeping our distance from each other. The next morning when I awoke, the spare bedroom door was open, and he was gone. It would be six years before I would ever see him again on that revealing night of dinner with the Robert.

A few days later I was just getting into bed at night when I heard a knock at the front door. Seconds later the yelling began.

"Changing the locks? Real mature, Joy. Let me in! This house belongs to me too." David was shaking and pounding on the door. I had gotten out of bed and snuck down the hallway, so I could hear.

"Go to Hell!"

"I just want my stuff. It will take five minutes." The pounding was getting louder and angrier. If the stuff belonged to him, she should let him have it. It wouldn't hurt us to let him have his stuff. It was his. He had a right to it, and maybe if he came in, he would decide not to leave again. I decided to try and step up and calm my mother down. When I came around the corner, she had her back to the door and the phone in her hand. As soon as she saw me, she used her other hand to grab the gold leaf bust of Beethoven off the piano nearby and fling it at my head while yelling at me to get back to bed, so I quickly went back out of sight.

"Get off my property. I'm calling the cops right now."

"Go ahead. I dare you. This is my property. I am the one paying the bills. I'll find a way in. I'll break this door down if I have to. You can't keep my stuff."

"I'm warning you. They're on their way."

Things seemed to go silent for a minute, before I heard rattling at the windows. He was trying to find a way in and circled the house checking every window to see it if was locked. The next thing I knew my house was glowing and flashing with the red and blue lights from the cop cars outside trying to settle the dispute. I remember hearing the police talking to Joy through a mega-phone, but I don't really know what happened. The reflections of the lights were there circling around and around on the walls of my room for a long time and as much as I wanted to stay awake and find out what happened, eventually everything got quiet and watching the reflections of the lights lulled me to sleep.

I guess the experience with David trying to get into the house made my mother nervous, so she hired a private security service to patrol the house. I don't know what was going through her mind, but I guess she thought if David approached me, I might let him in or something, so for the next three weeks I had a security guard take me to and from school each day. Of course, that made all the kids talk. No one was brave enough to actually ask me about it, but they were certainly quick enough to start making conjectures behind my back about why they thought I had a personal security escort. I must have done something to get in big trouble, or my parents had done something to get in big trouble. Someone must have gotten hurt or something must have been taken or destroyed. While it made most the kids keep their distance from me, I didn't mind. It was easier to let them believe the evil and sinister things rather than to tell them it was because my parents were fighting with each other and getting a divorce.

CHAPTER 10

"So how old were you at the time David left?" asked the Doctor.

"About nine."

"And after he left, that was when you moved to Maryland?"

"Yes."

"You said your life changed dramatically after he left."

"Yes."

"How did it change?"

My mother was never the type of person to let on to anyone that her life might be less than perfect. After the second divorce, for a while she went on like everything was normal and not telling anyone about what happened when they would call. I don't think she really believed that David wouldn't come back. But the weeks wore on and she started to crack. She would come home and call her friends, or her Aunt Cheryl and they would talk for hours. She would go on and on about how cruel and evil David was and how she didn't know how we would survive financially, but she never cried, and she never appeared to be anything other than angry. By the time two months passed by, she was a completely different person. Every night she would come home from her secretarial job with the National Park Service, poor herself a glass of vodka, put on some Barry Manilow, and begin to cry. I think she picked vodka as her drink of choice, so I couldn't tell when she was drinking and when she wasn't. She'd always tell me it was water, but if I smelled it or sipped it when she wasn't looking, it was never just water. Every night it was the same routine. Every night she eventually played the same song, *Mandy*. I didn't know who Mandy was or what she had to do with our lives, but I was getting really sick of hearing about her night after night.

I remember all my life rainin' down as cold as ice
Shadows of a man
a face through a window

Cryin' in the night
the night goes into morning,
Just another day
happy people pass my way
Looking in their eyes I see a mem'ry
I never realized how happy you made me
Oh, Mandy
well you came and you gave without taking
But I sent you away
oh Mandy
Well you kissed me and stopped me from shaking
And I need you today
Oh Mandy

I didn't even know that my mother had a diary, until she accused me of reading it. One Saturday afternoon, in fourth grade, I was sitting in my room listening to the record Robert had given me for Christmas. To me the record was like a secret message between us. Sure, it was about a relationship between a loving couple, but the simple part of it could also be between a father and a daughter. Lionel Ritchie's, *Three Times a Lady* was my song to play over and over. In my mind, it was the love my father was expressing to me, but at the same time, it was the realization that our family, our relationship was over. Our time together was just a memory too.

Thanks for the times
That you've given me
The memories are all in my mind
And now that we've come
To the end of our rainbow
There's something
I must say out loud
You're once, twice,
Three times a lady
And I love you
When we are together
The moments I cherish
With every beat of my heart
Yes, you're once, twice,
Three times a lady
And I love you

As life with my mother was deteriorating, the idea of living with my father was becoming more and more appealing. He had gotten married that previous summer to a woman who had a son and a daughter. I envied their stable family life enormously. Was having a loving family with a mother and father, brothers and sisters too much to want?

Sitting in my room, listening to my record, I tried to enjoy the song by singing along to it really softly, because any time Joy heard me sing, she would yell at me to shut up. Out of the blue I hear my entire name echo down the hallway. Here came trouble with a capital T. She had been drinking the night before, so I had been sitting in my room all morning, desperately trying to avoid her. My brain raced trying to remember what I might have done or even left undone the night before that I could possibly be in trouble for now.

I peered out of my room to see her standing at the end of the hallway with the dreaded spoon. "Don't you hide from me you little brat. Get out here."

"I'm not hiding," I stammered. Sure, I was trying very hard to avoid her, but I wasn't *hiding*.

"You know damn well what you did. That's why you're hiding, so get out here."

"I have no idea what you are talking about."

"Sure. Try to deny it. You can't hide anything from me. I know everything you do. I know damn well you read my diary."

"Read your diary?"

"Don't play stupid with me. I know damn well what you did. You weren't even smart enough to put it back." (Or maybe she was just so drunk, she passed out and didn't put it back?)

"I don't know what you're talking about. You have a diary?"

"It won't do you any good to keep lying to me. You're only making it worse. Now get over here."

During this whole conversation, I had been slowly inching myself down the hall towards her, not wanting to get closer, but not wanting to anger her by not going towards her either. Even though I was getting closer, her anger was still growing, and she was getting louder and louder, so that even though I was standing almost right in front of her, she was screaming at the top of her lungs. I was not about to willing go to the slaughter for something that I had no idea what she was talking about. When she could tell that I wasn't going to come any closer, she lunged to try and grab ahold of me, and I dodged her and went under her arm out into the living room. She started chasing me around the room, and I began dodging in and out of the furniture trying to avoid her hands or the spoon. Every time I jagged away and forced her to change directions, she would grab whatever she could get her hands on and throw it at me. If I tried to beeline towards a hallway so I could make it to a bedroom to shut her out, she would block me. After circling through the living room, dining room, front room, and back around to the living room four or five times, she knew there was no way I was going to let her anywhere near me. It was a physical showdown and we were both equally as stubborn. She wasn't going to lose this battle. If you don't consider the time in first grade when I threatened to run away, this was the first time she really kicked me out of the house. I was in fourth grade.

"Fine. If you aren't going to accept your punishment and apologize, you can just get out."

"Get out?"

"You heard me. Open that door and get out!"

That sounded good to me. By the time I had undone the locks and was stepping out onto the porch, she had covered the distance between us quickly, she slammed the door behind me clipping my bare heels. I cried out in pain and fell to the ground, nursing my now scaly scratched ankles as I heard the deadbolt to the front door lock behind me. I sat there crumpled on the ground for a while before I stood up and tried the door. I hadn't heard any sounds coming from the locking mechanism again, so I wasn't surprised it was still locked. We were living in Arizona on an acre of pure desert. Other than our small front and back porches, our entire house was surrounded by rough rocky dirt. Rough, rocky, unlandscaped dirt that did not feel pleasant on the bottom of my tender feet, but nevertheless I tip-toed around to the back porch hoping I would find the sliding glass door open. As I got closer to the handle, my mother stepped up to the other side of the glass and said loudly enough for me to hear, "You're not getting back into this house unless I want you to, so you had better apologize."

My mother just stared at me as I turned and leaned my back against the window and melted down to the ground. I was going to be out here a long time. I was already starting to regret not leaving my room that morning to eat breakfast. It was probably about eleven or so by then and I was starting to get hungry. I sat there for a long time because I didn't know what else to do. After all, this was just another form of the waiting game. I couldn't go very far in the desert without shoes, and the closest house to us in any direction was over an acre of pure desert away, and I mean pure desert. We were always finding creepy crawlies in our house: snakes, scorpions, tarantulas. You could hear the wolves howl at night. Not even a month ago, we had let our toy poodle out to do his business and he never came back. I was told that my neighbors found the remains. Quail, rabbits, roadrunners and bats were always coming up to our back door. During recess at school, we would go out and catch snakes and pull the tails off lizards and bring back eggs from bird's nests. Our teachers were always yelling at us to leave the wildlife alone, but we didn't really have a playground, so what else were we supposed to do? At least three or four times a year, I would find myself tripped up and crying out in pain because I found myself literally lying in a prickly pear cactus after tripping during a game of tag. We didn't have a playground. We had nature, and I knew being out in the desert without shoes was nothing short of dangerous.

I sat on the back porch for a long time, but eventually I got bored. Dangerous and painful walking or not, I had to find something to do, and I did not want to be anywhere near the house anymore. Our gravel driveway was at least a little less painful because the rocks were mostly smooth and predictably similar in size, so I went back around to the front and tiptoed down the driveway and across the street, through the soft sand river wash, down through the cactus and yucca, palo verde and mesquite trees until I found my favorite tree. Climbing up to my perching spot, I had a good view of my world: my house, my school, the neighbors, and the street. The tree brought me a certain sense of comfort and familiarity.

An hour or so ago I had been in my room minding my own business happily reminiscing about my father, only to be rudely awakened and brought into a nightmare. After the initial shock and anger wore off, I began pondering what I was going to do. Should I just run away? When I was dumped outside in first grade, I was beaten after they brought me home again. Should I go to the neighbor's house who had a couple of boys my age I knew from school? If I do, what will I tell them? Do I tell the truth and tell them my mother kicked me out or do I just try to pretend like I want to play for a while? If I tell the truth, will they just call her? I know I will get a beating if they call her, so maybe I shouldn't go to the neighbors and risk getting in more trouble. How long should I just wait for her to calm down? There wasn't any sort of real civilization within a thirty-minute walk, and I didn't know what to do.

The only reasonable option, it seemed, was just to wait her out, so I sat in the tree, played in the wash bed for a while, then went back to the tree. I tried to entertain myself to make the time and the hunger pass faster, but it wasn't easy. I didn't have any way to track time other than my growing hunger and the growing shadows. When the sun started to go down, figuring I had waited long enough, I wandered up to the sliding glass door at the back of the house and tried to open it, but it was still locked. I went around to the front door; it was still locked. Just as I was turning away from the door I could hear the lock turn and her voice through the slit in the open door: "Are you going to say you're sorry?"

I looked at her in disbelief. I had been stuck outside all day in the desert with no food, water or shoes because she wanted me to say sorry for something I didn't do. I couldn't believe she still wasn't going to let me in. Words couldn't even come to my mind. Even if I had read her diary, so what? What could it have possibly said that would have made her this mad? I had no idea.

"Well, you had better figure it out because I am not letting you in until you say you're sorry," and she slammed and locked the door again.

When the door locked for a second time, it was like my heart was locking too. Hearing the bolt latch, was like a switch being thrown in my head, and I knew I could not, would not give in to her this time. If I had done wrong, and I knew it, I would take the punishment, but this was too far, and I couldn't let her win this one because if I did there would be nothing stopping her from coming after me at any given moment for no reason at all. I couldn't give in. I wasn't sorry. I had not done anything to deserve this. Resolved to not giving in, I stood there and stared at the door.

As the darkness increased, so did my fear of it. The desert became wilder at night. Animals became more restless, and so was I. I was growing more and more afraid of the creepy crawlies that come out at night. I was panicking trying to figure out what I would do if she didn't open the door. I couldn't sleep sitting up in a tree because I would lose my balance and fall out so that was out of the question. I couldn't find any way of getting on the roof, so that was not an option. The only thing I could think of to raise me off of the ground was the green utility box on the side of the house. I dug through the trash and found a cardboard box. I broke it down so it would lay flat as best as I could make it, crawled up on the green utility box, tucked myself in with my cardboard box cover and tried to go to sleep as the night temperatures dropped rapidly. In the desert, the difference between daytime and nighttime temperatures can be wildly different, as much as fifty degrees different.

After a fitful night waking every so often, afraid of rolling off the box or the animals that might get me, I awoke starving. Seriously starving. I was shaking and weak. Sure, it was less than twenty-four hours since the last time I ate, but I wasn't used to it. The solution was simple. Not even ten feet from the utility box was the garbage can. I was too hungry to care about the grossness of the intermingling of dirty rags and scraps of food. I began rummaging through the garbage to find something to eat. I was sitting on my green palace throne, munching on my discoveries, starting to feel the shakiness subside, starting to feel more confident in my ability to survive on my own, when I saw my mother come storming around the corner of the house. She didn't even seem surprised to see me sitting there eating breakfast. She didn't even ask me where it had come from, nor did she appear to be worried or concerned that whatever food I had found to eat might make me sick. In fact, she seemed angry that I was resourceful enough to find food. I think she was mad that my hunger did not drive me back to her. We sat staring silently at each other until she came over, grabbed me by the hair and drug me back into the house. She tossed me down the hallway and told me to get dressed. Neither of us ever said we were sorry, and it was never mentioned again.

After David left, the drinking increased, and she became completely unpredictable. Experiences like the one being accused of reading her diary and being thrown out of the house started to happen on a more regular basis. When the summer finally came, I was so thankful to go spend the summer with my dad and his new family because it was reliably uneventful. One day during the summer, my mother called me. I knew something was up because I visited my father every summer and once she sent me down the airplane ramp, we didn't talk again until I came back off the ramp a few months later, so to hear her voice on the other end of the phone line in the middle of the summer was a shock. She had called to tell me that because of the divorce she had found a new job that was an awesome promotion. The only downside was that it was in Maryland and she only had a few weeks to get out there and settle in. I begged to just stay and live with my father, but she wouldn't have it, so when I returned to my mother at the end of the summer, it would be to a new home in a new state.

I understood that without David we wouldn't have the same amount of money we'd have had before, but what waited for me in Maryland was incomprehensible. When she came to the airport, we picked up my suitcase from baggage claim and went out to the same car she'd driven before in Arizona. We drove for an hour or so until we arrived in a town called Easton on the eastern shore or Maryland. Compared to the cities I had lived in before this place was tiny. Tucson had a population in the hundreds of thousands and Easton didn't even have ten thousand people. Easton wasn't always like that though. In the early 1700's it was considered the eastern capital of Maryland. Easton had the areas first newspaper, first federal offices, and first brick hotel, but to me I might have well as been in a foreign country. Everything about being in Maryland was different. As opposed to the harsh desert of Arizona, Talbot County, Maryland had 600 miles of tidal shoreline. Everything was about water and seafood and the history of our nation. But the foreignness of the state was nothing compared to the foreignness my life I was about to experience.

We drove into the center of town, and it was exactly the postcard image of small-town America with the Woolworth and art deco single screen movie theater in the center of town. We pulled up to a small two-story building that I was told used to be a firehouse that was converted into apartments. She opened the door to our apartment and had to kind of shove me inside because I froze at the sight. It was a studio apartment, so I could see everything in the entire apartment from the door, and it was basically empty. There was a small television set on a T.V. tray, a folding card table with two chairs and a mattress on the floor in the corner all boxed in with starch white empty walls.

We'd had a fully furnished four-bedroom house in Arizona. She hadn't warned me, and I didn't understand. "Where is all our stuff?"

"What stuff?"

"Our beds, our couch, our table, our piano. You know, our stuff?"

"I told you. I drove the car out."

"Okay, but didn't a mover bring all our stuff?"

"I couldn't afford that. The only things we have is what I could fit in the car."

We had a 1981 Toyota Starlet hatchback, so basically, we had nothing. The only things that belonged to me in that apartment were the clothes I had in my suitcase that I had just walked in with which also meant I basically had nothing because they were Utah summer clothes not suitable for Maryland falls and winter.

Back at my father's house my stepsister had a year or so left of high school and then I could have my own room in a three-bedroom house on a hill overlooking the whole valley. They had a dog and I had begun to make friends with the neighborhood kids and best of all I was never hit or yelled at or kicked out. Realizing that by refusing to let me live with my father she had condemned me to live in this hell hole with her, I became a very bitter, sullen, insolent child. She had incarcerated me. Forcing me to live with her, stole my happiness and my childhood.

"So, if you couldn't afford to bring our stuff, where is it?"

"I sold most of it to afford the move."

"What about the cats?"

"I gave them away to a lady at work."

"You could have at least told me. You could have warned me."

"Why? None of the stuff actually belonged to you. You couldn't have done anything about it. It wouldn't have changed anything."

"What about the things in *my* room? My clothes? My record player? My blankets? Those were presents. They were mine. You can't just get rid of my stuff without asking or telling me."

"Look. I have already told you; they weren't your things. You didn't have a say in the matter. I only had room for the necessities, and all you have is what's here, so get used to it. I don't like it any better than you do."

I put my suitcase down and went to the closet to see about taking care of the things in my suitcase, but the small one-person closet was already stuffed and overflowing with her things: shoes and purses all over the floor, scarves on the door, heavy winter coats, sweaters, robes, dresses, skirts, tops, sweaters and her multiple pair of Gloria Vanderbilt Levi's. She used to have a closet that spanned the length of the entire master bedroom just for her, and it looked like she hadn't tried to leave any of it behind. Where did she think I was supposed to put my things?

Seeing my frustration at opening the closet, she said, "Oh, you'll just have to keep your stuff in your suitcase for now."

"Great," I mumbled under my breath. It wasn't like it was even a full-size suitcase. It was a little kid's travel suitcase. The same purple paisley one I had been using since first grade.

When my mother and David were married most of the chore expectations for me were my room and bathroom. Often, I would have other things added to my Saturday list: vacuum the rest of the house, empty the kitty litter, load or unload the dishwasher, sweep the porch, take out the garbage, but they weren't always me, so it was okay. Then David left, and everything changed. When she was married to David, it was he and I who did all the chores, and now there was no David, I became responsible for everything because "she was the mommy and the daddy now," and that made her "too tired." Granted it wasn't hard to keep a studio apartment with no furniture clean, but it was more the premise of it. She had been able to pack the vacuum and the ironing board across country, but not a single thing I owed. The vacuum and ironing board sort of became mine though because I was the only one who used them. The apartment had no dishwasher or washer/dryer. I became the dishwasher and at ten years old, twice a week I would put all our clothes in a basket on wheels and walk two blocks to babysit our clothes at the laundromat. I had to go to the laundromat twice a week because not only were the clothes I had brought with me not appropriate for Maryland winters, but I only had a few. Sadly, providing me a whole new wardrobe was not exactly a priority for my mother. Her new job required her to dress in suit dresses, which required a whole new wardrobe for her, along with now, ever more frequent, weekly hair and nail appointments to keep up appearances.

School started for me a week after I arrived in town and realizing my summer shorts and flip flops weren't appropriate for school, she took it upon herself to make sure I was at least minimally prepared. Shopping with her was a like visiting a house of horrors. She always liked the shortest, tightest, floweriest, ruffliest, sparkliest, glitteriest, gaudiest stuff she could find. Trying on whatever hideous thing she picked out always made me feel like I was the center ring attraction at the freak show. I hated it. What I liked didn't matter since I wasn't the one paying for it and picking out clothes almost always ended in a battle that I lost, so maybe I should have been grateful that this time she ordered my clothes through a Sears catalog: two pairs of non-descript jeans, exactly the same kind, and two pullover sweaters, one green and one maroon and one button down plaid shirt.

Those two pairs of pants were the only bottoms I had to get through the whole school year, and they looked exactly the same. She told me, "I got you the sweaters so then you can layer your outfits and have more looks." How many "looks" can you have with only three tops to choose from? I may have hated the clothes she picked out for me before, but at least I didn't have to wear the same thing every single day. It made me feel embarrassed and ashamed to go to school. I didn't get a winter coat that year until my dad sent me one for Christmas. It was a beautiful fluffy white one, until I washed it with my mother's red robe. No one ever taught me how to do laundry, so that was a tough lesson about how clothes bleed. Wearing the pink coat to school made me want to bleed from embarrassment too. To make matters worse, I had a huge growth spurt that year. In fact, I haven't grown an inch since I was in fifth grade, but by February the few measly clothes I did have didn't fit well either. Describing the pants as highwaters would be generous. My one pair of shoes had holes in the bottom and the necks of the sweaters were starting to fray and the pink coat had holes in the pockets.

But if I ever cried or whined or complained about my clothes, she would go on and on about how important her job was because it was the only thing providing for us, and it was so important that she looked professional, so her clothes and appearance were the priority over mine because I was just lucky to have a roof over my head. It was a great speech, but it didn't make me feel any better about how I looked.

We lived in Maryland a year. After a few months in the studio apartment, we moved upstairs to a one-bedroom apartment. Now there was a wall that separated our mattress on the floor from the card table where we ate. There still wasn't a dishwasher or washer/dryer. We lived there for a few more months before we moved again to another apartment on the outskirts of town. The only thing I remember about the third apartment was that it was green.

Nevertheless, living in Maryland was an exceptional learning opportunity. My mother couldn't stand being locked up with me in those tiny apartments all weekend, so there were many weekends she would drive us into Washington D.C. and we would do all the appropriate touristy things: Arlington Cemetery, National Archives, The Smithsonian. It always amazed me because I would come back to school and talk about it and find out that the other kids in my class had never even been to the District of Columbia – not even once in their whole lives when it was only two hours away.

Either because she was concerned that I would get in trouble in my unsupervised hours after school, or because she wanted to have more time alone with the married man she was a mistress for, my mother got me a big sister from the Big Brothers/Big Sisters organization. Bridget was a horse groomer on the Wye plantation and would take me there sometimes. They would have rabbit hunts with the hounds and jousting tournaments. She would tell me about the history of the plantation. Fredrick Douglass had lived there a few years in his childhood. She would tell me how the main house still had shackles in the basement and there were still little blackface statuettes around the property. It was a different world. Out West, it was a rare occurrence to run into a person of color. When I rode the school bus in Easton. I was the one of only a couple white students on it. My life on the East coast was challenging me in every way possible. It was an important lesson in the idea that things can always get worse.

At least in our house in Arizona, my mother and I were separated by the distance of our bedrooms being on the opposite sides of the house, now I had to share a bed with her. Every night was the same. Come home from school, call her so she knew I was home, do homework or chores until she gets home, heat up some T.V. diners, watch as she drinks herself into a crying mess listening to sappy, crappy music until she falls asleep. Wake up and repeat. Day after day.

Maybe it wouldn't have been so bad if there was a greater variety in her musical rotation, but we were limited to *Mandy* (Barry Manilow), *Always on My Mind* (Willie Nelson) and *Memories* (From the musical Cats as sung by Barbara Streisand). On an interesting night I might be lucky enough to hear Olivia Newton Johns *Let's Get Physical*, but she would listen to these songs over and over and over. Each artist is a legend in their own way, but there is only so much repetition one can handle before even a note or two of the song can begin to make you revoltingly, regurgitatingly ill.

One night, overcome with my own depression as to the lows in which my life had sunk, I was curled up on the mattress crying my own self to sleep when my mother overheard me.

"What the hell is wrong with you?"

Silence. I knew better than to say what I felt.

"Why are you crying?"

More silence. I knew that to her there was no acceptable reason for my tears.

"Oh, is it because you think your life is so miserable? You poor baby. You think your life is so hard? You have no idea what a hard life is. Everything I do in my life is to make your life better. You ungrateful brat. You have clothes on your back and a roof over your head. You think you are owed more than that? You aren't owed anything in this life. Do you know how lucky you are to go to D.C. every weekend? You are a spoiled little brat!"

She starts to walk out of the room, and I thought it was over, but she came back in. "You have no reason to cry. You have no idea what a hard life is. You have a family that loves you. You have no idea what it feels like to hate your parents. You have no idea what it is like to be afraid to come home every day. You have no idea what it is like to be afraid of your father. Until you have lived in my shoes you have no right to be crying, so you better shut the hell up or I will give you something to cry about. Do you hear me?"

Silence.

"That's what I thought; you little spoiled brat. If you want something to cry about, I'll give you something to cry about."

It was around this point I learned the only control I had was to show no emotion at all. I would never let her see me cry again. I had a much harder time controlling my anger, but she would never see the tears again.

My mother started losing her hearing while we were in Maryland and she blamed it on the climate and used it as an excuse to move us back West. This time, I got to drive for four days across country in the car with her, with all of our stuff. Maybe it was sign of what was to come, but for only the second time in history, driving into

Vegas in the middle of a rain storm, water was spilling over the Hoover Damn as we drove into Las Vegas. The place I would call home for the next three years.

Not including the hotel on the strip, we lived in for a couple of weeks until we found a more permanent place to live, from the time we left Arizona until the time I left my mother the summer before ninth grade, we had lived in six different places in four years, going to a new school every year from fourth through ninth grade. But I didn't have anything to cry about. It was my mother who had a hard life, living in the same house surrounded by beautiful rose gardens and apple and cherry trees with a swing in the backyard her whole life, with her own bedroom, with her own closet full of her own clothes, with her close neighborhood friends, with financially well off, married parents, going to only three schools: elementary, junior high and high school. It was a hard life walking less than a mile to school, with her younger brother, in good winter boots that fit without holes, in the snow, both ways on the days she didn't get a ride.

CHAPTER 11

"It sounds like living with your mother was difficult," said the Doctor.

Really? Is his understatement an attempt to be funny or sympathetic? I really haven't even covered the most difficult days. It felt like he was just appeasing me, so I return the sentiment with a flippant, "Yep."

"I think you should read up on a website run by Danu Morrigan entitled daughtersofnarcissisticmothers.com. It lists twenty-four personality traits with examples of experiences someone who has had a mother with NPD might combat. It seems you have shared many of those experiences. Finding other people who have shared similar experiences can often help survivors to find ways to cope."

The worst part of being a child of someone with NPD is not being believed. Sure, he can tell me to visit a website about people who have had a similar experience, but that doesn't remotely mean he understands or believes me. Heck, even the American Psychological Association considered removing the NPD diagnosis from the Diagnostic and Statistical Manual of Mental Disorders. In my experience, people like therapists, teachers, other family members were always eager to defend her and explain away her behaviors, but finally, this was someone who at least acknowledged that I may have been living with someone with an identifiable mental disorder. "Hum, okay. I will check it out."

Quickly switching the subject, he says, "Good. One of the things we try to do in order to make sure you are ready to be released on your own recognizance is to make sure you are well supported once we let you leave."

Well supported? Oh, foolish doctor! Maybe you haven't listened to a word I said.

"We need to bring in your family and we all need to sit and talk together. Is that going to be okay with you?"

Confirmed. He is on autopilot. He didn't hear a word I said. "Go right ahead. I don't see the point. It isn't going to make a difference."

"Oh, I think you underestimate your family. I have already talked to them. They are very concerned about you and have already agreed to come in."

Here we go again. Always the assumption that parents actually love their children. In my mind, my unspoken response went, "No, doctor. They just want me out of here. They don't believe in depression. They think psychologists are quacks, and now my stepmother has been left to take care of a two-month-old on her own 24 hours a day. She doesn't want to care for the baby of a stepdaughter she barely tolerates. We had already spoken the day before when they brought Tom for a visit. They still did not understand why I am here and why I can't go home if I want. They do not understand the law that if a doctor believes you could do harm to yourself or others that the doctor is required to have you involuntarily committed to a psychiatric ward for observation. They were told the hospital would let Tom come twice a day for an hour, but my parents haven't brought him that often or stayed that long. Bringing my son to me, my son who was providing me my only sense of a reason to live, isn't even a priority to them. My health and sanity aren't important to them. It is their life and reputation they care about. They can't have a family member in the psych ward. They can't suddenly be expected to be the sole caretakers of a two-month-old. It's my availability to care for my own child that matters to them." I knew the spiel Robert and my stepmother would have told the doctor would make it seem like all would be fine between us when I got out. Everything in their life was always perfect and put together. Problems didn't exist. There was nothing the doctor could say that would make them understand the real place I was in mentally and the help I would need, so I thought maybe I should speak up, so he could see this relationship for what it really was, so he could understand that in my life, there is no such thing as familial support. "Well, before they come in, maybe we should talk a little about what it was like for me to live with them, just so you can understand our relationship, before we call them in and all meet together because ours isn't the best familial relationship either."

"Oh?" replied the doctor, a little stunned and taken aback since he appeared to have bought their story of all their concern and worry about me being here. "What is it that you think I need to know about them?"

While I firmly believe that many of my demon's stem from my relationship with my mother, I know there were aspects of life with my father that played just as important of a role in why I was sitting in that hospital having that conversation to begin with.

Life with my father was very different from life with my mother. Yes, the grass was definitely greener on the other side, but it wasn't without weeds. My stepmother was the stereotypical Cinderella –esque type stepmother. I am a shadow in her world that barely exists. My father inherently knows it, but never does anything about it. Once, when discussing the realities of my life he said, "you basically raised yourself from the time you were thirteen." Yep.

Sure, once I moved in with my father, at thirteen, I was able to live in a house that he had already been living in for six years, and I was fed a home cooked meal almost every day, and no one ever raised their voice or their hand to me, but weeds can still grow when the basics of yard care are ignored. So rather than someone looking over my shoulder and judging me with every breath I took, I was basically ignored.

My place in the new family is best illustrated through my relationship with my stepbrother. I was a freshman in high school, and he was a senior at the same school. He was a homecoming court, three-sport jock who ruled the school with his cheerleader girlfriend. My parents never missed a single game - whether it was home or away; one of them was always there and they frequently made me tag along too. He pulled a low B/high C grade point average. When our parents would go away for some weekend time alone, Brad would invite all his buddies over to drink beer and sit in the hot tub. Of course, my parents never knew about the friends or the drinking, and so in their eyes he was the perfect child who could do no wrong.

Regardless of his drinking buddies, I saw things from a different perspective. We lived a mile away, uphill, from our high school, and every day I would walk home as he would race by me in his car and ignore me – regardless of what type of weather it was. Never once did he stop to offer me a ride home. I had a low A/high B grade point average and was never late to class. I would sit in math class and watch him drive by the school in his red VW Beetle with a booming bass as he either skipped out early or showed up late. One day, I was at home in the basement watching T.V. and he was not aware I was home. Later that day we were supposed to go to my father's family reunion. At some point the phone rang and he started talking to his friend saying, "Yeah, I am supposed to go to some dumbass family reunion, but those people are poor white trash. They aren't my family, so I don't care." Thirty years later, nothing has changed. The stepfamily all still think they are too good for my father's family because they clearly are in a higher social class than my father's family. The step siblings haven't gone to the twice-a-year family reunions in decades and my stepmother tries to go late and leave early as often as she can.

There was another time I remember coming home for Christmas when I was married to Richard. We were staying at my parent's house and the doorbell rang. When I answered the door my stepbrother was shocked to see me standing there. No one had told him I was coming. When we exchanged presents later, Brad received season ski passes (easily averaging over $200 per person) for him and his wife and a grocery store gift card for $200. Richard and I got *a* book (to share), and we each got a shirt and pair of socks. The first few years I lived in California, I would always send Christmas presents home to Brad and his wife and Lacey (the older sister) and her husband. They never sent me anything, not even cards. Another year, when I had come home for Christmas, I told Ann, my stepmother, and the rest of the family that

I couldn't afford to participate in the family gift exchange that year. When that time of the evening came around Ann went to the back room and came out with a bag full of gifts and told everyone they were from me. However, since I had told everyone I couldn't afford to participate that year, none of them had actually gotten anything for me. Ann just used it as an excuse to buy everyone else two presents.

But I am jumping ahead. I should really go back to when I first moved in with my father. The first few weeks in Utah, I wasn't allowed to leave the house at all and we had to leave all the blinds closed and no one, not even close family, was allowed to know I was there. I had to hide to make sure my mother or anyone she might hire, didn't try to come to Utah and forcible try to make me return. After a few weeks, all the legalities were finalized, and we were safe to move around and announce to all the family that I had come to live with my father.

My first year living with my father was my freshman year of high school. The first few months of trying to figure out where I fit in was rough. On the first day of school, in a class called Freshman Orientation, the teacher, a coaching buddy of my fathers', said after calling my name on the roll, "Elizabeth Hunt! I've known you since you were knee-high to a grasshopper. I remember you coming to school with your dad when you were just a baby." That was all it took for everyone in the freshman class to know who I was. I was Coach Hunt's daughter.

I tried to live up to the expectation of being his daughter too. My senior stepbrother was the all-star jock competing in football, basketball, and soccer, so I tried to follow along and went out for Volleyball. I made the team and had a great freshman season. I scored seven straight ace points against our biggest rival and when volleyball ended, I tried out for basketball. My father's entire life was built upon his ability to play or coach basketball. I had never really played a day in my life before tryouts, so I didn't make it. Not wanting to be a disappointment and still wanting to still be that three-sport star, I went to the swim team. No one ever got cut from the swim team. I had never formally been taught to swim either, but I did okay. I could perform all the strokes with reasonable success. I mean, I could do a 50-yard butterfly without drowning, but after a few meets the coach decided to change things up. He put me in the 500-yard race. I about died. After the first 200 yards, I started to switch back and forth between freestyle and backstroke. After another 100 yards, when everyone else had already been for some time, there was just me and another competitor. I was barely a lap in front of her, which would have been okay except for when I realized she had no legs. Here I was as a fully able-bodied human being and I was going to get my butt kicked by someone with no legs. Regardless of the lecture regarding lack of commitment, letting down my team and the clear disappointment from my father, I quit the swim team the next day. I had no business being on a competitive swim team if I could get my butt kicked by someone without legs – even if she was really good. I didn't even bother trying out for a spring sport. My high school sports career was over, and I was okay with that, unlike my stepbrother, no one came to watch me compete anyway.

The friends I had made through sports weren't really the kind of people I wanted to hang out with either. Everything was a competition – not just sports. If I told my volleyball friends I thought a boy was cute during first period, one of them would be wearing his letterman's jacket by fourth period. My teammates weren't really interested in school or the sports they played. It seemed the only thing that mattered was the social status acquired from playing and the accompanying parties. Every party had free flowing alcohol, and every opposite gender relationship held an expectation of sex. It only took one or two invites to parties after the games or the meets for me to realize I was hanging with the wrong crowd, so once I quit the swim team, I didn't really have anyone left to talk to. I was afraid to look like a loner, so during lunches I would take a long lap around the school, always trying to walk with a purpose, so it looked like I had a place to go, and I would never just sit down alone.

A couple of guys asked me out on dates, and I went. I was nice, and I thought we'd had a good time. A few of the relationships developed into more than just a couple of dates, but when I wouldn't even kiss them, I was dumped. It turns out that just going out on a date for fun was considered rude. If the boy paid for the date and it didn't result in at least a goodnight kiss, I was apparently taking advantage of them. A couple of these guys were friends and they started the EHH club, which stood for the Elizabeth Hunt Hater's. Any time I walked past one of them in-between classes they would call me a "Bitch" and tried to shoulder check me to make me drop my books. They would leave nasty notes in my locker or have their friends pass them to me in class.

I was lucky enough to have my father as the teacher for my gym class. I was never a typical girlie girl, so I loved P.E., and I loved to participate to the best of my abilities. I was not a girl to hang out on the side or run away from a ball coming at me. I thought gym was fun, and I got to spend time with my father. Class was all well and good until the day we played dodgeball because one of the EHH founding members, Scott, was on the opposite team from me. I usually just tried my best to avoid him and it never really caused a problem, but having him on the opposite team in dodgeball, I knew his single-minded focus would be to hit me as hard as he could. I tried to protest playing against him, knowing it was just setting me up for the slaughter, but my father just said, "I can't protect you just because you are my daughter. You have to take your hits just like everybody else does. Now get out there."

Five minutes later, when Scott got the ball, I knew what was coming. I looked to my dad to step in and help me, but he did nothing. And while I was looking at my dad, Scott took the ball and drilled me in the head, and I was laid out flat on the gym floor, ears ringing and tears welling up in my eyes from the sting of the ball on my face. Head shots were supposed to be completely against the rules. But all I heard from across the gym was, "Get up, Elizabeth!"

I stumbled to my feet, to go take my obligatory time out, but I stayed out the rest of the game. When a new round started, I went and sat with all the kids who sat against the wall because they didn't dress or refused to play.

My father came over to the side and said, "How do you think it looks when my own daughter refuses to participate?"

"I am no different than all the other girls sitting over here."

"You are my daughter, and you will get your butt back out on that court now. I don't care who's on the opposing team. Do you understand me?"

I could tell this was not the time or place to challenge him, so I went, but I paced the back line, way too far out of reach for another punishing shot, but not shying away from easy bounce outs either. I would rotate on and off the court, but I never picked up another ball to actively participate.

By the time the middle of my sophomore year rolled around, my father started to worry about me because I didn't seem to have any friends. He was never even aware there was an EHH club, but a year later as I started to isolate myself even more, he started to notice. The good church girls shunned me because my family didn't go to church and party crowd didn't want me because I wouldn't drink or put out. One night my dad came into my room to harass me for not going to a school dance. He said, "You should go with Deb down the street."

"You mean the girl who just got pregnant?"

"Then how about Gillian?" (The cheerleader across the street.)

"You don't know what she's like, Dad."

"What are you talking about? She's a good girl. You two used to hang out all the time."

"That was before she started drinking."

"Well, you have to know someone you can go with."

"Nobody I want to go with."

"Well, you should just call Gillian and go anyway."

"Whatever." And so, I did.

Gillian and I drove to the dance together, but once we were inside, she ditched me to go hang with her own friends. For most of the rest of the dance, I sat alone on the one row of bleachers they had put out for the kids to sit on, until a group of seniors came up to talk to me. They were performing arts kids that I idolized, and they came to talk to me.

I don't know why they chose to come up and start talking to me, but it changed my life. Their inclusion of me that night led to opening a whole new world. It started with auditioning for the next play, and I got one of the leading roles. From, that point on, I was in every production the school ever did. I found a new group of friends and new role models. One of those seniors who came to talk to me that first night had the lead role in the musical, was a member of student government, had won every award he could win in math and science at the school, had every girl clamoring to date him (even though he was gay) and received the highest scholarship from the state that was possible. I knew there was no way my parents were going to help me pay for college, so I spent a lot of time trying to watch and learn from the seniors that were getting the big scholarships. I spent a considerable amount of time with Nick and asked him an abundance of questions about how he was able to accomplish all those incredible achievements.

"First, it starts with good grades. You have to study and work hard. You have to get the best grades you can. Second, you need to be well rounded. You have to participate in lots of things, not just one. Third, you have to do service. Find what you like to do the most, what has the most meaning for you and find a way to give back. Fourth, enjoy life. It will all be meaningless if you don't enjoy it." Nick's advice clearly served him well in his life because he grew up to get his Doctorate in cell biology and became the Dean of Students at a prestigious research university and lived happily ever after with his life partner.

Nick's example and leadership served as my model for success for the rest of my high school career. My senior year I was selected as a student director for the theater department. I was the debate and choir president; the color guard captain and sole instructor/show designer for the color guard, traveling to California with the band and the choir. In fact, I was so successful in band I had spent the summer traveling and preforming all over the country, culminating in a semifinalist placement in a World Championship competition. I was elected as a member of student government and was admitted to the early college program. Finally, I was the leader of the program called the Governor's Youth Council which strove to prevent drug and alcohol abuse in children by traveling throughout the state making presentations at schools. While I didn't earn a scholarship, I did receive a four-year teaching incentive loan. As long as I promised to teach for four years, the state would pay for four years of my college education.

During my eighth-grade year, I was walking down the road, putting a razor to my wrist ready to end it all. Four years later I was on top of the world, but I had done it entirely on my own.

Robert and Ann didn't know how to relate to the performing arts. I was lucky if they would show up to one show in the run of a play, and I never received flowers or gifts. Other parents would come every night and give girls flowers or candy on closing night. Not my parents.

Of the hundreds of band competitions I performed at in four years' time, all around the country, they came to one local show one year. They didn't see the point of participating in band. They didn't see what purpose competing in band served in my life, or how I could use the skills later. I auditioned and was invited to tour with the five-time World Championship winning (drum corps) band – an opportunity allowed to only 40 people in my section from the entire country – an opportunity band students around the country could only dream about. It was the opportunity of a lifetime. I had auditioned and made it, but my parents didn't "get it," so there was no help or support to make the tour happen by helping me get to rehearsals or pay for instruction. I was relegated to the minor leagues of a semifinalist band closer to home because that was all I could make happen on my own by arranging my own transportation and funds. I wanted to make a career out of teaching band. I wanted to be the next Scott Chandler – the reigning instructor of the World Championship group (the equivalent to Michael Jordan in the sports world). If I had gone to perform with that group, like I was invited to, it would have changed my entire life, but my parents didn't understand what difference it made between one group and another. I tried explaining to them using sports analogies they could understand. Touring with the world champions was like playing for the World Series championship winning team and touring with the other band was like playing for the local farm team. With the world championship team, the treatment was better, the talent of my peers would be better, the coaching staff would be better, the lifetime opportunities would be better, the chance for me to win a national title would be better. From an academic perspective it was like be admitted to Stanford as opposed to attending the local junior college. The two groups just weren't the same, but it was music, so no analogy I could provide even mattered. My parents just didn't understand. To them all groups were all the same. They were all a waste of my time and money because a band was a band, and a show was a show. Robert had won the Junior College Basketball National Championships in 1958. That paved the way for his scholarship to a four-year university and he went on to become a P.E. teacher and high school basketball state champion coach. What did sports do for his life? Is every sports franchise, regardless of competitive level the same? Is every college the same? Of course not, but my father refused to see what being a member of the World Championship band could do for me because "performing arts are *not the same* as sports." It was a battle I could never win. The kids who took my spot on the pro team are still teaching in the activity today, because people value the name of the organization on their resume, but my little farm team folded and no one recognizes the name of the group I performed with, so no one values my experience. It was just a farm team after all.

I was competing on the national stage in band and couldn't get them to come to a show, regular hometown performances weren't any better. No grandparents or stepsiblings ever saw any of my shows.

It was always the most heart breaking on opening and closing nights when all my peers would be surrounded by their family, extended families, friends, neighbors, and church members receiving gifts and flowers, and I would stand there being awkwardly congratulated by complete strangers who would feel sorry to see me standing there awkwardly by myself. Eventually, I stopped participating in post-performance meet and greets. I would be changed and gone by the time the rest of the cast returned backstage. It was hard to see all my friend's families and supporters come to multiple shows, especially the state, regional and national championships, sending care packages to our stops around the country, and there I was - never anyone or anything there for me. Even as just a semifinalist competitor, I was part of the nationals sweet sixteen. I was performing and competing on the national stage, equal in talent to my father's basketball prowess, and even though I was the sole director, designer and instructor for my championship winning high school team, while I was still in high school myself, my father still saw the performing arts as nothing but a waste of my time.

But if there was one time I thought I wouldn't have to specifically ask for my parents to attend something for me, it was my high school graduation, after all attending graduation was an expected part of my father's teaching contract. He was obligated to be there by his employer, but he wasn't there.

You see doctor, being completely alone on what I thought was one of the most important nights of my life pretty much sums up my life: I am always alone. Even though I am surrounded by people, I am still essentially alone.

CHAPTER 12

"That's great, Elizabeth," replied the doctor.

"Huh?" What was he talking about?

"Look how successful you were able to become."

Yeah, on my own – without support. Did he miss that part?

"Look at all those wonderful things you were able to accomplish, you performed all over the country and you graduated from college. Aren't those good things?"

"Yeah, sure, but..."

"There is no 'but,' those are good things. Accept them for what they are."

Realizing that he was missing the point of why I shared all of that, I just resigned to acquiesce to the conversation. "Okay, you're right. I did accomplish some amazing things."

"See? That's much better! Maybe the medication is starting to help a little this morning." The doctor seemed pleased that I had finally come around, even though I had only agreed to one positive thing.

"If you say so."

Or, maybe not. His positivity instantly drained with my response. "Do you really not think that you were able to come a long way and do amazing things?" the doctor questioned.

"No, I do, but what difference did it make."

"What do you mean?"

"Nobody cared what I did, so what difference did it make?"

"It made a difference for you."

"No, it didn't. Nobody cares about semifinalists. My life didn't change. Nothing in my life today is better or different because of what I did then. I would be the same person one way or the other."

"I don't think so. Doing those things made you a better person. Do you think someone has to recognize everything you do before it matters?"

"No, but..."

"Elizabeth, there is no 'but' here. You aren't always going to be recognized every time you do something great. Does it mean that just because you aren't going to be recognized, you shouldn't do it?"

"No, but..."

With frustration the doctor's tone and volume increased. "There is no 'but' here."

Grrr... "You're the butt here," I thought after he wouldn't let me complete my sentence for the second time. All I wanted to say was "just once." Just once it would be nice to be seen and recognized from my family – to feel supported, to feel like the things that mattered to me, were important and mattered to someone besides just me. Just once it would be nice to be seen and loved by my family. But he wasn't going to let me get that part out. Just once I wanted to finish my sentence.

The doctor continued, "There will be plenty of times in your life where you will do great things, and no one will notice. That doesn't mean you stop trying to do great things. We do great things just because it is the right thing to do."

"Yes. I know," I responded defeatedly. That was the only lesson I had taken away from life – keep doing the good things, even if no one notices because that is just the right thing to do. That was seriously the one thing I didn't need anyone else to lecture me about.

"Then stop saying 'but,' and stop worrying if anyone notices and just keep on doing great things."

"It's hard."

"Of course, it is. Life is hard. Who told you it would be easy?"

I don't respond. There were too many angry, negative, sarcastic, zinger retorts racing through my head that I knew I should never say, so I just sat there, silently.

"Look, Elizabeth, we know life isn't going to be easy. We know not everything we do is going to be recognized, but we have to do them anyway. The trick is to just keep going. Keep putting one foot in front of the other, one moment at a time."

He finishes, and we sit in silence for a while because I still have nothing to say. I mean that was kind of the whole point of why I was there. I was tired of going. I didn't want to fight to keep going anymore. I didn't want to put one foot in front of the other. I am tired of always doing the good thing and right thing and the better thing. I am tired of being walked on and ignored and taken advantage of and downright abused. Once, just once I wanted someone to love me for being me.

Inherently, I knew what the doctor said about putting one foot in front of the other was the only choice I had, but it didn't make it any easier to swallow when I felt like I was sitting at the bottom of a well that was only two feet in diameter. It doesn't do you any good to put one foot in front of the other, if no matter which direction you travel, you run into a wall. At the bottom of the well, I couldn't see the light at the top. The sheer vertical rockface climb just seemed too daunting to keep trying because climbing takes way more strength than just putting one foot in front of the other. Your arms get tired and shaky. Sometimes, you really can't grasp the wall anymore. It's not like I have everlasting superhero muscles. I just needed time, a rope and someone to give a little tug when my body gives out.

"I am going to let you sit and think about what it takes to keep going while I go out and talk to your parents about what we need to do to get you out of here, okay? They may not have supported you then, but they are clearly supporting you now because they are outside waiting for me."

"Yeah," I mumble. "Okay," feeling defeated because it was clear he didn't see my point. Other than allowing me to leave my mother and giving me a place to live after leaving Richard, Robert and Ann had never been there to support me in anything meaningful or important in my life. Why where they suddenly going to be different now? What difference would these days I have spent in the hospital make to our relationship? They didn't even believe in depression. But the doctor still only saw wanted he wanted to see – whatever it was that allowed him to move on to the next patient. Other than getting a great prescription, there would be no real enlightenment found from this hospital stay to help anything in my life be better. I was just someone taking up a bed that now needed to be used by someone who was in more trouble than me.

During the weekend, I learned what I could about postpartum depression and the benefits of antidepressants. After a few days on medication, I wasn't consumed with thoughts of killing myself and I started to feel better and was allowed to go home. I had taken my little time out from trying to grasp the walls to climb out of the well, and it was time to hold on again. I do not necessarily think leaving after only a few days was the right thing to do, but my son needed me. My parents had called Richard to tell him I was in the hospital, but he had no reaction or response to that information at all. He made no attempt to check on me, and that spoke volumes to me about what his real feelings towards me were.

After getting out of the hospital, I finally began to call my friends. Surprisingly, they actually understood more than I thought they would as I opened up with my story because suddenly other people started to open up about their lives too. I was shocked at the stories that started coming out of the woodwork. So many friends and family members had stories to tell about spouses that had cheated on them, except in most cases (but not all) they stayed married. But it totally shocked me how all of this was going on around me and I never knew it. I was living through it, so I understood why people were afraid to talk about it but seeing how much knowing their stories helped me to get through, I wished people would not hide their experiences so other people don't go around thinking they are alone, when they really aren't. Infidelity was something I had never heard discussed around me before and suddenly I was surrounded by it. I learned my stepmother's previous husband, my Aunt, my brother-in-law, and one of my friends had all cheated on their spouses. It was everywhere, and I hadn't known any of it before.

After I got out of the hospital my parents began to drag me with them all around the valley. Prior to being in the hospital, even though I was at my parents' house, they lived their life and I lived mine. Before, they didn't really include me in their daily plans. They would just get up and go. When the doctors released me from the hospital, my parents were given a lecture on how to keep better tabs on me, which included keeping me in sight, so even though I didn't really want to be taken all over town to do whatever they were doing, I had to go because they wouldn't leave Tom and I to be home alone. Up until that point I was pretty much just staying home with Tom and waiting for Richard to call.

But then came the holidays. I hated holidays even when it was a good year. Everywhere people are talking about being with family and all the joy of the season. Holiday joy and family were never things I associated together. But from the middle of November until the end of December it seemed like my parents had a different party to go to every day. I put on a smile and went from house to house while my insides were being chipped away with every cheesy couple under the mistletoe. Tom was the only thing that made it tolerable, seeing him in the snow and surrounded by all the lights, wrapping paper and bows and everyone fighting over who got to hold him next.

My life was like a junkyard, being swallowed by the piles of my messy life growing all around me. With one pile I was still talking to Richard on the phone every couple of days, begging him to reconsider his decision for hours on end. With another pile, I was trying to be a single mother of a three-month-old, and then there were my parents. Coming to Utah did not make my life easier like I thought it would. Rather than just leaving me alone to get my bearings in life, my parents were not really helping with the baby and they were pressuring me constantly to move on and get a job and my own place to live. It just piled more pressure on me. I was being swallowed up by the mess and I had to get out.

Even though I still desperately hoped Richard and I would get back together, I had now been at my parent's house for almost three months. I had to take the next steps and get out. Because of moving around so much in my childhood, I desperately feared moving from place to place as I raised my son. When I started looking for a single-family home to buy, instead of an apartment to rent, my parents thought they might need to check me back into the psych ward. They tried to get me to compromise by trying to get me to buy a townhouse or a condo. I knew I could not live in a place like that forever and with the real estate market in our area I knew it would be difficult to resell. Besides, I have known so many people who have bought a house with the thought that someday they were going to move into a better house, then life happens and that someday never comes. I wanted the best for my son, and I knew I could give it to him. I had a substantial amount of money coming from the sale of our home in California, so I wanted to buy my dream house. I found a perfect split level four bedroom house on a quarter acre fenced in lot in a cul-de-sac with a beautiful view of the Wasatch Mountains. A perfect place for a growing little boy to play and if I had to, I could live there forever and be happy. I went against everyone else's judgment when I bought my house, yet it was one of the best decisions I had made in a long time.

Even though I moved to Utah, Richard still hadn't signed the divorce papers, and even though I had bought a house, in the back of my mind I continued to hope Richard and I could still work things out, but I wasn't going put my life on hold waiting for him. Eight months after telling me he was divorcing me he still hadn't signed the divorce papers. He asked why finalizing the divorce papers made such a difference to me, like we could just go on with our completely separate lives without it. I guess I am just old fashioned in the belief that if I am legally married to someone, we should probably be agreed on the fact we love each other and are committed to each other. It would also be a nice bonus to live in the same state in the same house, but I guess that was just an outrageous thought. His inability to understand my reasons was just another indication he didn't get what the importance or meaning of what marriage was to me to begin with. Looking back, I remembered our early discussions about marriage. He thought getting the marriage certificate was stupid. He said it was just a piece of paper. Whereas, I feel the point behind the legal contract was because it was a sacred promise to love, honor and respect your spouse above all others. A paper that showed shared commitment to be faithful to one person, forever, but he clearly didn't see the value of the contract the same way, so having a legal document to recognize that commitment was meaningless. As soon as our house sold, he moved into her house, was raising her son and having sex with her as often as he wanted, yet he couldn't see why it was important that the legal bond created by that *piece of paper* needed to be broken. He obviously did not feel what he was doing with Scarlett while we were still married was wrong or immoral or else he would have been extremely motivated to sign the papers. He did not care or even realize the limbo his inaction placed me in. I couldn't move on and start thinking of my life as single person until the divorce had been finalized. His inaction in signing was just as painful as his initial adultery. I begged him to stop the procrastination and get my suffering over with, so I could just move on with my life, but he didn't.

Time passed and the next thing I knew it was April, time for my birthday. I prayed that my birthday present from Richard would be telling me this was all over one way or another. I prayed maybe he would show up on my doorstep. My parents asked me to lunch, and I hoped it was a ruse to get me out of the house, so Richard could surprise me at the house later. I prayed when I came home that I would see a rental car in my driveway. I even tried to make sure I looked my best, and I even went so far as to think about putting a note for him on the door when I left. That is how much I hoped it would be true. I waited all night to hear from him and I checked my email every couple of hours. Nothing. Absolutely nothing, and he didn't even say happy birthday to me when he called the next day. He had forgotten about my birthday just like he had so many times when we married. I had lived moment by moment for any word from him. I just wanted to have anything that said he was thinking of me. Just twelve months earlier, I was four months pregnant and thought I was so happy. There was no way I could have predicted that twelve months later my life would have been so entirely different.

A few weeks later Richard came for a scheduled visit. When I saw Tom with Richard, it reminded me how angry I was Richard could do this. How could he leave his son? How could he make someone else more important than Tom? Because Tom was only eight months old when Richard came to visit him, Richard would have to come into my new house that I bought by myself, alone, without him. And for the second time, I felt being a single mom was not such a bad thing, because you are the expert and get to make all the decisions about what is best for your child. Richard was worrying about all kinds of needless stuff and trying to tell me about stuff he read in books about how to raise children, but the reality was he had never lived day to day with a baby, so he had no idea what he was talking about and I tried really hard to let him be a dad without stepping in and telling him what to do, but Richard had no experience and it showed! Then there would be times Richard would just sit Tom down and Richard would lie down and ignore him by just staring out the window. I got the sense when Richard left that leaving his son behind didn't really bother him. He didn't know what to do with a baby, so it was okay only coming to visit every so often. That wasn't something I could understand because being in the hospital taught me there was no way I could leave my son for someone else to raise.

While Tom was taking a nap one day, I made Richard watch the movie "High Fidelity." I could see many similarities between that movie and us and hoped he might learn something when the couple got back together at the end of the movie. I was curious what kind of reaction he would have after watching it. The main character owns a record store. He defines his life using lyrics from different songs. He makes tapes that represent his feelings. His girlfriend dumps him, and he spends the movie trying to figure out why she dumped him by talking to older girlfriends. In the end, he realizes how stupid he was, and he gets his girl back. The part Richard liked the best, was not the end, but the quote at the beginning:

> *"What came first, the music or the misery? People worry about kids playing with guns, or watching violent videos, that some sort of culture of violence will take them over. Nobody worries about kids listening to thousands, literally thousands of*

songs about heartbreak, rejection, pain, misery and loss. Did I listen to pop music because I was miserable? Or was I miserable because I listened to pop music?"

Creating CDs that allowed him to wallow in his immature emotions is what led to some of our problems, those two CDs he created, the "I hate my wife and can't stand my life" CD and the "I have always loved you and can't live without you" CD. It goes back to what is it that really creates the miserable feelings in one's life. Does the music create the situation, or does he listen to the music because of the situation, but then the music only makes it worse?

Richard's birthday was about a month after mine. I called him and suggested that I bring Tom out to visit him for his birthday. Considering the problems it would cause him since he was living with Scarlett, I didn't figure he would even consider me coming because I told Richard that Tom and I were a package deal. Tom would always be in my presence, no taking him off alone. I thought it would be the deal breaker because he would want to take Tom off to Scarlett or to his parents, but he said he wanted me to bring Tom out.

While we were on the phone, I was taken aback by his music choice I could hear in the background. He was listening to "As If We Never Said Good-bye" from Sunset Boulevard. I was the musical theater junkie. This was not a radio song or something you just pop in. It was a conscious choice. I couldn't help but wonder if there was a meaning to it. Did he miss me? I was listening to it myself recently and thinking of us. I could only hope he was doing that too.

Feel the early morning madness
Feel the magic in the making
Why, everything's as if we never said goodbye
I've spent so many mornings just trying to resist you
I'm trembling now, you can't know how I've missed you
Missed the fairytale adventure
In this ever-spinning playground
We were young together

Then in a moment of clear thought I thought, "I must be vain! Why would I think his listening to that song would have anything to do with me?" Besides, it really isn't a love song. It is about going back to a long-lost career in entertainment. Maybe the line 'as if we never said good-bye' meant the song was about Scarlett? Maybe things are going so well for them - it was "as if they had never said good-bye?" Maybe he was just listening to a musical? Whatever! Could I ever listen to music again without reading something into it? Ugh! I had to stop doing that to myself.

Even though going to California for Richard was stupid because in my heart I knew we never going to be together again, in the end it turned out to be a great decision because it provided a life changing revelation. Going back made me realize that I didn't regret what happened. I was glad I didn't live in that small condo in the Bay Area. I was glad I didn't have to deal with traffic. I was glad I didn't have to deal with the feelings I had when he would get home late. I was glad I didn't have to deal with his alcoholic parents. I was glad that because I was in Utah, thanks to the sale of our house I could afford to not go back to work. I was glad because overall, I felt Utah was a better place to raise a child. I was glad my house was nice house and I was glad because I had so many people that had been supportive and loving to Tom. It took nine months, but I was finally starting to climb out of that deep, dark well I had fallen into and realizing that the light at the end of the tunnel wasn't as far away as I thought, and the light was getting brighter. Richard still hadn't signed the divorce papers yet, but I was starting to not care, I was starting to think of myself as separate AND happy.

Then one day in May, Adam (Scarlett's husband) called to tell me that he had received medical bills for Scarlett that indicated she had gone in for a pregnancy test. He didn't know the results but thought I ought to know about the test. As we talked, I learned he was also still waiting for her to sign their divorce papers. So, Scarlett and Richard had both initiated the separation from their spouses, were currently living together, and possibly pregnant, but neither one had enough courage to formally sign their divorce papers. But a month later, the confirmed pregnancy finally changed all that because eleven months from the time he told me he was leaving me, he FINALLY signed the divorce papers because her pregnancy became common knowledge to the rest of the family.

CHAPTER 13

There I was at the end of my first marriage with very little hope that I would ever find anyone that would ever be able to love me again. It was April, seven months after Tom had been born. I was tired of the gloom and doom and decided to take it upon myself to make myself happy. It was my birthday and I decided to have a party and invite all my all my friends. When I had my baby shower just ten months before everyone except for Mike and his wife, Jo, had come. They had just recently lost a baby, so it was completely understandable why they wouldn't want to attend someone else's baby shower. Mike did end up coming to my birthday party though, because our friends were working hard to make sure he was doing okay since he was also now in the midst of a divorce.

Mike and Jo had been married for about seven years and had just bought their first house when they lost the baby. After losing the baby all of Jo's emotions came to head. She let Mike know she had felt alone and unappreciated in the marriage for years. From her perspective she had tried to reach out to him many times to explain her sadness, but nothing seemed to ever change, so she turned to find friends online. One thing led to another and those online friends developed into relationships that became more than just online. Eventually, she started to meet and hook up with people in real life. At first, she tried to hide what she was doing, but then just came out and asked for a divorce right after the holidays.

By the end of my party, Mike and I had kind of separated ourselves from the rest of the group and were in deep conversation about our similar divorce experiences with cheating spouses. Asking questions like: How did you find out? How long had it been going on? It has been months now, has he/she signed the paperwork yet? When did you move out? What did your parents say? How are your surviving? What are you going to do now?

None of our other friends had gone through a divorce, so no one could really understand, and going through a divorce with a child is a very different thing than going through one without a child, but we found we had a lot in common – most significantly the painful feelings of betrayal.

After the party that night we found we both started to rely on each other for comfort. If I started to get too wrapped up in my thoughts and just needed to get out do something to get my mind off things, all I had to do was call Mike because he was most likely wanting to do the same thing. It didn't really matter if we had somewhere to go or something to do. It only mattered that we weren't home alone stewing in our sadness, and we could support each other during these trying times.

He had waited for five months for Jo to sign the paperwork. I went with him to the courthouse when he was finally able to file the papers. He drove me to the airport when I took Tom to see Richard that May. He could see the toll being a single mom of infant was having on me and would come over after work just to take care of Tom for a couple hours, so I could rest. It was amazing to have someone to help because once I had moved out of my parent's house right after the holidays, they essentially dropped out of my life again. Even though I was only a 20-minute drive across town, they only checked in every few weeks or so.

Little by little, Mike and I started to hang out with each other more often. By the time July came along, if we hadn't talked to each other that day, I felt something was missing from my life. I looked forward to any time we would spend together, and it made me happy. As my feelings for Mike continued to grow, it finally reached the point where it was beginning to be awkward. Because of my growing feelings for him, I started to become embarrassed to look him in the eye. Where everything between us used to be very comfortable and relaxed, things started to change, and all my senses were on high alert every time he was around. I was evaluating everything that either of us said or did for some hidden meaning. Wondering if it wasn't really an accident if he brushed my hand when we reach for the door at the same time. Just to think of him or hear his voice after a long day would bring a smile to my face, but at the same time I was afraid. I had been in this place before. I had felt these feelings before, and they didn't turn out well the last time. There was no way I was going to fall for this again. No way I was going to let myself be hurt again. No way I was going to trust a man again.

Then one day while driving down the street listening to a Disney movie music CD, a song from the movie Hercules spoke directly to me, and I knew I was a lost cause.

If there's a prize for rotten judgement,
I guess I've already won that
No man is worth the aggravation
That's ancient history, been there, done that
Who d'you think you're kidding
He's the earth and heaven to you

Try to keep it hidden,
Honey we can see right through you
Girl you can't conceal it
We know how you're feeling
Who you thinking of
No chance no way I won't say it, no no
(You swoon you sigh why deny it oh oh)
It's too cliche I won't say I'm in love
I thought my heart had learned its lesson
It feels so good when you start out
My head is screaming "Get a grip girl"
Unless you're dying to cry your heart out
Girl you can't deny it
Who you are is how you're feeling
Baby we're not buying
Hon we saw you hit the ceiling
Face it like a grown-up
When you gonna own up that you got got, got it bad
No chance no way I won't say it, no no
(Give up, give in, check the grin you're in love)
This scene won't play I won't say I'm in love
You're way off base I won't say it
Get off my case I won't say it
(Girl don't be proud it's okay you're in love)
At least out loud I won't say I'm in love

Yep. It was cliché; it was just like Journey said, I "just {couldn't} fight the feeling any longer." Face it, music speaks to you most strongly when you are either falling in or out of love. Bottom line, I couldn't pretend any longer that all I felt for Mike was friendship. If we were going to keep hanging out, I had to deal with these emotions. When it comes to sharing my feelings verbally, I have a difficult time. It has always been easier to express my feelings in writing than to actually speak, so finally one day, I mustered enough courage to write and tell him how I felt. Before this letter everything that had gone on between us was verbal. This letter was a turning point in our relationship where we began to include writing as an important part of our communication.

I don't know where to start. I am afraid of so many things. The last few weeks have been wonderful to me in many ways. For the first time I stopped being consumed by thoughts of Richard, which is great – only now I am consumed by thoughts of you. I think about you all the time. I check my email hoping to see a message from you. You always write something to make me smile. Every time we are apart, I can't wait until I see you again.

I don't want to scare you, make you feel uncomfortable or pressure you, but what I feel is deeper than just friends. It scares me. Even though nothing has happened between us, I don't want you to get hurt. I want to spend time with you, but I am afraid I will hurt you. After all you have been through, I couldn't bear to see you hurt again. I am also afraid you don't feel the same way about me. I don't want to be your rebound relationship and I don't want you to be mine, but neither of us have really had the time to emotionally work through our divorce, so I am afraid. I am afraid that what I am feeling isn't real, that I am deluded by how it is so nice right now. Life really couldn't work out this well, could it? You are so wonderful with Tom. I can't tell you what that means to me. I watch you holding my son and I can't help but love you.

When we were watching the movie the other night it felt so awkward having us sit on separate sides of the couch. I have wanted to hold you on more than one occasion, and partly because I think you have needed it, but I am way too chicken. I think you have the same feelings of trepidation towards me. Am I wrong?

His response:

No, Elizabeth, you are not wrong. There have been times I have wanted to hug you too, but I am also afraid – afraid of moving too fast. I am not comfortable with having these feelings before my divorce is even final. However, I could use a hug and a couple times I've felt you probably needed a hug too, but I have refrained. Normally, I am a touchy-feely kind of person and am comfortable with the whole hugging thing, but I just have some irrational fear about being too forward or something. I needed that hug last night as much as you did. Clearly, we are both a little chicken.

As can be expected, I was more verbose, but at least the lines of communication were now open.

I replied, "Try – a lot chicken! Our relationship is getting very hard for me, and I don't know what to do. I am cautious because I don't know what you really think. I am afraid because this is nice and I like it so much. I don't think I could trust anyone else. Until we can really move forward, I will probably continue to have strange bouts of moodiness while I try to work through exactly what I am feeling."

"I know," he wrote, "you can sense I feel the same way. We are both very nervous about being in a rebound relationship."

"I tend to doubt what I sense these days." I replied. "I don't want to hurt you. I trust myself not to hurt you, but I don't know... Sometimes you can hurt a person without even knowing it."

"I don't know what is best." He wrote back. "I do know I like to be with you, but I am afraid of how easy it has been for us."

"So, what now?"

"Six months ago, I was living one day at a time, with no real idea of what the big picture was and it was killing me. Some days taking life one day at a time takes a heavy toll, but I am getting better at it. The time I have spent with you has made the process easier."

In an oddly optimistic response, I said, "It is not that you don't have an idea of what the big picture is. It's just the roll of film changed unexpectedly and now it's a different picture. Shock is rough, but if this is the story the film was meant to tell, it will all work out."

We were married six months later. It was a surreal experience. Both of us were very wary and fearful of new relationships and being hurt, but at the same time we were so happy to be with each other. One day we were driving through the canyon and I said, "We should get married," and two weeks later we did, and nine months after that our twins were born and four years after that our youngest child was born. At the time of this writing, it is twenty years later, and we are still undergoing this adventure together.

CHAPTER 14

It would be great if the story ended there and Mike and I rode off into the sunset of happily ever after, but despite what Hollywood tries to portray, that really isn't how life works most of the time.

Marriage is hard. Marriage to someone with as much baggage as me is hard.

It is challenging to be aware of what your labeled problem is – to know what is wrong with you – but still not be able to make it go away. I know I have problems with depression and attachment, but even medication doesn't just make all the problems go away. I can be with Mike and want to hold his hand, but I am physically unable to reach out to him. I literally feel like my arms are lanced to my sides and no matter how much one part of me wants to, I won't reach out to him. I physically can't. My hands feel locked, like chains are wrapped around my body confining my arms to my sides, and it isn't something that I can just push through. The dissonance it creates in my brain refuses to let me reach out, and no matter how I try to explain the dissonance to him, he doesn't understand. He has always been a very affectionate person, so he has a very difficult time dealing with my lack of providing or desiring affection. Our marriage struggles regularly as a result. Our kids struggle as a result. I am not a warm, cuddly mommy. I find myself frequently needing to try to explain it to my husband. "It will seem like I am doing everything in my power to push you away. Don't let me do it. Don't fall for it. Keep fighting through whatever I throw at you, to still love me, and if you do love me, you can do it." And he does. There are ups and downs, but he works hard to try to be the man I need him to be. I can even watch myself pushing him away, aware of what I am doing, but I still do it. He has had to work hard to realize that often my behavior isn't personal, but a myriad of defense mechanisms built up as the result of years of mistreatment, and it's tough. I had never in my life had anyone who always had my back, who was always in my corner and wouldn't hurt me, so I never let my guard down and watch and judge every behavior warily. I have been taught over and over again to not trust anyone, so it doesn't take much for me to lose faith and find fault in everything around me. Things that might not even register on other people's radars as actions to pay attention to can cause me to go off the emotional deep end. As a result, there are very few people I trust, and even fewer that can call friends.

Other than when his wife left, Mike's world was full of people who loved and supported him all the time, so he frequently does not understand my fear and distrust of other people. I use an analogy to help him understand.

Imagine there was a puppy that had been beaten to within an inch of losing its life and left abandoned on the side of the road. Someone finds her and puts her in a kennel to take her to the vet. When they open the kennel at the veterinarian's office, is she just going to run into her savior's arms because she was rescued or is she still going to cower mistrustingly in the back of the kennel, even if you put food right outside the door? It will take a while for the dog to feel comfortable enough to come out, and if you spook or scare her at all, she'll run to the back again. At some point, she will come out, and at some point, she will let you touch her. She will be very skittish and will watch everything around her wryly all the time. If she is ever fearful, she will run right into the back of the kennel again and the process will start all over. It might take a little less time to get her to come out the next time, or it might take twice as long. You never know.

But marriage isn't easy. There will be challenges and sometimes those challenges have spooked me to the back of my kennel. Every now and then Mike will say, "Why are you looking at me like that? You are looking at me like you don't trust me."

The answer is obvious. Because I don't. No one is perfect and can say the right things and make the right choices all the time. I understand that, and even though my heart knows I should be safe with Mike, my brain doesn't always listen to my heart, after all I should have been safe with Richard. It doesn't take much to send me skittering to the back of my kennel to hide. The world has proven to be a big, bad, white, sterile vet's office with scary sounds and smells. There might be some safe people and places out there, but overall, I feel safest just curled up in the back of my small, dark kennel.

But sadly, as a parent, I don't get the luxury to hide. When your kids rush out into the world, you have to follow to make sure they're okay. And it isn't surprising, when people come after my kids, I tend to react much more like a wild, overprotective dog than a sane human being.

Dealing with relationship problems with your spouse behind closed doors in your home is difficult, but it is nothing compared to trying to make all the right decisions and fight all the right battles when it comes to raising children – especially special needs children.

When people see me and my family, no one ever thinks we have a special needs child or even more than one. Even people who have known me and my family for years don't think of any of my children as a special needs child, but in reality, our family has been repeatedly faced with the challenges of raising two special needs children. Having said that, however, our struggles are nothing compared to parents who have to raise children with the kind of special needs that requires constant medical intervention or support. At the same time though, that doesn't mean my family's struggles haven't been real. Sadly, in today's society, we are taught not to speak out about our struggles because we are told someone always has it worse than us, but when we get caught in the idea that someone always has it worse, it dismisses our reality and invalidates our experience.

I knew early on that my oldest child was different. I knew he was gifted, but I didn't truly understand the other signs and symptoms until he was around ten years old. At ten, Tom was diagnosed with high functioning Asperger's syndrome.

He was different from other kids his age. He wasn't interested in the same things. He liked to play with baby dolls and had imaginary friends, and he clung to me for dear life wherever we went: church, the store, family parties, etc. I enrolled Tom in preschool and the teacher would tell me stories of how Tom would go off to a corner and play all by himself and didn't care what the other kids did. She would tell me about the immaculate and intricate block structures he would make and that his attention to detail and focus were so single minded.

Tom missed the birthday cutoff for entering kindergarten by two days, I tried to petition the school to test him because he was academically so far ahead of his peers. I got the typical school run around, "Oh, Mrs. Mackie, every parent thinks their child is gifted."

"But you don't understand. I am teacher. I know gifted when I see it."

"Oh, Mrs. Mackie, yes we understand. We have parents in here every fall telling us how special their child is."

"I know he is different. Please just evaluate him."

"Every parent likes to think their case is different. If you still want, we can evaluate him next year when he is eligible for services."

"If you wait until next year, you're missing the point."

And I wasn't wrong, Tom ended up skipping second grade because he was so intensely bored with school. Tom was a teacher's dream: quiet, compliant, courteous, always finishing work on time with excellent scores, but at home he was nightmare. He would only sit in a certain chair at the table, when it was explained that we didn't have assigned chairs, Tom got a marker and wrote his name on the chair to make sure it was assigned. He would never wear certain clothes because he didn't like the feel, most notably anything made from a jean material. He would chew each bite fifty times, even it was applesauce or Jell-O. (I don't even understand how that is possible.) Mealtimes lasted for hours. Once a teacher told him to color his assignment, to him that meant every single visible part of the paper needed to be colored – on both sides. In fourth grade his teacher gave him the assignment to draw a picture of the Topaz Internment camp. Most students completed their drawing in class in about 15 minutes. Tom stayed in from recess all day and worked on it, brought it home and worked on it all night, after it was taken away to force him to go to bed, he snuck out of bed and stayed up until two in the morning to finish it. Every building, road, and tree had to be in the correct place and at the correct scale. And regardless what the truth actually was, if he believed something to be true, he would argue forever, even if facts proved him to be wrong. One time we argued over whether it was raining outside. I opened the door and held his hand outside.

"Did your hand get wet."

"Yes."

"Are the sprinklers on?"

"No."

"Can you see how the cement is a darker color than usual?"

"Yes."

"Is that the color it looks like when it gets wet?

"Yes."

"Do you see those heavy, dark clouds?"

"Yes."

"Did you hear the thunder?"

"Yes."

"Don't all those signs usually mean it is raining?"

"No."

"What made your hand get wet?"

"I don't know."

UGH!

Another time, he argued with me over what the state capital of California was.

"It's San Francisco."

"No, it isn't. Here look at the map. What does the star mean?"

"It means it is the capital."

"So, what does it say next to the star?"

"Sacramento."

"So, what does that mean?"

"It means the mapmakers made a mistake."

What do you do with that? If he wasn't always just saying the opposite of whatever you said, he would just non-stop ask questions and every answer you gave him resulted in another question. Every day, I was left exhausted from his questions. My battery was drained to zero. Finally, I took him to a psychologist and at first, they thought he had Attention Deficit Hyperactivity Disorder. Except, he could focus for much longer periods of time than his average peer. We tried medication, but it made no difference. Then they tried to diagnose him with Oppositional Defiant Disorder. Even to this day, almost anything you say he will contradict, even if he actually knows he is wrong. We have a hard time telling if he is doing it to be funny or intentionally trying to annoy us, or if he really just can't understand some issues, but his opposition was never mean or cruel. And when we would start to get frustrated with his questions or his opposition, he never got the cues, even if we blatantly said we were frustrated, he didn't understand why were frustrated. But surprisingly, he does best when you establish rules and structure because he will follow them to the letter. It is what has always made him so good in school, but even having what appear to be clear expectations can be difficult, like the example above of coloring his paper or the one time he nearly had a melt down because I walked a foot outside of the marked crosswalk when crossing a street.

I heard a saying once that if you have met one Asperger's child, you have met one Asperger's child because each is so different, and that is true. We had worked so hard with Tom to work through all these issues. He did well in school, and was participating in sports, participating in scouts, going to church, then in sixth grade he had a meltdown. I checked his grades at the beginning of May and he had straight A's. When I got his report at the end of the month, he had straight C's. I lost my mind. How could things devolve so quickly and no one at the school had noticed or said anything to me? When I confronted the teacher she said, "He always does so well that I guess I just didn't notice when he fell through the cracks."

"Fell through the cracks!" I was paying for my children to attend a private school specifically so my children would not fall through the cracks. Our neighborhood public school had no honors program and no special services they could provide for Tom, so it was decided that rather than return to the private school, Tom would be allowed to go live with his dad where the junior high had a gifted and talented program. In the meantime, while Tom was away, we researched and found where we thought the best public schools in our state were located and stretched our financial abilities to the limit in order to move within the boundaries of those schools.

At the end of junior high, Tom moved back, but he was a much different, more negative child. There would be no more scouts or church without long arguments and with normal daily battles I had to face, I wasn't willing to fight those too. He was still an academic star, but I had to babysit his teachers all the time. His last two years of high school were the worst. During his junior year, I would explain to his teachers that he had Asperger's and they would respond with things like "Well, he can come and talk to me anytime he needs help."

"No, you don't understand. The defining feature of Asperger's is difficulty with social interaction. Tom will never approach you with a question or problem, and I am telling you he is a gifted straight A student, so if he doesn't have an A in your class, there is a problem." I was not saying the teacher was the problem. I was not saying

I only expect my child to receive an A and you will give him and A. I know that parent. One comes to my honors class every year. I was saying if he didn't have an A, it is a sign there was a problem with him not being able to understand the teachers expectations and I needed the teacher to reach out to him to discuss it because he would rather fail a class than ask a teacher for help.

"Well, if he needs accommodations, he will have to ask."

"I am asking you."

"I can't do anything unless you have followed the formal accommodations process."

"Really?" I am teacher too, and that mindset boggles me. Is it really that hard to have compassion and understanding? Oh, I understand that class sizes in Utah are ridiculously overloaded and that effects a teacher's stress levels and ability to individualize and accommodate within their lessons. I also know how many times a day parents and students come asking for exceptions to the rules, but I wasn't for exceptions. I was asking for teachers to accommodate his communication issues with compassion.

Consequentially, his junior year, I felt I had to get a 504 for my son so that teachers would stop telling me this. A 504 is a plan set in place at the school to ensure that students with diagnosed disabilities receive the appropriate accommodations to ensure their academic success. The teachers needed to understand talking to them was not something Tom was capable of doing, and I worked in a town an hour away, and stayed after school to coach. I couldn't just walk into his school with him to talk to a teacher to work things out because they were never on campus when I was available. I got the 504 to clearly and legally explain to teachers that he won't ask for help and as such they are obligated to assist him and how do they respond?

"If Tom has a problem, he needs to talk to me about it."

"Did you read his 504?"

"I read all of my student's 504's."

"So, you understand that Tom will never approach you with a question about anything, ever?"

"He seems to do fine in class. He doesn't appear to have any problems."

"Have you ever seen him talk to another student in class or even in the halls?"

"Well, no, but..."

"Does he ever raise his hand or ask questions?"

"Well, no..." the teacher will invariably respond.

When Tom applied to an out-of-state college, the online application had him enter teacher's emails for recommendations. A process very different, at the time, from our in-state colleges. This is relevant in that only a miniscule amount of Utah high school students apply for out-of-state colleges. After waiting a few weeks, the online tracking showed one of his teachers still hadn't submitted a response. When I contacted her about it, she said she wouldn't fill it out because he didn't talk to her before he submitted her name. Normally, I understand. You should always ask someone if you can use them for a reference first. Tom sort of understood this. He sent an email to the teacher to inform her he had filled out an application and provided her email for reference. When I reached out to her to ask why she wasn't submitting anything and she said it was because he hadn't actually talked to her, I asked, "Why is the email request not sufficient enough for you to complete it considering his 504 accommodations?"

"Because all students are supposed to go talk to their teacher before they request a recommend."

"Did you understand the fact that Tom is deathly afraid of talking to teachers and will not approach you for any reason as stated in his 504?"

"Well, I understand that having Asperger's means Tom has problems with communication, but he should have talked to me first."

It was like having conversations with a dog that was running in circles chasing its tail. These teachers had no understanding that what they were asking him to do was the equivalent of asking a quadriplegic to stand up out of his breathalyzed powered wheelchair and walk up the stairs. They might as well have been asking him to leap over a building in a single bound. Sometimes, even after going into lengthy family history, diagnosis and explanation of his disability, teachers still refused to see the level of fear and anxiety the mere idea of speaking aloud in class would cause him, let alone the idea of having to talk to the teacher one-on-one. Why is it that I would have to go to such extreme measures just to obtain a little empathy?

"Oh, I know, Mrs. Mackie. We all think our children are different and deserving of special accommodations."

"He has a medical diagnosis with expected accommodations."

"Oh, we know Mrs. Mackie. We get your point. This is our job. We understand. Every student needs some kind of accommodations."

Yeah. This is my job too, and there is no way I would treat a parent like that, but with teacher after teacher and administrator after administrator this is what I would encounter. The assumption that just because he looks normal, he should be normal. That isn't how Asperger's works.

I agree. EVERYONE DOES NEED ACCOMODATIONS at some point in his/her life. The teacher will invariably continue as if they need to explain to me, "These students aren't going to get accommodations in the real world, so we have to teach them to deal with it now."

My easy to anger side kicks in because just like they face the demanding parent's hour after hour, I face the unsympathetic teachers year after year, and I think, "What kind of accommodations have people made for you today alone? What consequence will you face for showing up late to this meeting?" People have accommodations made for them all the time.

These teachers forget school is the real world for these students. The difference between a B+ and an A- can literally mean the difference between a four-year scholarship and a two-year scholarship. That 89.9% B+ in AP Calculus that the teacher feels so strongly is teaching that student a lesson on working hard, actually means that one of the smartest kids in the school is now not likely to finish college because his parents can't afford it. When Tom has passed fourteen AP tests, is graduating high school with his college Associates Degree and an unweighted grade point average of 3.8, is teaching him a lesson about asking for recommendations first really more important than his chance to go to the college of his dreams? Why is it so hard to treat students like real people instead of just numbers? (She lied and told us she wrote the letter. Online tracking showed she never submitted anything.)

Tom got a summer job as a janitor for the school district his sophomore year, and he loved it because he didn't have to interact with people – ever. However, he didn't get his first paycheck for months because he was too afraid to go into the office and pick it up (all the other checks were direct deposited). It was at this point I realized that I wasn't doing Tom any favors by trying mediate between him and his teachers because I wouldn't be able do that for the rest of his life if we expected him to go out into the world and function on his own. Because I believe school is the real world, I needed him to face these school battles, without me. I needed him to try to walk up those stairs by himself. The result was his grades dropped.

"Tom what happened to your AP Biology grade?"

"The teacher didn't grade my assignment. (Or the teacher lost it, or the teacher put the grade in wrong, or some other teacher mistake. It happens.)"

"So, what are you going to do about it?"

"Nothing."

"Tom, you need to talk to the teacher."

"No."

"But, Tom, you aren't receiving the right grade."

"I don't care. I would rather have a bad grade than talk to the teacher."

"Tom, that effects college and scholarships and everything."

"I don't care."

"Well, I care. Are you going to pay for your college?"

"I don't know. What difference does it make?"

"It makes a huge difference. The difference between a full-ride scholarship and partial scholarship."

"So?"

"So? So, I am going to go talk to your teacher."

"No. When you talk to my teacher, they know I am different, and then they look at me funny and talk to me funny, and I don't want anyone to know, so don't."

"You realize sitting here watching you take a lower grade than you deserve is killing me, right? You know you deserve the better grade?"

"So? Why should it bother you? It's not your life."

Except that it is my life, but he doesn't see that. And as challenging as learning to cope and live with Asperger's has been, my other children have had equally difficult health challenges.

By the time Tom was 21 months old, I gave birth to boy/girl twins. They were born a little early (normal for twins) and had to spend some time in the Neonatal Intensive Care Unit (NICU), but we were prepared for that because we were told that was a common experience for twins. One had to be on oxygen for a while and the other had to have a gavage tube for feeding, but both were home within two weeks. As they grew, my daughter seemed to have more issues than any of my boys. She turned her toes in and was told she had tibial torsion which caused her feet to point in (along with other issues). We tried to take her to physical therapy and construct various braces for her to wear to get her feet to turn the correct way. (I had always wanted her to be a dancer, but those hopes were quickly shattered.) Then she started having urinary tract infections. After ultrasounds and voiding cystourethrograms (VCUG's), we were told that she had kidney reflux problems in one kidney and the other kidney was basically completely non-functioning. As a young, new parent, seeing your little baby undergoing all these test and hearing doctors talk about medications and surgery, it can be overwhelming, but after months of repeated tests and many follow up appointments the reflux eventually stopped on its own. We were relieved. No surgery.

While celebrating the news our daughter didn't need surgery, it was discovered that both of the boys had inguinal hernias. Both boys required surgery. Again, everything went just fine but having to watch your children be put under anesthesia, and knowing that complications could occur with any surgery, makes it stressful, and to have two of your children in surgery on the same day doubles the worry.

Four years after the twins were born, my youngest, Drew was born. His pregnancy seemed much more difficult, but my doctor just said it was because I was old (34). When the twins were ready to be born one of them was laying transverse across the vaginal opening, so they had to come via cesarean section. Compared to the vaginal delivery I had with Tom, with whom I was the lucky winner of an epidural headache – one of the worst pain's I have ever experienced in my life, next to kidney stones and labor, delivering the twins was a breeze. So, when they recommended my last child should also be cesarean, I was all for it!

We kind of had a clue something was different when the staff was struggling to pull Drew out and when he finally came there was an audible gasp and comments about the size of his head. The staff in the room seemed surprised that his head size hadn't been observed during ultrasounds before he was born. While this OBGYN had also delivered my twins, this post-op experience seemed like he was trying to avoid me. Drew weighed 9 lbs. 6 oz. and was 21 inches long. His newborn head size was: 44.38 cm, which was in the 98th percentile. They were so concerned that they look him off to be observed and studied. They took him to the NICU for 24 hours and did a CT scan. They brought him back and said, "Nope. He just has a big head. No big deal. He's fine." We went home the next day. However, after a couple of days, we noticed he seemed to slowly turn yellow, so back to the doctor we went, and he ended up having to spend three days under the bilirubin light to prevent jaundice.

But at the well child check-ups his head kept growing and growing. At his two-month well child check his head circumference had jumped well above the chart to 48.5. They decided to request an MRI, in which they found a subdural hematoma (collection of blood outside the brain) and hydrocephalous (fluid accumulation around the brain sometimes causing brain damage). In our state, it is required that every infant with a subdural hematoma be reported to the Department of Child and Family Services (DCFS) because most of the time the reason for an infant to sustain a subdural hematoma is shaken baby syndrome. One doctor suggested it might have been the OBGYN who caused it by yanking him out of my tummy, and that is why he was avoiding us. So while we were in the midst of worrying about our son because subdural hematoma's can be life threatening and can sometimes require surgery, DCFS had to come do a required home visit. Granted they determined we were fine, but it was a perfect example of adding insult to injury.

As for the hydrocephalous, they were going to keep watching (CT's or MRI's) to see if the fluid began to build up or drain naturally and thankfully, after a few months, it began to drain naturally.

But even though the blood and fluid were draining, his head size continued to grow off the charts and he started to show signs of gross motor delay. He didn't really sit up or roll over at the expected time markers, but we supposed it was because his head was too big for the rest of him to support. The pediatrician arranged for Early Intervention physical therapy specialists to come in and work with him on physical types of skills once or twice a week. When the time came to transition him from formula to baby food, he would not eat baby food. They said he most likely had problems with different kinds of textures and again had other therapists working on different oral textures with him. He essentially went from formula to solid foods because he wouldn't take anything mushy.

When Drew was 18 months old, his head circumference was 54.8 cm. Not only is this above the graph, but 54 isn't even listed on the doctor's chart paper. We took him down to the specialist at the children's hospital that was watching his head size and evaluating his hydrocephalous. They couldn't figure out why his head size was continuing to grow without any buildup of fluid, so the doctor took urine samples and drew blood tests to try and figure out what was wrong. Drawing blood or getting IV's with Drew has always been difficult. Nurses had a hard time finding veins and frequently had to turn out the lights to use flashlight to shine through the skin and still ended up poking him four or five times and moving around to other parts of his body like his foot or his head. It is heart wrenching to watch your screaming infant be treated like a living pin cushion, appointment after appointment.

Within a week of visiting the doctor this time around, Drew got very sick. He was having difficulty breathing, so our babysitter took him to the emergency room one day while I was at work. Once she called to tell me where she was, I called an administrator to come take my class while I rushed off to the emergency room. He was instantly admitted and put on oxygen. He was diagnosed with RSV, but the doctors were surprised that 1) he was such an old child to be having such a hard time with RSV 2) the standard RSV treatment wasn't working. Drew was getting worse. After a week in the local hospital, they had to life-flight him an hour away to the state's dedicated Children's Intensive Care Unit (ICU). They wouldn't let us on the helicopter with him. The nurses sent us home to pack and drive to the other hospital.

I don't remember the drive home, but I remember getting out of my car in my driveway, tears streaming down my face, as I watched the helicopter with my deathly ill son, fly over me. When Mike and I arrived at hospital forty-five minutes later and saw him for the first time, my baby boy looked like an alien with all the ventilator tubes, wires, and attachments strung all over his body.

We lived in the ICU for a week. I took the day shift with Drew and the night shift at home with our other kids. My husband, would take the kids to school in morning, work most of the day, take a short nap, then stay up with Drew all night. One of us was by his side twenty-four hours a day.

It took a week before the ICU staff decided he must also have a complicating pneumonia. They started guessing all kinds of various things that might be wrong, and eventually settled on the easiest answer, which was asthma. Once they started treating the pneumonia and the breathing issues with asthma medications, he started to get better and was moved out of the ICU. Altogether, he spent three weeks in the hospital and was beginning to fear anyone who wore a yellow protective gown. We were sent home with a nebulizer and a slew of medications. Nebulizer treatments multiple times a day would become a regular part of his life for a long time to come.

We were just kind of emotionally settling down from our grueling three-week, experience with our son, thinking that all was going to be better now, when we got a phone call asking us to come in and discuss the results of the head specialists' urine sample that had been taken the week before Drew ended up in the hospital. We were told that his urine came back for MPS III otherwise known as San Filippo syndrome. It is often a terminal diagnosis because it is a degenerative metabolic disorder that makes the body unable to properly break down long chains of sugar molecules which build up in the body over time and eventually causes all the organs to shut down. We had just gotten out of the frying pan, and now we were back in the fire. A terminal diagnosis? Really? It is hard to even begin to explain what you feel when you are told you son is very likely never going to reach his teenage years. Books and books have been written about what it is like to experience such a thing. But we couldn't jump to conclusions. In order to confirm this diagnosis, they had to do a skin biopsy, so back to the hospital we went. It would take six months for the results to come back.

Granted, I still had to wait six months for the diagnosis to be confirmed, but I flipped out. I cried almost every day. I had to wait *six months* to find out if my son had a diagnosis that meant whether he would live or die. I was an emotional wreck.

Suddenly, I would get very angry when I went to the grocery store and was asked to donate money to the Children's Hospital or the Muscular Dystrophy Association or the Multiple Sclerosis (MS) Society. I just spent three weeks at the children's ICU. Didn't they already have all of my money? There is no cure or even anything helpful to assist a San Fillippo child. I wanted every person who asked me to donate to their cause - to donate to my cause. I was mad because you can live with MS or muscular dystrophy, and I was in debt to the children's hospital up to my ears. San Fillippo's Syndrome would kill my son, and no one had ever even heard of it before. It isn't like people wear signs saying my family is struggling with a terminal diagnosis. Cashiers didn't understand why I would suddenly stop talking and start crying when they asked such a simple question. Having your child diagnosed with a terminal illness felt like it does when someone close to you dies. You don't understand how the world can go on. You don't understand why time can't stand still and why everyone just doesn't "know" what you are going through.

It was hard to get up and go to work as a teacher every day. I worked at a school in a tough neighborhood, with children who it would seem had a death wish with their gang involvement and disrespect of adult authority. Students who did things every day that put their lives and future in jeopardy because they didn't care what happened to them. Watching those students, I started to question how God could take away a child that was so loving, thoughtful, caring and kind with such a bright future ahead of him, but leave all these other disrespectful, hurtful kids who didn't care about themselves or anyone else. I just wanted to be at home with my son, but every day I had to put on a brave face and pretend everything was okay and to go to work.

My other children knew Drew was different because he was constantly being seen by doctors, but I never explained terminal or degenerative to them, so at times I would watch my children play together and any time they left him out or beat him in a game or teased him, I just wanted to scream out, "Don't do that. He won't be here forever. In a year or two, when he can't play, you'll be sorry." But we didn't know for sure, and I didn't want to scare them, so I said nothing, and it broke my heart.

We lived in typical home for our state, a tri-level split. I began looking for a new home because there were no bedrooms or bathrooms that were on the main level of our house and we were going to need a handicapped accessible home because as the proteins built up in your system, it robs you of the ability to even walk. I was preparing for my life to change dramatically.

There are five different kinds of MPS, San Fillippo's is just one, and they have a very well-developed national support group and we were able to connect with local people in our state to talk about how this was potentially going to change our lives. I went to support events to meet their children and I was very frightened about our future. Doctors and their staff started to introduce me to Medicaid and what it could do for my family.

I was preparing for my life to be altered forever, but in the meantime, I still had to take care of my other children as well. My daughter was starting to complain every day of stomach problems, but I tried to write them off: "You are just growing," or "You didn't eat enough," or "You ate too much." I made excuses for a long time; besides I just didn't want any more doctors' appointments, but when I finally took her in, they instantly diagnosed her with Celiac Disease. The results of her blood draw were so definitively conclusive they almost decided not to do the scope, but they did it anyway.

Celiac Disease means my daughter cannot ingest gluten of any kind because not only does her body instantly try to reject therefore quickly making her pukingly ill, it also kills the lining of her stomach. When the lining of the stomach is injured vitamins and nutrients cannot pass through her stomach lining correctly. Failure to get these vitamins from food deprives many parts of her body from getting the fuel they need to function properly. This malabsorption can lead to cancer, a weakened immune system and other autoimmune diseases - even premature death.

So, unlike the people who don't eat gluten because it is the trendy paleo, keto, whatever-o diet to follow at the moment, or the people who don't eat it because it gives them a tummy ache, eating gluten can literally be a life-altering, life-threatening thing for my daughter, but because it has become a fad, people tend to dismiss her illness. They don't understand that Celiac Disease isn't something she could grow out of and isn't something that she can have a little of whenever she wants. Some people treat gluten contamination like it is no big deal, but to her body it is.

The first time I went shopping after the diagnosis, back in the early 2000's, I stood in the middle of the grocery store aisle and cried. At the time of her diagnosis there was not the great push in the general society to go gluten free, so there weren't all kinds of products in every store. I had to go to a specialty grocery store with very few options and gluten free products were boat loads more expensive. Even today, a loaf of her bread costs triple what I pay for a loaf for the rest of the family. Her diagnosis instantly doubled our grocery bill and cut our ability to go out to eat in half. She was in first grade, and how difficult her life would become was instantly clear. We were still getting used to the diagnosis and how to work with the limitations at home, when she received her first birthday party invitation. She could not eat any of the traditional birthday party menu: no pizza, cake or most ice creams. No donuts, no cereal, no cookies, no bread, no pasta, no everything our family ate for every meal. Parents and teachers would bring donuts and cupcakes to the school for birthdays or rewards and my daughter could never participate. She would just sit to the side, politely say no thank you and just watch. A few times when she felt left out, she thought she would just try to sneak a bite or two, but she realized how quickly it made her sick. She learned just as quickly the price she had to pay for trying to sneak a bite wasn't worth throwing up and having to leave early. It was heartbreaking.

There were some gluten free replacements, but most of them did not have even remotely comparative texture or even an appealing taste. Since 2012, things have really started to change. Rather than gluten binding agents, more companies are starting to use Xanthan Gum, so more and more products like cereal, bread, cake, pizza and pasta are products that we can easily find and prepare, but it didn't start off that way. It took us awhile to learn what products she liked, and which were worth spending money on.

About the same time as her Celiac diagnosis, her twin brother was having problems with tonsillitis. One of his lymph nodes on his neck was way bigger than the other and they were concerned it could be cancerous, so he was going to go in for a tonsillectomy and biopsy. All of my children were under a doctor's care of some kind. Tom was in the middle of the Asperger's diagnosis, my daughter had Celiac Disease, her twin possibly had cancer and my baby might have terminal degenerative illness. I felt like our lives were just an endless stream of doctor's appointments and our medical debt was climbing daily. In total, the checks we cut to doctors each month were more than our house payment and car payment put together. It was all an overload. I didn't want to get out of bed. I just wanted to hide under the covers all day.

Within a few days of the tonsillectomy/biopsy results coming back benign, we got Drew's biopsy results as well. It wasn't MPS. The elation I felt was overwhelming. I had been holding my breath for six months and I could finally exhale with relief. Maybe there was a light at the end of this tunnel. I had been on an emotional roller coaster for six months and now the ride felt like it was at least slowing down. But now we were back at square one with Drew and no one knew what was causing his head to grow, so back to the doctor we went.

They started asking all kinds of questions, but one question stopped the whole room. "We know this is kind of awkward, but does Drew have any spots on his penis?"

"Y-y-yes." I stuttered out. "Is that strange?"

"Not really, but do you mind if we take pictures?"

"Um... no." I mumbled as I gave the doctor an extremely strange side glance.

The doctor left the room and came back with a polaroid and four other doctors. That was when we really knew, spots on your penis really was strange. That was when they decided to look into something called Banyan-Riley Rubaclava Syndrome (BRRS) as a diagnosis. We were told this was an extremely rare genetic mutations that was not terminal or degenerative. It just had a tendency to predispose him to certain cancers as he got older, so we went home with a much calmer heart. Having a predisposition to cancer isn't the same as actually having cancer. BRRS wasn't an instant terminal diagnosis. We didn't even pursue confirming the diagnosis through testing right away because we couldn't afford it (I had lost my job since I had to take so much time off do deal with all these medical issues.)

A few months passed and Drew graduated out of Early Intervention and everything was going just fine. Now that he was older there didn't seem to be any indication that Drew was any different than any of my other kids, but then we started seeing all these large fatty bumps on his stomach and he started growing quite a few large moles. They were worrisome enough we had to take him to the doctor, again. They turned out to be nothing but fatty lipomas and another symptom of BBRS, but now the doctor highly recommended we follow through on confirming the diagnosis through testing, so we did and after six more months of waiting the DNA sequencing test confirmed the genetic mutation for BRRS.

At this point in 2009, if someone did a google search online for BRRS, there were a small handful of rather uninformative websites to visit. We could hardly find any information on what BRRS actually was, so when the Cleveland Clinic called and wanted blood and tissue samples to study and understand more about it, we agreed.

Today there are dozens of websites to visit and many different support groups. Bottom line is that BRRS is a genetic condition caused by the mutation or deletion of the PTEN gene. This gene produces a protein that is a tumor suppressor, so without this genetic information it makes certain kinds of tumor growths (like cancer or fatty lipomas) more likely. It is such a rare diagnosis that doctors can't even tell how many patients there may be in the general population. With such a rare diagnosis, the doctors want to follow him closely so they can learn more about the condition, so the first few years we took Drew to his appointments every few months or so, but as he started to grow, he was no different than the rest of kids, so we only started to take him to appointments only when he was actually sick, but after the last few years of constant medical attention for all my children, even that was more than enough trips to the doctor for us. The RSV, Pneumonia and Asthma meant Drew's lungs were very weak and his Asthma trigger was illness and bad air. For the first few years, no matter how well we tried to stay on top of his asthma, at the height of flu season he would end up in the hospital for a couple days during the winter as we tried to get the asthma back under control.

For a while, it seemed every time I took a child in for a doctor's appointment, it resulted in more appointments. For example, a couple of years ago, the other kids needed junior high shots, so everyone was scheduled for a well-child visit. That visit resulted in four more visits. My daughter is very athletic and had a heart murmur, so we went to check it out. It was an innocent murmur that she eventually grew out of. It was also suspected that she had scoliosis. That required x-ray confirmation and it resulted in being told she had 7% curve. On her second follow up appointment a few years later, they said she didn't have it all. For Drew they wanted thyroid ultra-sounds and another MRI of his head. Of course, getting these test means traveling to the children's hospital an hour away, but the point was baseline tests for the early detection of future potential cancer, so we couldn't really say no. By this point, Drew at eight years old, had been through more MRI's and CT scans than most people will experience in their entire lifetime.

Sometimes I wonder if less health care would be better. Sometimes I wonder if it would just be better not to know any of this. Over the years, we have undergone so many tests, x-rays, scans, biopsies, whatever, and most of it has been for nothing because we either couldn't do anything about the diagnosis anyway or whatever the problem was ended up being something they eventually grew out of. We have undergone thousands and thousands of dollars of tests to be told everything is fine. You reach a point where you have to wonder if the tests are really worth it? Is the knowledge and worry really worth it?

I dread taking my children to the doctor because I know it will just result in the request for more trips to the doctor. It has gotten to the point that I don't take myself to the dentist or eye doctor or regular well checkups for me because I am so tired of spending my entire life in doctor's offices for my children.

Then my friend calls me to complain, "I am so annoyed. I have to take Janey [her only child] to the doctor for her junior high shots."

"Yeah. That sucks. It's too bad they can't just get them all done when they are little kids, right? Not to brag or anything, but I am on my 8th appointment this month. I'll trade ya!"

"Why do your kids need to go to the doctor? Nothing looks wrong with them."

And there it is. The judgement. The assumptions that because you can't see it and I don't talk about it doesn't exist and everything is fine.

"Welcome to my world." I laugh in my head. But the issue of my kids' appointments ends there. She doesn't ask why I have eight appointments because she assumes that is the natural result of having four kids instead of just one. It really isn't, but she doesn't bother asking. I have spent so much time at doctor's offices I haven't had the time, energy or money to maintain any kind of social life. I have only talked to my friends sporadically for months now. She has no idea what the details of my children's medical conditions are or what my life has been like and we can't really relate to each other anymore.

To this day, all my kids have to do is mention they have a sore throat or a headache and I cringe, then cry a little inside about scheduling another appointment and what it could possibly mean and what it will potentially cost us. For the first fourteen years of our marriage, I think I knew my pediatrician and Children's Hospital geneticist as well as I knew my husband. I was beginning to know the imaging staff at both of the major hospitals by name and sight.

Things started to settle down with serious medical diagnosis's once everyone hit their teenage years, but then there were different kinds of problems to face. As the kids reached puberty, they developed cystic acne. Besides the social implications of being cast out, it is something that can scar your face for life, so that meant rounds of trips to the dermatologist. All of this is in addition to our regular vision, dental, and orthodontist appointments, too. Three out of the four kids have had braces, and two of the four have glasses.

Being female, my daughter had additional issues. The pain my daughter would face when it was her time of the month seemed ridiculously over the top and having learned my lesson from ignoring her stomach complaints when she was younger, I took her to be checked. She was diagnosed with polycystic ovarian syndrome at just 14 years old.

And, of course, considering all my children have played recreation or competitive sports year-round, we have had our fair share of the typical scrapes and cuts that have required stitches and twisted ankles and torn muscles and just the plain old regular flu.

Sometimes, I just feel like we live at a doctor's office.

Sometimes, calling for one more appointment makes me want to cry.

Sometimes, calling to deal with one more insurance company that screwed up our claim sends me over the edge.

Sometimes, my arms are just too tired to want to do this parenting, adulting thing anymore.

Sometimes, I just don't want to do anything, anymore.

But if you were my child's teacher, chances are you wouldn't know about the medical challenges my child is facing because I go out of my way to schedule every appointment outside of school time. If you were the waitress who served us after we just left our most recent doctor's appointment, you wouldn't know any of this. If you saw us all walking together in the grocery store, you wouldn't know any of this. But if you did, would you be a little more understanding if Drew didn't want to run the mile in P.E. class or if Tom asked for his third new set of silverware at the restaurant because none of the others were clean enough? But here is the thing, our family isn't that different from anyone else. Our problems may be different from other families, but everyone has problems. Everyone deserves empathy, even if you don't know their story.

EPILOGUE

Being a parent is hard and unpredictable even for the most stable and intelligent people, but I don't consider myself very stable or intelligent. While very few people I interact with on a daily basis might not be able to suspect it, I struggle every single day to take my medications and hold myself together and function normally in society. I struggle every day to get up, go to work and do a good job. I struggle every day to stay engaged with my own children to try and give them the best chance to get the most out of their life. I struggle every day not to push my husband away and pull the covers over my head and hide in the back of my comfy kennel. My life really is a daily emotional struggle. I face the depression, the attachment disorder, and the triggers for my Post Traumatic Stress Disorder every day. But if you just met me today or any time in the last ten years, you aren't likely to know any of the stories in this book because they are all in the past, and I don't go around talking about my past on a regular basis. But these stories define who I am. They define my struggles I still face every day.

But here is why I chose to write this book and tell my story - because I'm still here. I work with teenagers every day who think they are the only ones to have ever experienced whatever pain they are going through. They think whatever they are going through is worse than everyone else. They think nothing in life can be harder than what they are experiencing right then, and it is always the end of the world, and they want to give up.

I teach in a pretty rough area and some of my students have some rough stories. One girl I started teaching in eighth grade was absent because she had been raped by her stepbrother and was going to have an abortion. She was living with her grandmother because her parents had been jailed for making and selling Meth. In ninth grade she tried to kill herself. In her eleventh-grade year, she became a yearbook editor. Over the summer she was diagnosed with cancerous tumors in her spine, and in the first few months of the year, the yearbook advisor died of a sudden heart attack. I have had students write stories about their siblings being arrested for murder or finding their brother after he killed himself. Students who can't come to class because they have to take care of their younger siblings so their parents can work. Students who became parents themselves. Homeless students. Illegal immigrant students. Every single one of these students graduated. The hardest thing isn't to learn calculus. It is how to is to push through life. Just this last summer, the news outlets have been discussing how suicide rates are up by 30% across the nation, especially among women and teens. I get it. I understand why people make the choice to check out.

When I reached out to my family as a teenager, I was told depression wasn't real and psychologists were quacks. I was told the pain I was feeling was imaginary because kids can't feel that kind of pain and adults knew better. When suicide touched my own family, they were so embarrassed and ashamed they hid the truth from everyone. And once, as a teacher, I was quietly asked to resign immediately because while teaching *Romeo and Juliet*, I gave a choice of journal prompts to answer, and one of them was, "Have you ever thought about killing yourself?" When I was called into the office, I was told I was encouraging suicide and I quote the principal when she said, "Our children don't think about those kinds of things." When I walked out of the building the next day for the last time, I left the large stack of journals on her desk of every student who had written that they, in fact, HAD thought of killing themselves. I knew there were children who thought about it and wanted to be found because when I was their age, I was one of them.

My last year as a debate coach, I frequently felt like I needed to have an emergency social worker on call for my classes because I had a number of students who told stories of how they were on antidepressants and they all seemed to want to play a game of one-upmanship of "my life is worse than yours." I was worried that we wouldn't be able to make it through the year with all of them still there in the end. When I would talk to administrators, they didn't have the time. I started to question if my experiences and feelings had made me overly sensitive. But when it comes to saving a life, isn't that the point? We need to pay attention and be sensitive. When someone calls out, listen! I spent an inordinate amount of time listening to my students rather than shoving state standards and busy work down their throats. We made it to the end of the year and on the bus ride home after winning our region conference, every single one of them was crying and talking about how they had found the family that had *literally* saved his or her life.

I am thankful that for some the strength to go on came from hearing my story.

"You amaze me, Mrs. Mackie. You have gone through so much and you are still here, and so normal."

AH-HA-HA-HA-HA! Oh, my innocent darlings! How fooled you are! That is my acting skill! That is my teacher face! That is because you have no idea what goes on in my life outside of the classroom. You have no idea the depression I fight on a daily basis. But yes, I am still here.

With the epidemic of suicide on the rise, our State Board of Education has mandated we teach a 10 to 20-minute suicide prevention lesson with a prescribed provided video every year. The lesson boils down to recognizing the signs of depression and telling depressed students to find someone to talk to. Um, newsflash, if withdrawal is one of the signs, they aren't going to find someone to talk to.

Elizabeth Smart, the young woman held captive and raped daily for nine months by Brian David Mitchell once said, "Those with shattered souls find it very difficult to speak." Even within this book, I haven't shared some of my most difficult stories. I still struggle to find the strength to share those stories, so some years, I feel strong enough to be able to teach the mandated suicide lessons, and others I don't. But one of the problems with the lesson is that not everyone displays the signs. I can stand in front of room full of students talking about the need to be aware of the signs of a suicidal person and inside just laugh at the irony that no one ever clues in to the suicidal teacher in front of them, because to the students I am just a talking head without feelings, emotions or my own personal journey. And sadly, I see too many of my peers treat the students in the same reciprocal manner - as just a body in a desk expected to regurgitate whatever is thrown at them. In the pressures to achieve and prove accountability we have lost the sense of humanity, empathy and understanding of each individual's journey.

But here's the thing, a depressed person shows people what they think others want to see precisely so as not to arouse suspicion because they don't want the attention focused on them because they don't think they are worthy of saving. They don't think they have anything to offer and they do think the world would be better without them in it. Suicidal people are not selfish. They actually think they are helping other people by removing the burden they inflict on the world.

People who know my story will sometimes say, "You're so strong." No, I am not. Strength is an illusion. You just don't see what happens behind closed doors when I go home at night. After the recent suicides of Kate Spade and Anthony Bourdain, friends or family members of theirs came forward to say that just the day before, both of them had been talking to friends and family and talking about things they wanted to do in the future. Social media pointed out that sometimes it is the "strong" ones that need more attention. I propose the idea that maybe there is no such thing as strong ones. We are all vulnerable to pain and suffering. If my husband were asked to describe me, he might pick the word resilient, but he probably would not pick strong because my husband has a front row ticket to watch me fight the demons of my past. He sees the truth of how weak I really am.

He sees how I sleep all the time as a way of avoiding everything. He sees how I close myself off from him and the kids when things get too rough. He knows how many times he has held me when I cried for no reason. He knows how hard it is to be married to someone who is depressed, to someone who can't give back, to someone who doesn't even want to get out of bed in the morning, to someone who sees and reads problems into everything, to someone who is always negative, to someone who, no matter what he does, doesn't feel loved, to someone that he constantly has to try to evaluate their current mental state. "Is today a day that I can leave her alone or is today a day I have to stay by her side? What level is the depression meter hitting today? What triggers are around today that could potentially set her off? What do I need to shield her from today?" My appearance of strength and sanity are largely a reflection of how well he is doing navigating that minefield on any given day because without him in my life I wouldn't be much more than a quivering mass of tears.

But he still sees only what I allow him to see, and heaven forbid he and I have a rough patch because then the struggle is even worse. There are times when I am living in a whole other world that he doesn't see, so there are times even he doesn't know when those suicidal thoughts are running through my brain.

One of the things I hate about how people approach depression and childhood trauma is when people say, "That's the past. Just forget about it. Move on." It is a very typical attitude of the people who live in Utah. It's inbred. Trey Parker and Matt Stone, authors of *Book of Mormon: The Musical* wrote a song all about how people are told to just ignore things society considers bad called *Turn it Off*:

When you start to get confused
Because of thoughts in your head
Don't feel those feelings!
Hold them in instead
Turn it off, like a light switch
Just go click!
It's a cool little Mormon trick!
We do it all the time
When you're feeling certain feelings
That just don't seem right
Treat those pesky feelings
Like a reading light
And turn 'em off

Granted the song is referring to a character who is gay, but the concept isn't different. Cue social media meme from *Game of Thrones*, "You can't simply forget about being abused (or gay)." The experiences of my childhood made me who I am today, and trust me, I would love to forget many of them, but it doesn't work that way. I can't just "turn it off." The experiences of my youth literally changed the hardwiring in my brain by changing the way the neurons in my brain fire when faced with certain experiences. Scientists have actually discovered that depending on the size of alleles on the 5-HTT gene, different people will react differently to the triggers of childhood trauma. But childhood trauma, can in fact, change the way things trigger or react in your brain. I will see and seem to overact to things that wouldn't even tend to phase most other people.

Let me provide an example.

Some days of the year are more of a problem for me than others. Keep in mind I am no gentle snowflake. I have an exterior that is thicker than most concrete barriers for nuclear safe bunkers, but a few times a year all it takes is the tiniest grain of sand to crumble that concrete to pieces and the past comes flooding back. Mother's Day just so happens to be one of those days.

I avoid to going to the doomsday beaches of social media or anywhere else particularly difficult I might find sand, but it seems to find me, no matter what I do. One year, I cancelled all the obligatory family get-togethers and didn't open my social media accounts in an attempt to ensure I kept anything abrasive away.

Mother's Day is a day to think about your mother. A day to honor all the nice, soft, warm fuzzy feelings that society says a mother is supposed to give you. To give thanks that she brought you into this world and does her best to make your life better. The woman who made Mother's Day a recognized holiday in the United States said that the purpose was the sentimental recognition of motherhood.

There is no sentimentality in motherhood for me. All the women in my life with the title of mother, the ones responsible for raising me, all failed me. And every time Mother's Day rolls around and everyone is posting about how grateful they are for their mothers and how wonderful these women are and what great people they have all been – all it does is remind me about all those difficult relationships, so I approach the holiday differently. In the weeks leading up to Mother's Day, I have to spend time mentally preparing myself for all the triggers and PTSD that I know are likely to occur.

I have to prepare and steel myself against the onslaught of marketing and social media. I have to start pouring my concrete foundation around me early, so that I can make sure the concrete has settled and cured before Sunday, so when the inevitable memories occur, I can take it in stride without breaking down and falling apart. And how great is this conversation every year. "Oh, are you going to celebrate with your mother?"

My mind instantly jumps to, "Well, which mother?" but that opens a whole can of worms that isn't appropriate for casual conversation, so I answer simply, "No."

"Why not?"

Now, I guess, I could start to anticipate this conversation, and come up with a nice social avoidance line, but instead I answer with, "Because she is dead." Sometime that makes other people uncomfortable enough to back off, but not always.

Sometimes they follow up with, "Oh, that's too bad. What happened?" Thinking that my mother, having clearly died so young that her death must be due to some tragic accident or terrible illness are usually never prepared for my blunt answer.

"She killed herself."

No better way to kill a casual conversation, but some might keep trying with, "So what are you going to do?"

"Nothing."

"Oh, well I hope you enjoy your day."

Now, what I want to say is, "Yep. That is not likely to happen." But again, I stay with the more acceptable, "Okay. You Too!"

When driving with my oldest son this year, the week after Mother's Day, and he realized he missed it, he said, "Why should it matter? It is only one day out of the year." I would agree with him if my children showed respect and appreciation the other 364 days of the year. However, other than a means to service their desired ends – laundry, meals, rides, vehicles, cash - I am mostly ignored.

Mother's Day is no different. I don't get breakfast in bed or flowers or cards or hugs or dinner out or any special plans at all. Not even a verbal "Happy Mother's Day." Nothing – from anyone, not even my husband. (This is exactly not the kind of way families should interact with someone who has attachment disorder problems. While some people would be okay and say, "Hey, it is just another day." I see it as a screaming reinforcement of the idea that says no one loves or cares about me.)

Then when I try to talk to other people about my feelings - about no one recognizing me on Mother's Day, I am met with the following reactions: Don't be such a drama queen. You're making too much of this. Your overreacting isn't going to solve anything. You just want to be the center attention.

These reactions are one hundred percent the wrong things to say and exactly why people don't talk about what they really feel. These types of reactions are exactly why when someone commits suicide people will say, "I didn't see the signs."

Passing in the halls, administrators, teachers, and students ask me all day long, "How's it going?"

They never want to hear the real answer. They don't have time for the real answer. It is just a socially acceptable platitude, so I also answer with the corresponding, "Great" or "Fine." Anything less than that means people feel forced to stop and give you attention, and then you get a reputation for being negative and complaining. People really don't want to hear the truth or get involved in other people's problems, but then they act so shocked when someone has a break down or worse. But when people take the time to know my story, my answers seem less like being a drama queen, but very few people I encounter on a daily basis know anything about my past.

When people look at me, when they see me right now, they have no idea what I have been through, where I have come from and what I have overcome. They make so many assumptions. I appear to have a stable job, successful children, a happy marriage and a nice house, so I must have always lived a nice, happy life of middle-class white privilege. Never mind that I have never worked anywhere longer than four years or that every relationship in my house is a constant struggle. All people see is the cover to my book, not what is actually inside. There is this whole story people don't know so even now when people see me smiling and laughing, assuming I am happy and well-adjusted would be a mistake. I am very good at letting people see only what I want them to see. Don't assume that just because everything in my life seems all put together that it actually is or that it means I am actually strong. My strength is an illusion I crafted and created for an audience.

A skill I teach in debate is "fake it until you make it." Often students are forced into the world of competition without all the skills they need to know. I just don't have the time to teach everything, but that doesn't need to hold them back from their ability to be successful and achieve to the best of their ability. If they go into a round and appear worried, scared or intimidated, even if their ideas are better, they are likely to lose the round. Whether or not they *feel* confident is irrelevant. They need to portray strength and confidence regardless of what they feel. Often times this portrayal of strength can take them quite a long way in competition even if they have no idea what they are doing. This mantra is more than just a competitive skill to be used in debate. It is a life skill. It is my version of putting one foot in front of the other and just pushing through. Not only do you have to push through, but you have to fake that you're doing it in a stable, normal, strong, confident, happy way, until the day that you do have all the knowledge and all the skills so that you won't be faking it anymore, and stable, confident and happy will actually be reality. It's hard. It's very hard, but it is why I am still here.

One of the reasons suicides are becoming such an epidemic is because of the fakeness people present through social media. The social media illusion, as it has been called, is when someone's life has been taken, edited and photoshopped, so that followers only see what the poster wants them to see. People create edited highlight reels of their lives and when others compare themselves to their friends highlight reels, they are left feeling inadequate. For the most part, all that can be found on social is other people's successes. People don't usually post pictures of them sitting around on a Friday night doing nothing, and all it takes is seeing even just two friends out doing something exciting and suddenly you're throwing a pity party for how sad and boring your life is. What you didn't see was the last two months of those same two friends sitting around doing nothing having their own pity parties.

We have to stop comparing our day-to-day moments to other people's highlight reels; stop judging people on what is happening at one moment in time and learn to always look at the bigger picture and not make assumptions. When I go into work after Mother's Day people ask, "How was your Mother's Day? What did you family do for you?" They have no idea the baggage that comes along with such simple questions, so I will answer the first question with "fine" and ignore the second one because I already know what happens when I tell the truth. When I tell someone who doesn't know me well I was bothered because my family ignored me they will say something like, "It will get better. You're making a big deal out of nothing." But if you knew me, it is a big deal, and how many years do you need to be forgotten before it is acceptable to become a big deal? It was already the fifth year in a row where my family did absolutely nothing for me.

Sure, this is an overblown and ridiculous example, but it shows how we end up living in this very surface level world. If people don't have perfect lives, they feel they can't discuss their real lives and real feelings and that leaves people feeling unvalued and lonely. In a world where the only part of your life that matters is the highlight reel posted to social media, people become too terrified of judgement to share with one another anything but perfection, but reality is life is anything but perfect. Life is messy. People are complicated; emotions are complicated. A photoshopped, layered Snapchat photo of a single moment doesn't show reality. Sit anywhere teens are likely to take photos and watch. They go along doing mundane things, then suddenly stop and perfectly pose gigantic smiles then instantly return again to the mundane. They have honed and practiced each pose that they fall into and out of at will. That isn't reality. That is acting.

For much of their youth the twins did many things together, but as they started into junior high things started to change. My daughter became very social and was participating in more and more extra-curricular activities, while her brother started becoming more and more antisocial. Even though he played competition soccer and was one of the best players around, he would talk about how horrible he was, and how he didn't care if he played. Even though he got straight A's in his full honor's class schedule and did better than his sister in school, he would always talk about how stupid he was and then his grades started to slip. He would never allow me to hug him, and he started using KMS (Kill myself) as one of his gamer tags. Every time something went wrong - like accidently spilling a drink, he would say things like "I should just kill myself."

This generation has a huge problem with joking about suicide. I hear students say KMS or see them write it on papers regularly. They even frequently outright say it to each other. "You should just kill yourself." I think the use of the phrase started from the idea of rage quitting in video games. In my youth, when you played video games, you had three or four given lives before you would lose the game and have to start over. In today's generation, there is no such thing. They have infinite gaming lives. Sure, a player can die, but they pick up right where they left off and keep playing. If things aren't working out in a game, a player can kill themselves to reset to a more favorable starting point. I would love to restart my life from a more favorable starting point, but that isn't how real-life works. But this generation talks about life as if it were just a game they could reset by "killing myself." Likewise, horribly losing in a video game is referred to as being "raped." I heard a student talk about how she had cut a class and her parents had found out and she was afraid to go home because they were going to be angry with her. She said, "Pray for me. I am on my way home to get raped." Of course, I couldn't let her leave and had to talk to her, only to learn that using the word rape in that context was common among her peers. I cross checked Urban Dictionary after she left the room to make sure I didn't need to call child protective services.

In this world of expected perfection, people don't think about the inflammatory and triggering use of their words. Getting yelled at by your parents for ten minutes is not the same as rape. Dropping that word in casual conversation in a classroom, comparing a victimized act to a normal expected outcome (the parents should be angry and reasonably punish the girl who cut class) suddenly sends the student who was violently raped last year reeling into a flashback of emotion, feeling denigrated by this twisted acceptance of rape culture.

Words Matter.

Every time I would hear KMS or other 'jokes about suicide' and tell students it was not a phrase that should be used as a joke because they never know what other people are thinking and feeling around them, they would write me off as an old woman who wasn't hip with the times. It goes back to the idea, that the students don't know my story. They don't know about the student who shot himself in the bathroom, so that I do know with direct experience just how harmful those words can be. It is all just a joke to them, and sadly something bad has to happen before they figure that out.

One of the reasons I like to teach *Romeo and Juliet* is that we can take an honest look at how young teenagers look at problems they encounter in their lives and how today's teens are still experiencing very similar types of problems to the main characters. Romeo begins the play wandering around in a melancholic stupor bemoaning the fact the Rosaline won't have sex with him (Act 1 Scene 1 lines 206-215). Romeo goes from the beginning of the play in love with another woman to married to Juliet in less than four days, and what is the first thing he does when he meets Juliet? Starts making out with her. Was he in love or in lust? Face it, how quickly do love interests of thirteen-year-olds last? Because let's not forget that was how old Juliet was.

Then when Romeo is banished, his first thought is to ask the Friar for a different way for Romeo to kill himself because to him banishment was like death. When Juliet hears she has to marry Paris, her first thought is that if no one can come up with a solution she will kill herself. But the best part of the play is the end, the actual deaths of Romeo and Juliet, the representatives of supposedly the best love story ever told. The second Romeo hears Juliet is dead, his first thought is to kill himself – not to even confirm the story of her death. (Because even in Shakespeare's time they apparently had fake news.) If he had taken an extra twenty minutes to check in with the Friar, Romeo wouldn't have needed to die. And if the Friar hadn't stopped to talk to the servant outside the tomb, he maybe could have prevented both deaths, or even if Juliet had woken up ten minutes earlier neither of them would have had to have died. In my class, we talk about how stupid the timing of everything is, and how the truly over dramatic nature of the whole thing is really comedic and doesn't lend itself to the opinion that this is the most romantic, tragic, love story ever told because Romeo and Juliet were just two horny teenagers that couldn't wait five minutes for anything. Just because almost everyone dies it does not make it a tragedy.

At that point, I teach my students a quote from Phil Donahue, "Suicide is a permanent solution to a temporary problem," because every problem in the play was temporary. Every problem had a solution. Sometimes the solution is nothing but time. So next, I teach a concept called the three-day rule. Every big life (or death) decision should take a minimum of three days to decide. There is such a thing as buyers regret and certain industries make allowances for when that occurs, but there is no such thing as buyers regret on a successful suicide attempt. Research says that 48% of people who attempt suicide had thought about it for less than ten minutes before making the attempt. For many people it is an impulsive decision, so for many people the idea of taking it one day at a time is too long a time frame. For a suicidal person, the adage may need to be one moment at a time. There is a very powerful video on BuzzFeed by a man named Kevin who tried to kill himself by jumping off the Golden Gate Bridge. He said the second his hands and feet left the bridge, he felt instant regret. He was one of the very few who was lucky enough to be saved.

The lesson Romeo needed to learn was to go moment by moment for three days after hearing of Juliet's death. If at any point in those three days there is any moment of joy, glimmer of hope, or someone who reaches out, the three-day clock has to reset. If Romeo would have had a three-day rule, he and Juliet could have lived happily ever after. Chances are that within three days, there will be some moment of joy or glimmer of hope, and if at any time the thoughts are just calling out too strongly to resist, get help. When I went to the mental hospital, I was there for three days. Did I know about the idea of the three-day rule then? No. But those three days made a difference in my life. What was my life saving moment? Realizing I was the only one I could trust to raise my kids to have a better life than mine. But you have to wait three days and you have to be strong enough to ask for help if you just can't shake it no matter what you do.

And what if it isn't you? What if you are watching someone you love struggle? What can you do? At first, when my son would make the comments about soccer and school, they came across as jokes and trying to be humble, but the more he persisted with the comments the more concerned I became, and I started to watch and listen more closely. It got to the point that when he would go to his room, I would have to regularly check on him because I was afraid of what he might do. Then over Thanksgiving break, his tone changed even darker, and I was worried, so worried that I called the mental health hotline and they sent social workers out to our house to evaluate his mental state. The whole time I sat watching him talk, silent tears were running down my face. They decided he would not need to be taken in for observation as long as we took him to a psychologist as soon as possible. (It was the holidays and offices wouldn't be open for three more days.) They also suggested that we not leave him alone, and we allowed him to pick the family activities for the next little while. We set up his computer in the family room and that is when I learned how to play League of Legends. It actually became a great family bonding experience when we created our own team of five. After the social workers left, I wrote my son a letter in which I explained that I understood his feelings and explained my own battle with depression. For the most part, my husband and I did a great job of hiding my illness from the kids, so once my son knew he looked at me differently and we started to bond on a deeper level. We took him to the doctor, and he was put on medication. He did not want to take it and I would have to hover over him to ensure that he did every day.

But what if it isn't a family member? What if it is the random person in class, or the guy in the cubical down the hall, the cashier at the grocery store? You can still make a difference. When you start to focus less on yourself and more on treating those around you with kindness, you can make a difference. Because, in reality, your life isn't about you. It is about all the people around you. The Center for Disease Control considers suicide to be contagious, creating what is referred to as cluster events - when there are large areas where there is an increase in the number of attempted suicides. In other words, if you know of someone who has committed suicide, the chance that you might also commit suicide increases. This is one reason why people are hesitant to recognize and discuss suicide when it happens, which is completely understandable, but we can't hide from other contagious diseases like AIDS and just hope it goes away, so we can't hide from a society inflicted with an increasing number of suicides. We have to find the preventative medicine, and I prescribe that the medicine comes from realizing that your life is about the people around you. Every interaction with every person you know adds a drop in their bucket of mental health. Is the drop you are adding composed of acidic rain or a pleasant aromatic fragrance. Is that drop going to contaminate the well or preserve it? In my class I demonstrate this with a sheet of paper. I go around the room and ask each student to tell me about a bad experience they had that day.

"I was late getting up."

"I was late to school."

"I forgot my homework."

"I didn't finish my homework."

"I didn't have time to eat breakfast."

"I dropped my books in the hall."

"I accidently spilled my drink on Sam."

These are kind ones, usually there are things like: "My parents yelled at me."

"My teacher yelled at me."

"My friends yelled me."

"People made fun of me."

The list goes on and on and it is not usually that difficult to get an answer from everyone in the room. With each answer, I take a full sheet of paper and rip a small piece off.

While we are doing this, I have each student take their own piece of paper and if their life was also impacted by one of the comments, they have to rip a piece off their paper too. For example, if the student who says I was late to school was responsible for giving another student in class a ride that day, so they were both late, the other student also has to tear his paper. Or, when the student didn't do their homework, did the whole class get yelled at? If so, they all have to rip their paper. Or, when the student spilled his drink on Sam, they both have to rip their paper. When we have gone around the room and there is a pile of ripped paper at my feet, I pick it all up and hand it to a student and ask, "Can you put that back together for me?"

Answers vary; sometimes yes and sometimes no. Then I say, "I want it to look exactly like it did before I ripped the first piece off, okay? Is that possible? Oh, and I need you to put it back together in the same amount of time as it took me to tear it apart."

If they are smart, they will say they can't do that.

"Why not?" I ask.

"Because in order to put it back together it will take time to figure out where all the pieces go and then I have to put tape all over it, so it can never look the same."

"EXACTLY! Each and every time something bad happens a little piece of you breaks off. One by one, over a long period of time, it may seem like no big deal. Some bad things like spilling a drink may only tear off a little, but bigger things like your friends ditching you and calling you a loser, tear off a much bigger piece, but either way, little by little these little pieces add up. When you interact with someone in a negative way, you are tearing them apart, and repairing them is time consuming and difficult and sometimes isn't even possible." It is a lesson they have known since kindergarten, but yet every time I do that demonstration, I feel they are just understanding the concept for the first time. The idea that their words and their choices really can make that much of an influence in someone else's life starts to sink in. The idea that your life really is about all the people you impact, all the people you influence and all the people you emotionally touch, daily.

And really, that is probably why I became a teacher, not because I love my content area and wanted to teach it to others, but because I have hope for our youth. I want to make other people's lives better. I just happen to use my content area as the vehicle to make it happen.

The things that I think helped the most on the road to my son's recovery was the fact that we listened and took action. I didn't tell him to suck it up or just stop saying those things. I didn't say, "Oh, you won't really do that" or "You're just trying to get attention" or "Just get over it" or "Your life is perfect. What do you have to be depressed about?" We acknowledged his pain and we brought people to the house to make sure he was safe. We took him in to get medication. We listened to him when he said he couldn't handle all of the pressure at school and allowed him to take less rigorous classes by going to the counselor and changing his classes the next week. What we did say to him was "We'll get through this together." Four years later, it is still a struggle. He still takes medication and we still watch him closely. We always will. The minute something seems off we address it. He still plays soccer, has developed a group of friends he has over for games on a regular basis and even has a girlfriend. He is taking things moment by moment, and at this moment he's okay.

Elizabeth Smart said, "I like to think that we're not defined by what happens to us...because so many times they're beyond our control. I like to think that we're defined by our choices and our decisions." It is our choices and decisions that make us strong. A different person who might have lived through Elizabeth's gruesome experience, might have come out on the other side as a very broken person, but she says she is not broken. She realized that through all the many months she has spent on this planet, her time in captivity was only nine months, and that those nine months should not override all the other wonderful things in her life - an amazingly, positive, optimistic way to choose to approach her ordeal. So, when people say to me, "Oh, you are so strong." Maybe I am, but unlike Elizabeth, I do feel very broken, and even though I feel I have a shattered soul, I still choose to speak and share my story in an attempt to help others see that they are not alone and there is always hope – and that those aren't just platitudes. Maybe I am strong because it takes courage to not succumb to the demons, to make the decision to get up and live every day, and to try to not let my life be defined by the experiences in my past, to get up and be the light and hope that my students need on a daily basis. Maybe to be strong is just to live the best life I can and help others along the way.

Have you ever felt like nobody was there?
Have you ever felt forgotten in the middle of nowhere?
Have you ever felt like you could disappear?
Like you could fall, and no one would hear?
Well, let that lonely feeling wash away
Maybe there's a reason to believe you'll be okay
'Cause when you don't feel strong enough to stand
You can reach, reach out your hand
And oh, someone will come running
And I know, they'll take you home
Even when the dark comes crashing through
When you need a friend to carry you
And when you're broken on the ground
You will be found
So let the sun come streaming in
'Cause you'll reach up and you'll rise again
Lift your head and look around
You will be found

- From "You Will be Found," from the musical *Dear Evan Hansen*

Being found might take time. It might take months and months of time or even longer, but you will be found, and the rewards will be worth it. At the bottom of my well people told me about those rewards all the time and I never believed I would find them, so I didn't reach out my hand. I stayed at the bottom of that well longer than I needed to, but with a lot of time and a little help I eventually found my way out, and even with all its struggles, life on the outside of the well really did contain those rewards and was better than I ever believed it could be. You can't see the light at the bottom, but just keep reaching out and climbing. Eventually, there will be light again and you will be found.

www.ingramcontent.com/pod-product-compliance
Lightning Source LLC
Chambersburg PA
CBHW032110280326
41933CB00009B/783

* 9 7 8 1 7 3 3 3 4 1 5 0 9 *